Caroline Tee is a research associate at the Faraday Institute for Science and Religion, St Edmund's College, University of Cambridge. She was previously a postdoctoral research assistant in the Department of Archaeology and Anthropology, University of Bristol, and Research and Policy Adviser at the Centre for Turkey Studies (CEFTUS), London. She has been the recipient of a major John Templeton Foundation Grant (2013–15) and has published numerous articles on Islam and society in modern Turkey.

'Caroline Tee has produced an ethnographically rich and highly readable book on the social impact of Turkey's Gülen Movement. Carefully building upon preceding scholarship, Tee usefully explains how for over 40 years, Fethullah Gülen and his followers in Turkey were able to develop significant political and economic influence as a faith community by relying upon science education as a primary organisational approach. Indeed, Tee is at her best when she explains how one of Turkey's largest and most influential religious communities managed to unite piety and science education in such a way as to develop a recipe for national (and ultimately, global) expansion. In so doing, Tee provides readers with a scholarly account of the ways in which modern religious identity can both compliment and be contradicted by the rationalisation of knowledge and the inevitable desire for status, influence, and prestige.'

Joshua D. Hendrick, Assistant Professor of Sociology and Global Studies, Loyola University Maryland, and author of *Gülen: The Ambiguous Politics of Market Islam in Turkey and the World* (2013)

THE GÜLEN MOVEMENT IN TURKEY

THE POLITICS OF ISLAM AND MODERNITY

CAROLINE TEE

Published in 2016 by
I.B.Tauris & Co. Ltd
London • New York
www.ibtauris.com

Copyright © 2016 Caroline Tee

The right of Caroline Tee to be identified as the author of this work has been asserted by the author in accordance with the Copyright, Designs and Patents Act 1988.

All rights reserved. Except for brief quotations in a review, this book, or any part thereof, may not be reproduced, stored in or introduced into a retrieval system, or transmitted, in any form or by any means, electronic, mechanical, photocopying, recording or otherwise, without the prior written permission of the publisher.

References to websites were correct at the time of writing.

ISBN: 978 1 78453 588 9
eISBN: 978 1 78672 027 6
ePDF: 978 1 78673 027 5

A full CIP record for this book is available from the British Library
A full CIP record is available from the Library of Congress

Library of Congress Catalog Card Number: available

Typeset by Newgen
Printed and bound by CPI Group (UK) Ltd, Croydon, CR0 4YY

Table of Contents

Acknowledgements		vii
Note on Turkish Spelling and Pronunciation		viii
Abbreviations		ix
Introduction		1

PART ONE: BACKGROUND

1	Gülen: Leader and Community	13
2	A Nursian Spiritual Framework for Modernity	35

PART TWO: SCIENCE AND EDUCATION

3	The Gülen Movement's Science-focused Schools	53
4	Islamic Creationism in Gülenist Thought	78
5	Higher Education, Networking and Careers in Science	99

PART THREE: THE WIDER CONTEXT

6	Intercultural Dialogue	119
7	Globalisation of the Movement, and Gülen in the USA	140
8	Political Influence and the AKP	162
	Afterword	183
	Notes	189
	Bibliography	214
	Index	224

Acknowledgements

I gratefully acknowledge funding for this book, which was provided by the John Templeton Foundation under grant ID 38749. The research was undertaken while I was postdoctoral research assistant in the Department of Archaeology and Anthropology at the University of Bristol, 2013–15, and the book was completed during my tenure at the Faraday Institute, Cambridge.

I wish to thank the generous individuals from the Gülen Movement in Turkey and the UK who allowed me to research their lives and communities as well as the institutions in which they work. The book could not have been written without their willing co-operation, and I am extremely appreciative of their help. Most of them remain nameless for purposes of anonymity, but I express my thanks to the Journalists' and Writers' Foundation in Istanbul along with the Dialogue Society in London for welcoming my inquiries and providing introductions that were most helpful.

I am indebted to David Shankland of the Royal Anthropological Institute, and formerly of the University of Bristol, for his valuable insights throughout the research. David Barchard and Salman Hameed provided comments on particular chapters, and Joshua Hendrick shared with me general points of wisdom concerning the Gülen Movement. I am also forever grateful to the various personal friends who remain anonymous here but whose enlightening conversations and kind hospitality during my stays in Turkey were greatly appreciated.

My editor at I.B.Tauris, Baillie Card, has provided invaluable feedback and support throughout the process of publication, and I thank her along with the two anonymous peer reviewers who provided insightful comments on the manuscript.

The book is dedicated with affection to my parents, Tony and Joanna Tee.

Turkish Spelling and Pronunciation

The modern Turkish language uses the Roman alphabet, with the exception of the letters 'x', 'w' and 'q'. The letter 'c' is pronounced like the English 'j', 'ç' is 'ch', and 'ş' is 'sh'. The letter 'ğ' is silent, and elongates the vowel that it follows, for example *sağ* (right/healthy) is pronounced 'saah'. The letters 'ö' and 'ü' are the same as in German, and 'u' is a long sound as in the French 'où' (where). The dotted 'i' is pronounced like the French 'i' in 'il', and the undotted letter 'ı' is similar to the ubiquitous schwa sound in English (for example, the letter 'a' in 'about').

The plural form is arrived at through the addition of 'ler' or 'lar' to the noun (e.g. *kız* for girl becomes *kızlar* for girls). For ease of understanding, I have generally pluralised in English throughout the book, so *abla* (older sister) is *abla*s (older sisters) rather than *ablalar*.

Abbreviations

AKDİM	Antalya Kültürlerarası Diyalog Merkezi (Antalya Intercultural Dialogue Centre)
AKP	Adalet ve Kalkınma Partisi (Justice and Development Party)
BAV	Bilim Araştırma Vakfı (Scientific Research Foundation)
CHP	Cumhuriyet Halk Partisi (Republican People's Party)
CUP	Committee for Union and Progress
DİB	Diyanet İşleri Başkanlığı (Directorate for Religious Affairs)
DP	Demokrat Partisi (Democrat Party)
FP	Fazilet Partisi (Virtue Party)
GYV	Gazeteciler ve Yazarlar Vakfı (Journalists and Writers Foundation)
HDP	Halkların Demokratik Partisi (People's Democratic Party)
LYS	Lisans Yerleştirme Sınavı (Degree Placement Exam)
MHP	Milliyetçi Hareket Partisi (Nationalist Movement Party)
MİT	Millî İstihbarat Teşkilatı (National Intelligence Organisation)
MÜSİAD	Mustakil Sanayici ve İşadamları Derneği (Independent Industrialists' and Businessmen's Association)
PKK	Partiya Karkerên Kurdistanê (Kurdistan Workers' Party)
RP	Refah Partisi (Welfare Party)
SETA	Siyaset, Ekonomi ve Toplum Araştırmaları Vakfı (Foundation for Political, Economic and Social Research)
SGK	Sosyal Güvenlik Kurumu (Social Security Institution)
TED	Türk Eğitim Derneği (Turkish Education Association)
TIMSS	Trends in International Mathematics and Science Study
TMSF	Tasarruf Mevduatı Sigorta Fonu (Savings Deposit Insurance Fund of Turkey)

TÜBİTAK	Türkiye Bilimsel ve Teknolojik Araştırma Kurumu (Foundation for Scientific and Technological Research of Turkey)
TÜSİAD	Türk Sanayicileri ve İşadamları Derneği (Turkish Industrialists' and Businessmen's Association)
TUSKON	Türkiye İş Adamları ve Sanayiciler Konfederasyonu (Turkish Confederation of Businessmen and Industrialists)
YGS	Yükseköğretime Geçiş Sınavı (Examination for Entrance to Higher Education)
YÖK	Yükseköğretim Kurulu (Turkey's Higher Education Board)

Introduction

Fethullah Gülen is a Turkish imam and preacher, and the driving force behind one of the world's largest transnational, religiously inspired social movements. Resident in the USA since 1999, he provides leadership to an amorphous entity known variously as *Hizmet* ('service') to its affiliates, *Cemaat* ('religious community') to its critics and detractors in Turkey, and the Gülen Movement to its observers in the English-speaking world. The movement emerged in Turkey in the late 1960s, and today – although it continues to be supported primarily by individuals of Turkish origin, and is still strongly characterised by Turkish culture – it has become a global entity and is present in an estimated 120 countries on five continents.

Gülen's followers are devout practitioners of Hanefi Sunni Islam, which is the majority religious tradition in Turkey.[1] While faith plays a very central role in their lives, however, it is not usually the focus of the movement's public activities. Instead, its major field of engagement is modern education, and it runs a global network of mostly secular, science-focused schools and universities. Gülen's followers are also active in other areas of civil society, including intercultural dialogue, business, the media, private healthcare and charity work. Over the past 50 years, the movement has accrued a significant presence for itself in these various fields, and its total global assets are thought to be in the tens of billions of US dollars.

Islam, Politics and Society in Turkey

Since its foundation by Mustafa Kemal Atatürk in 1923, the Republic of Turkey has been an officially secular state,[2] although almost the entire population identifies as Muslim, following either the Sunni tradition of the majority or the Alevi tradition of the minority.[3] Secularism was disputed by some from the beginning, but only began to be seriously contested in the late 1980s with the rise to power of the Welfare Party (Refah Partisi) under Necmettin Erbakan. Erbakan espoused a political philosophy based on the reintegration of religion with politics and the implementation of the Sharia in place of the secular order. The Welfare Party's ostensibly more moderate successor, the Justice and Development Party (Adalet ve Kalkınma Partisi, AKP), has been in office since 2002, and during that time political Islam has gained further momentum.[4] Today, while Turkey remains mainly secular in official orientation, religion is resurgent in the cultural sphere as well as in many aspects of political life.

The Gülen Movement's emergence has run in parallel to this broader Islamic revival in Turkish politics and society. It has, nevertheless, historically maintained an ambiguous relationship as a religious actor with political power, and in this way is quite distinct from either the Naqshbandi Sufi Order in Turkey or the Muslim Brotherhood in neighbouring Arab countries.[5] Gülen instructs his followers against open political activism, and they are not formally represented within the party-political system in Turkey. This does not, however, mean that either he or his followers are not interested in an Islamised national order. Indeed, this endeavour lies at the very core of the Gülenist project. Rather than pursuing power through the usual, public parliamentary channels, Gülen encourages his followers to attain leverage in areas of civil society and to exert their influence on the political process in indirect ways. They have done this very successfully and, until a crisis with the AKP in late 2013 that has subsequently seen many followers of Gülen dismissed or reassigned, they were strongly represented in the police force, judiciary and media as well as in Turkey's economic sector.[6]

The Gülen Movement has pursued an alternative way for Muslims in modern Turkey to be political, and in so doing has followed in the path of the early twentieth-century Ottoman thinker, Said Nursi (1877–1960).[7] Nursi realised that the opportunities for Islam to assert itself in the Turkish political arena in his day were very few. He lived at a time when Kemalist secular hegemony was at its height, and Atatürk and his associates held a firm grip on political power. Accordingly, in his major theological work, a Qur'anic commentary called the *Risale-i Nur* (Epistle of Light), which he wrote between 1910 and 1950, Nursi advocated a kind of civic activism – referred to as *müspet hareket* (positive action) – that was both non-political and non-violent, yet which actively sought to reintegrate Islam back into the daily fabric of national life. His methods were thus quite different from the open political activism espoused by his contemporary in Egypt, the Brotherhood ideologue Sayyid Qutb (1906–66), as well as by other Islamist thinkers across the wider Muslim world.[8]

Şerif Mardin has spoken of the way in which Nursi worked *through* the cultural framework that had been largely imposed by the republic, restoring the usage of a 'traditional Islamic idiom' through which he sought to re-democratise Turkish society. Nursi thus recognised the need 'to mobilise Muslims as individuals and as members of a community but not as subjects of a political order'.[9] Drawing on its heritage in Nursian philosophy, the Gülen Movement functions today as an ostensibly apolitical community, but one which has managed to accrue significant power and influence. It is the major transmitter of Said Nursi's religious and political ideology in the present day, and the *Risale-i Nur* is the key spiritual and intellectual influence on Fethullah Gülen.

Science and Education in the Gülen Movement

Like Said Nursi before him, Gülen is profoundly interested in the relationship between religion and modern science. Concerned about the relative lack of scientific progress that has been made by Muslim-majority societies in recent times, he exhorts his followers to become familiar with the modern field in order that Muslims might compete on equal terms with their non-Muslim counterparts, mainly in Western nations, while retaining their Islamic faith. Seeking the reinvigoration of religious faith in Turkey specifically, and the modern Muslim world at large, he recognises the major challenges posed to literal religious faith in an age of scientific scepticism.[10] Gülen draws on a Nursian philosophical framework to reconcile the two fields, and legitimises modern scientific enquiry in Islamic terms, arguing in favour of a kind of 'Islamised science'.[11] At the heart of his argument lies the idea that science has been corrupted in the modern era by the Christian Church, which oversaw the emergence and development of secularism in Europe. According to Gülen, the enforced separation of the two spheres that resulted has led to the association of science with atheism, whereas, in his view, there is no contradiction between religious and scientific ways of knowing.

The outworking of his views on this subject can be seen in the dedication of his followers, wherever they are found in the world, to teaching modern science. The schools that the Gülen Movement runs are characterised by their focus on science and mathematics, and, while there are multiple reasons behind their success, they generally achieve high standards in these subjects.[12] Staffed and run by Turkish followers of Gülen who exhibit high levels of personal piety, the schools nonetheless follow a secular model and religious instruction takes place outside the classroom rather than as a staple part of the curriculum.[13]

The Gülen schools represent a way of teaching modern science to apparently high standards within a cultural and religious milieu defined by Sunni Islam. In this sense, they are noteworthy phenomena in the Muslim context, where, notwithstanding substantial regional variations and some notable exceptions, modern experimental science has not developed at the same rate that it has in the West and elsewhere.[14] While a complex web of historical, social and economic factors may be responsible, global league tables nonetheless show that Muslim nations generally rank lower in standards of science education than do their non-Muslim counterparts.[15]

In many Muslim societies including Turkey, the reception of modern, Western science has been bound up with broader and more complex encounters with modernity.[16] Gülen, like many Islamic thinkers before him, has wrestled with the task of separating modern science from its positivist and often atheistic associations, in order to make it a legitimate field of engagement for his devout Muslim followers. In so doing, and in extolling the importance of modern education in parallel, he has opened up a strategic sphere of influence. Modern scientific education is a major feature of globalised, twenty-first-century society, and is a prerequisite for successful participation in a rationalised knowledge economy.[17] The Gülen schools have proven to be able competitors in this contemporary global market, and have done so while retaining their socially conservative and religiously observant outlook. This is a key aspect of their identity, and one which this book explores in some detail.

Aims and Theoretical Approach

The overarching theme of the book is the encounter between Islam, secularism and modernity in the twenty-first century. To this end, I focus on the Gülen Movement and its interaction with the realm of modern science and science education as an illustrative study. The movement has attracted the attention of scholars interested in its significance vis-à-vis Turkish politics, and Gülen's politico-economic philosophy has been explored in detail by Joshua Hendrick.[18] Hendrick identifies 'strategic ambiguity' as the movement's central organisational characteristic, and considers this essential to its successful accumulation of power both in Turkey and abroad. The true scope and operational structure of the Gülen Movement are peculiarly opaque to outsiders, and neither Gülen nor his followers admit to its existence as an organised entity. It is precisely this structural ambiguity that allows the movement to operate within the 'grey area' between the political, civic and economic spheres, and which makes it a unique entity in the study of modern Muslim politics.

The political context provides an essential framework for the present study, yet I am not *primarily* concerned with joining Hendrick in analysing the Gülen Movement from the perspective of its political or economic significance. The subject of my enquiry is, rather, the movement's engagement as a pious Muslim group with the field of modern science and science education. As such, I take as my starting point current discussions in the burgeoning field of the sociology of science and Islam, wherein the reception and application of modern science in Muslim contexts have been the subject of some scholarly enquiry. Both Salman Hameed and Nidhal Guessoum have highlighted the intricacies inherent in translating 'Western' science for a Muslim audience, while at the same time recognising the vast range of views that exist in Muslim societies on subjects such as cosmology, divine action and evolution.[19] Stefano Bigliardi has brought together different attempts to 'harmonise' science and Islam by various contemporaneous

Islamic scientists and philosophers, highlighting a recent turn towards evolution acceptance by a 'new generation' of Muslim scientists and thinkers, although neither Said Nursi nor Fethullah Gülen feature in his analysis.[20]

My approach diverges from these philosophical and sociological studies, and utilises the methodology of social anthropology in order to understand the particular strategies that Gülen's followers employ to negotiate the field of modern science as pious Muslim practitioners, and how they achieve success in it. More broadly, I seek to understand *why* science plays such an important role in the movement, and thus I situate this question within a broader investigation of its civic activities as well as its political ambitions in Turkey. The broad research questions that frame the book are therefore as follows: What are the particular challenges posed to Islam by modern science, and how are these challenges negotiated at an individual and institutional level in the Gülen Movement? In an age of hyper-rationality, how is participation in a modern knowledge economy predicated on access to science education? How has the Gülen Movement's investment in education specifically, and the civil sector more broadly, allowed it to accrue societal as well as political influence in Turkey?

Methodology

The research was carried out in Turkey between the spring of 2013 and the winter of 2014–15. During the research period, a major row developed between the Gülen Movement and the AKP Government under the leadership of then-Prime Minister Recep Tayyip Erdoğan, the dynamics of which are explored in detail in Chapter Eight. Tensions had been rising between the two groups for some time, but reached their full maturation in December 2013 after high-profile corruption allegations were launched against senior figures in the AKP, apparently by prosecutors loyal to Fethullah Gülen. Gülen has since turned from ally to arch-enemy of now-President Erdoğan. Erdoğan, for his part, has launched a comprehensive retaliation, and the movement's assets and activities in Turkey and elsewhere face serious pressure to close down. In the case of the Gülen-controlled Bank Asya, they have been forcibly appropriated by the State.

The failure of the Gülenists public challenge to the AKP government, and the ensuing rupture of their unofficial alliance, has left followers of

Gülen in a much more vulnerable position than they were before the end of 2013. The ramifications of the crisis are still being worked out as this book goes to print, and the movement faces an uncertain future in Turkey. The political situation had implications on my research with movement insiders during this time, and, while I was able to establish contacts and conduct much valuable fieldwork in the preceding months, I noticed a marked change in the climate from the beginning of 2014 onwards, and some participants were less available and generally more guarded in conversation after that time.

My research took place in four different cities in the west of Turkey, and focused on the following collection of Gülen-run institutions: two locally affiliated groups of primary, middle and high schools; two private universities; and three different dialogue platforms. The material was obtained through participant observation and semi-structured interviews with school students and teachers, parents, university students and academics, professional Gülen research scientists, and staff and participants at dialogue events. The two school communities that hosted my research were located in different cities, and in order to preserve the anonymity of my fieldwork participants, I refer to them using the fictitious names Kelebek and Yunus. Each contained a number of mixed-gender primary and middle schools as well as separate high schools for girls and boys. On account of the strict gender segregation practised within the movement, the most fruitful research was undertaken at the girls' high schools – and, for this, the best opportunities presented themselves at Kelebek. It was relatively easy there for me to integrate informally into the (almost) all-female staff and student body, and also to participate in social and religious activities.

It also aided my research at Kelebek to have been introduced through a personal contact, which was very valuable in helping me to quickly gain trust in the community. At Yunus, I was introduced and escorted by a senior member of the movement whom I had contacted to request access, but with whom I had no previous relationship. While this individual was very helpful in facilitating my research, I had considerably less freedom to move around the school premises and talk to individuals than I had at Kelebek. The material obtained from Yunus was nonetheless valuable as a point of contrast and comparison with the other site.

Using the same methods, I also conducted research at two Gülen universities in different cities, where I spoke and interacted with students, administrators and academic staff. Only one of these universities is referred to directly in the text, and I use the fictitious name İrfan – again, for purposes of anonymity. I had had no previous contact with either of these institutions, but at one, its public-relations office was happy to facilitate my research and at the other a senior professor whom I had contacted in advance did the same. At both institutions, I was given freedom to visit the campus at my convenience, participate in classes and other activities and speak privately with students and staff. Gender restrictions were not an issue at the universities in the same way that they were in the school communities, and I engaged with an equal number of male and female interlocutors.

At three other universities, not all of them Gülen-run institutions, I carried out semi-structured interviews with a focus group of five research scientists. These individuals were all affiliated to the movement, and I was introduced to them by a contact at the Journalist and Writers' Foundation (GYV), the movement's main dialogue institution in Istanbul. I also interviewed various senior members of the GYV at its base in Istanbul and in other cities, as well as individuals from different Gülen dialogue institutions elsewhere in Turkey. Some of the discussions that arose from these interviews were continued by email later on. I participated in various dialogue-related activities in Turkey, and also carried out some supplementary research in the UK, where I did the same as well as visiting one of the movement's schools.

Names of individuals have all been changed in order to protect their identities. Locations and institutional names have also been changed as much as possible, although some have been retained out of necessity (e.g. the GYV in Istanbul and the Dialogue Society in London, which are both well-known Gülen institutions). The languages of research were English and Turkish.

Structure of the Book

The book is divided into three parts. Part One is entitled 'Background', and it provides the historical and philosophical context for the Gülen Movement, looking first at the life and times of Fethullah Gülen himself and the structure of the movement that he inspires. It then sets the movement in its wider historical context by analysing the life and work of Said Nursi, in whose tradition Gülen follows, focusing on Nursi's spiritual rationale for worldly engagement generally and science education specifically, and drawing on illustrative extracts from his *Risale-i Nur*.

Part Two is entitled 'Science and Education'. It explores the practical engagement of Gülen actors in science and scientific education, and presents material from fieldwork in Turkey to this end. In Chapter Three, I focus on the strategies for teaching and learning science within an Islamic milieu, and show how the schools achieve success in this field with particular respect to their engagement in international competitions called 'Science Olympiads'. In the following chapter, I consider the Gülen Movement's rejection of human biological evolution, and examine Gülen's teachings on the subject in the context of the emergence of a powerful Islamic creationist movement in Turkey in the 1980s. Chapter Five surveys the futures that graduates of Gülen science-focused schools are being prepared for, with respect to careers in science as well as their continued affiliation with the movement. As such, I investigate the role of alumni networks, and a broader culture within the Gülen Movement of patronage and informal networking.

Part Three, which is entitled 'The Wider Context', examines other aspects of the Gülen Movement in order to show how its activities in science relate to its broader engagement with secularism and modernity. I begin with an analysis of the movement's interest in interfaith and intercultural dialogue, which I explore in light of a threefold nexus of opportunities that these activities provide. I then consider the movement's globalisation with particular reference to the presence of Fethullah Gülen in the United States. Besides being the organisational hub of the movement in the twenty-first century, the USA has also become a major cultural influence on Gülen's followers in Turkey. The book concludes with a chapter dedicated to the subject of the movement's political involvement, which focuses on the rise and fall of a Gülen–AKP alliance over the past 15 years with particular respect to the corruption scandal of 2013 and its aftermath.

The afterword surveys developments since the Turkish general election of 7 June 2015, presenting the implications for the Gülen Movement along with its future prospects in Turkey and around the world.

PART ONE
BACKGROUND

1

Gülen: Leader and Community

Fethullah Gülen is the reclusive and enigmatic figure behind the Gülen Movement. He is an Islamic preacher and qualified imam of the Turkish state who hails from the central-eastern Anatolian province of Erzurum. Since 1999, however, he has lived in self-imposed exile on a rural estate in Pennsylvania, USA. From this secluded location, Gülen provides spiritual direction to a transnational network of followers that has built up, over approximately the past 30 years, a formidable global presence.[1]

Gülen's teachings are transmitted to followers and other interested parties around the world through a variety of media and in multiple languages. He rarely appears in person except to deliver a weekly sermon, which is videoed and streamed on the internet for his close followers.[2] His reclusive lifestyle, and choice to maintain residency in the USA, has been the subject of much speculation and debate. Gülen is reported to live the simple, ascetic life of a Sufi contemplative, and thus to eschew any kind of personal public engagement. This reputation for contemplative piety is greatly admired by his followers, who refer to him as *Hocaefendi* (respected teacher), and is an essential element of his charismatic persona. It is not, however, without its tensions and ambiguities, and detractors question the complex relationship between the pious esotericism of its leader and the accumulation of worldly power and wealth by which the Gülen Movement is easily recognisable.

This question of precisely who Fethullah Gülen is, and what defines the multifaceted movement that he inspires, has puzzled many observers. Who, then, is this man, and what has led to the emergence of a global movement in his name? The brief survey of Gülen's biography that follows will show how he has adopted and developed Said Nursi's ideas concerning science, faith and modernity. It will illustrate how, shaped by the social and political contingencies of twentieth-century Turkish society, these ideas have emerged to define the Gülen project today.

Early Life and Career

Fethullah Gülen was born in the village of Korucuk, Erzurum in 1938.[3] Erzurum is a socially and religiously conservative province, located high on the central Anatolian plateau, within a few hours' drive of Turkey's eastern frontiers with Iran, Armenia and Georgia. Erzurum is therefore a strategic city and has a long military history, dictated in large part by its frontier position in both Ottoman and Republican eras.[4] Military skirmishes with neighbouring powers have been a feature of life in Erzurum for centuries, and have contributed to the development of a regional identity built on strong national as well as Muslim religious sentiment. One of the most recent of these military excursions, the occupation of Erzurum during the Ottoman–Russian wars in February 1916, took place in the living memory of Gülen's older relatives; so too did the first national congress of the new Turkish Republic, held by Mustafa Kemal Atatürk in Erzurum in 1919 during the War of Independence (1919–23).

Typically for the time and place in which he was born, Gülen's childhood in the 1940s and 1950s was characterised by rural, Turkish Sunni Muslim practices and ways of learning. His mother and grandmother appear to have played a particularly important part in shaping him in Islamic piety, and he learnt to recite the Qur'an at home as a child. He attended the first four years of primary school, but thereafter had a traditional religious education in local Sufi *tekke*s. He would complete his primary-school education later on, and graduate in 1958.[5] In the *tekke*s, Gülen received religious instruction from sheikhs of the Naqshbandi Order,[6] of which his father was a member, as well as from the Qadiri Order. On leaving the *tekke*, Gülen continued to pursue his study of Sufism under the guidance of various local sheikhs in Erzurum, where he also embarked on the formal study of Islamic jurisprudence (*fiqh*).

While he was still a young man, Gülen became familiar with the teachings of Said Nursi, the Kurdish-Turkish Islamic thinker whose intellectual tradition he would go on to follow.[7] Nursi was a paradigmatic Turkish modernist thinker who lived between 1877 and 1960. While Gülen never met Nursi personally, he was greatly attracted to the latter's teachings in his seminal text, the *Risale-i Nur* (Epistle of Light).[8] Gülen started to read the *Risale* as a young man at a time when, after many years as an active and influential public figure, Said Nursi had emerged as the inspiration of the so-called Nur Movement. The principle tenet of Nursi's teachings is his vision of a revitalisation of Turkish religious culture, which he saw to be under threat from the rise of scientific scepticism and secularisation in the modern age. He envisaged this religious revival taking place, not through the medium of political activism or violent revolution, but rather through a principle that he defined as 'positive action' (*müspet hareket*). This principle allowed for pious believers to engage with and contribute to society at large in all of its constituent parts, and through it Nursi foresaw a peaceable and effective way of reintroducing Islamic mores back into the public sphere with the ultimate aim of reinstating Islam as the guiding principle of Turkish society.

Nursian principles and the core intellectual themes from the *Risale* are clearly visible in Gülen's own teachings, and his exposure to the text at a young age was a highly significant part of his intellectual formation. Indeed, the *Risale* is a central text for the Gülen Movement today and is read on a regular basis in *sohbet*s (reading groups), which themselves emulate aspects of the Nur tradition from which the movement emerged.

At the age of 18, Gülen passed the exam to become a state-appointed imam, and was sent soon afterwards to work in a local mosque in the European province of Edirne. He remained in Edirne for two and half years, and was posted shortly afterwards to the nearby town of Kırklareli for eight months. After this, in 1965, he was sent to Izmir, where he assumed the directorship of a Qur'anic school attached to the Kestanepazarı Mosque in the city centre. Gülen would remain in Izmir until 1999, when he would leave Turkey to settle in the USA.

Izmir

Life in the urban centres of the west of Turkey was markedly different from the rural, socially and religiously conservative surroundings of Erzurum with which Gülen was familiar. He was uncomfortable experiencing the relatively liberal atmosphere of these western provinces, and particularly the easy availability of alcohol and the freedoms demonstrated in the lifestyle and clothing of women. Indeed, his preference upon leaving Kırklareli was to be posted back to a more conservative part of the country, rather than to Izmir, and he is reported to have objected to his employer, the Directorate of Religious Affairs, saying, 'Izmir will swallow me up. If it's possible send me to a small province in the East.'[9] He was sent nonetheless, and it was in Izmir that the vision of a reinvigorated Islamic society – which had its genesis in Erzurum when Gülen was a young man, and in his reading of Said Nursi – would reach its full maturation.

Gülen began to attract a following as a result of his public preaching and teaching in the late 1960s. As well as preaching regularly at the Kestanepazarı Mosque in Izmir, he began to visit local coffee houses to preach, and his message started to reach a wider demographic than the already religiously observant sectors of the community. By reaching out beyond the traditional catchment of pious individuals, Gülen sought to take his message of moral and spiritual reform to a broader group of listeners in the public sphere. The teachings of Said Nursi constituted the foundations of his message but, significantly, Gülen's presentation of those teachings focused on their practical enactment in the local context of 1960s Izmir. He set out to show his early audience of students, small-business owners and tradespeople how religious piety might complement, rather than compromise, their professional activities and successfully be enacted in their various spheres of worldly influence.

A major factor behind Gülen's success in these early years was his charismatic oratorical style, which is still very much in evidence today in his online sermons; his use of a rather archaic Turkish is quite distinctive and he has an extremely emotional style of delivery, which often results in him being overcome and crying while preaching. This tendency to display emotion, for which he is well known, is greatly admired by his followers and is interpreted as a sign of sincerity and spiritual depth.

The Genesis and Growth of a Movement in Education

In the late 1960s, Gülen and a burgeoning group of followers who were attracted to his teachings started to organise summer revision camps in Izmir for local high-school and university students. These early camps, which were the prototype for the global network of private schools that the Gülen Movement operates today, were inspired by Gülen's vision for the education of a 'golden generation' (*altın nesil*) equally well in modern science as in knowledge of Islam and Islamic ethics.[10]

This distinctive educational vision can be traced back to the thought of Said Nursi, who attempted in his own lifetime to establish a university teaching both the secular and the religious sciences in the eastern city of Van. This plan encountered opposition from the State and was never realised, but the philosophical seed for the conception of such a project is contained within the pages of the *Risale*. Gülen articulates this educational vision in the following way:

> As stated by Bediüzzaman [Nursi], there is an understanding of education that sees the illumination of the mind in science and knowledge, and the light of the heart in faith and virtue. This understanding, which makes the student soar in the skies of humanity with these two wings and seek God's approval through service to others, has many things to offer. It rescues science from materialism, from being a factor that is as harmful as it is beneficial from both material and spiritual perspectives, and from being a lethal weapon. Such an understanding, in Einstein's words, will not allow religion to remain crippled. Nor will it allow religion to be perceived as cut off from intelligence, life, and scientific truth and as a fanatical institution that builds walls between individuals and nations.[11]

The Izmir camps were initially all-male; they were staffed by volunteers and their publically stated aim was: 'To ensure, in the setting of the natural world, the spiritual and physical development of students who are scattered to their villages for three months, and [thus] to continue their education without a break over the summer months'.[12] They were characterised by a culture of strict discipline. The inculcation of Islamic ethics is a crucial component within Gülen's educational vision, and typically takes place through the lived example of Gülen educators and their demonstration of meritorious ethical practices:

> The future of every individual is closely related to the impressions and influences experienced during childhood and youth. If children and young people are brought up in a climate where their enthusiasm is stimulated with higher feelings, they will have vigorous minds and display good morals and virtues.[13]

In Gülen pedagogy, then, the role of the teacher is twofold. The transmission of scientific knowledge is one aspect of the teaching vocation, but of equal importance is this informal mentoring of students in Islamic ethics and morality. The latter endeavour is not limited to the classroom setting but extends to extra-curricular time and space where close personal relationships are formed between teachers and students.[14]

Early Expansion of the Movement

In the 1970s, Gülen's fledgling group of followers began to establish a presence outside Izmir, and opened further summer camps as well as dormitories and after-school revision centres (*dershane*) in other Turkish cities. In the 1980s, changing circumstances in domestic politics and their impact on Turkish society at large had an important effect on the development and growth of the young movement. Its activities expanded dramatically during this decade following the military coup of 1980 and the new constitution of 1982, events which ushered in an era of economic liberalisation under the leadership of prime minister Turgut Özal.

The tenor of Turkish society shifted markedly in the 1980s, and the previously hegemonic authority of the self-consciously secular state began to concede to counter-hegemonic voices, namely those speaking for Islam.[15] This followed a decade of severe unrest and social polarisation in the 1970s, during which time violent clashes between right- and left-wing factions were common and the loss of life had been considerable. The military coup of 1980, under the leadership of General (subsequently, President) Kenan Evren, sought to bring an end to this chaotic situation, and did so by ushering in an intellectual doctrine called the 'Turkish–Islamic synthesis'.

Conscious at the time of internal currents of leftist dissent exacerbated by the keenly felt threat of Soviet communism on Turkey's near borders, the 'Turkish–Islamic synthesis' paved the way for Islam to re-emerge in the public sphere, and to be recognised as the key unifying feature of the Turkish nation. The size and scope of the Directorate of Religious Affairs (Diyanet İşleri Başkanlığı) was accordingly increased during this period, and religious themes began to resurface in various areas of national life.

During this decade, therefore, the followers of Gülen benefited from new social and economic conditions that were highly favourable to the flourishing of their schooling project. Private 'Gülen schools' were established in cities all over Turkey during this decade, including those that are still considered the most prestigious and academically successful today.[16]

Followers of Gülen were also active in the 1980s in other fields. It was during this decade that they began to invest in business as well as the media, interests which today represent a significant share of the movement's total financial and cultural assets.[17] In the 1990s, the group started to branch out overseas, primarily in the field of education but also in these other constituent areas. The first countries that the movement expanded into were the newly independent states of Central Asia, where Gülen's followers capitalised on the emergence of new markets following the collapse of the Soviet Union in 1991.[18] They did so to some extent in collaboration with the Turkish state, which, under the prime ministerships of Özal and later Tansu Çiller, was itself seeking to build on the cultural ties between Turkey and the Central Asian peoples and to establish itself with a diplomatic and trading presence in that part of the world. The movement grew rapidly internationally during this time, and by the end of the 1990s it had schools and business interests in approximately 80 countries around the world.

During the 1980s and 1990s, Gülen attracted support from a new generation of pious Anatolian businessmen who established themselves during this period as successful manufacturers and exporters. Known colloquially as the 'Anatolian Tigers', they emerged from religiously and socially conservative, medium-sized towns such as Kayseri, Adana and Afyonkarahisar. These pious entrepreneurs successfully capitalised on newly liberal economic conditions instigated after the 1980 coup, and joined a financially elite class in Turkey that had previously been largely off-limits to religiously minded people in the Anatolian hinterland.

This new phenomenon in Turkish business and industry was, in turn, institutionalised. In 1971, TÜSİAD (Turkish Industrialists' and Businessmen's Association), a staunchly secularist business confederation dedicated to the principles of Kemalism, had been established by members of Turkey's old industrial class. In 1990, MÜSİAD (Independent Industrialists' and Businessmen's Association) was founded by a new group of pious Turkish businessmen. It served as a religiously minded alternative to TÜSİAD, and has focused particularly on cultivating closer trade links with the Muslim countries of the Persian Gulf and the wider Middle East. Industrialists who were followers of Gülen later established their own Gülen collective known as TUSKON (Confederation of Businessmen and Industrialists in Turkey) in 2005. The Gülenists thus separated from MÜSİAD, and TUSKON has become a transnational organisational umbrella, under which the businesses that are affiliated with the Gülen Movement come together for regular trade summits and networking.[19]

Gülen's Move to the USA and the Globalisation of the Movement

Partly as a culmination of domestic political shifts in the 1980s, the 1990s saw the rise to power in Turkey of the Islamist Welfare Party (Refah Partisi), which was in office between 1996 and 1997 under the leadership of prime minister Necmettin Erbakan.[20] Erbakan and his government left office after a so-called 'post-modern coup' in 1997, which aimed to restore Turkey's constitutionally secular principles to the national order. Gülen had not openly lent his support to the Welfare Party, choosing to retain his distance from the political Islamism of Erbakan's group in much the same way that Nursi had kept his distance from Adnan Menderes and the Democrat Party (Demokrat Partisi) in the 1950s.[21] However, in the tense atmosphere of the anti-Islamist period that followed the 1997 coup, Gülen was also implicated. He was wanted by the authorities for his involvement in what were perceived as anti-secular activities of his own, and a warrant was issued for his arrest.

In 1999, Gülen left Turkey for the USA. The charges against him were later lifted yet he has chosen not to return, always citing poor health as his reason for preferring to remain in the US. A popular additional narrative amongst his followers, which he himself endorses, is that he chooses to stay away in order not to risk the 'destabilising' effects on the country that his return might invoke. Certainly at the time of writing and particularly since late 2013, when the Gülen Movement became involved in an ongoing and acrimonious public conflict with the ruling AK Party, the complexities surrounding Gülen's possible return to Turkey are greater than ever.

The decade following Gülen's move to the USA witnessed the movement's fuller global expansion, as well as the rapid development of its activities in the US itself. While Turkey remains central, the movement now manages a sizeable portfolio of interests in the USA, including a number of major dialogue platforms (namely, the Rumi Forum in Washington, DC and the Gülen Institute in Houston), and somewhere in the region of 150 charter schools.[22] In the past decade and a half, it has also expanded its global activities to an estimated 120 countries around the world, ranging from Europe[23] to South America and from Southeast Asia to Sub-Saharan Africa,[24] where it now runs a global network of schools, medical facilities, dialogue platforms and business interests.[25]

Gülen's Teachings: Core Themes

Gülen is a social activist and in some senses an entrepreneur, but primarily he is a teacher and preacher of Islam. His interpretation of the Sunni tradition is distinctive in a number of ways, and it is strongly influenced by the mystical conceits of Anatolian Sufism.[26] He has written four books that address Sufi themes directly, although the same Sufi idiom pervades all of his writings and sermons on other topics.[27] This is an area of Gülen's work in which he diverges somewhat from the precedent set by Said Nursi. The heavy emphasis on Sufi themes, and especially on the Sufic concept of love, is particular to Gülen and not something that is developed in the same way in Nursi's *Risale*.

Gülen's followers point out, however, that his reliance on mystical themes and ideas in order to communicate with his readers is entirely consistent with the Turkish cultural and religious context from which he emerged. Sufism has been a central component of the Islam practised in Anatolia since Ottoman times, when *tarikat* (Sufi brotherhood) activity characterised every level of society for hundreds of years. The official abolition of the *tarikats* in the 1920s may have dramatically reduced their presence in public life, but the language and motifs of Sufism have continued to occupy a central place in Turkish Muslim consciousness, be it through familiarity with the Anatolian folk poetry of Yunus Emre or the learned wisdom of the great Konya-based mystic Mevlana Rumi.

It is therefore within this framework of a broadly familiar Sufi cultural tradition that Gülen communicates. Central to Sufi thought is the concept of love: love for God and the desire, ultimately, to be united with him. Love is also a central motif in Gülen's theology:

> Love is the most essential element of every being, and it is the most radiant light, and it is the greatest power; able to resist and overcome all else. Love elevates every soul that absorbs it, and prepares those souls for the journey to eternity. Souls that have been able to make contact with eternity through love exert themselves to inspire in all other souls what they have derived from eternity. They dedicate their lives to this sacred duty, a duty for the sake of which they endure every kind of hardship to the very end, and just as they pronounce 'love' with their last breath, they will also breathe 'love' while being raised on the Day of Judgment.[28]

Through the prism of this Sufic interpretation of love, Gülen articulates his vision for the betterment of humanity. This is a key concern that underpins his social and religious teachings, and which has become gradually more expansive and ambitious over the past 50 years of his life and career. Love of God plays a crucial role in Gülen's thought, and love of others for the sake of God is also ascribed great importance. Altruism, which is highly praised, is therefore rooted by Gülen in Islamic spirituality and defined as, 'devoting oneself to the lives of others in complete forgetfulness of all concerns of one's own [;] it is self-annihilation in the interests of others'.[29]

While Gülen draws frequently on Sufi-inspired ideas, and often references poetry from the mystical canon in order to elaborate his teachings, he is clear to distance himself from the organised nature of Sufism, namely its *tarikat* structure. His followers are also often at pains to point out that their movement is not a Sufi order, appealing to two points of evidence: first, the absence in the Gülen Movement of any kind of ritual religious practice, something that is a central element of the Sufi orders; and second, the lack of initiation rites or clear demarcation of membership or belonging. Indeed, Gülen's vision far exceeds the scope of a Sufi *tarikat*. Rather than being introspective in the traditional way it is outward-looking and preoccupied with the engagement of pious Muslims with the world around them rather than esoteric seclusion from it.[30]

The trope of love for God and humankind in Gülen's thought provides the context for his articulation of Said Nursi's doctrine of positive action (*müspet hareket*). This concept provides the essential framework for Gülen's understanding of how Islamic faith might best be enacted in the modern age, and is based on the moral responsibility of believers to make a positive contribution to society in the service of Islam. The ultimate aim of positive action is the restoration of religious values to modern society, which is perceived in the Nursian (and Gülenist) imaginary to be under threat from secularisation and accompanying forces hostile to religion. Unlike other modern Muslim revival ideologies, however, which have espoused political activism and even violent revolution, positive action is a peaceful, apolitical and non-confrontational endeavour. It therefore requires of believers that they contribute to the preservation of public order and stability rather than directly challenge the status quo. The principle of positive action is explained in the following terms by a movement insider in Turkey:

> In every society you might find radical challenge and violent movements – in the USA, Africa, Russia, everywhere [...] But, speaking about this movement, it is not anti-systemic. It is not a protest to the existing norms, authorities, state, tradition – and I am talking about every country in which it is present. In every decade of its maybe four-decade lifespan it has been non-contentious, non-violent. This is *müspet hareket*, in Hocaefendi's terminology.[31]

Structure and Organisation: Defining the Gülen Movement

The Gülen Movement defies easy categorisation, and points of comparison with other religious organisations or ideologies are hard to find. The movement is ambivalent about labelling itself, and tends to reject the suggestion that it is an organised movement (*hareket*) at all. Insiders talk instead of the movement as *Hizmet*, which literally means 'service' and refers, in this usage, to the application of the abstract, philosophical concept that they say lies at the heart of Gülen's vision of a better world. The Islamic rationale for this concept is sometimes made explicit and sometimes not.

Gülen's own role within the movement is also the subject of considerable ambiguity. He is presented not as the head of an organised, hierarchical structure, but rather as an 'inspiration' to a loose network of altruistic volunteers who are united only by their commitment to universal principles of civic and humanitarian service. Insiders typically play down their connections with one another, and a common assertion is that there is no 'organic connection' (*organik bağlantı*), by which is meant an official tie, between them.

Joshua Hendrick has called this tendency towards opaqueness about the movement's operational structure 'strategic ambiguity', and links it to its emergence in late-twentieth-century Turkey when limitations were in place on public religious identities.[32] It has attracted scepticism amongst detractors, who find it hard to countenance the spread of institutions and initiatives all around the world that bear the hallmark of Gülen and yet recognise no central organisational structure and have no official affiliation.[33] These sceptics tend also to question the presence of an Islamist agenda at the movement's core, and find unconvincing the claim that its interests and aspirations lie purely in the realm of civil society. In this vein, in Turkey it is common for unsympathetic outsiders to use the term *cemaat* (religious community) to refer to the movement, in a somewhat pejorative sense. The term *cemaat* has connotations of subversion, in that it refers to religious groups that are still legally banned under the 1925 law that forcibly closed the Sufi *tarikats*. Movement insiders argue that it is an inappropriate label partly because of its association with religious ritual activity, which is not a feature of the movement, and partly because of its closed, sectarian implications, which Gülenist actors invariably seek to play down.

The ambiguity surrounding the movement and the identities of its affiliates has lessened to some extent since the eruption of a public conflict with the AK Party at the end of 2013. Insiders have become rather less insistent on stating publically that the movement is not, in fact, a movement at all, and have discarded some of their earlier guarded reserve on this subject. They still, however, refer to *Hizmet* rather than using the term Gülen Movement, which is largely an appellation used in external, English-language sources – and for this reason is the one used here. Insiders fluent in English might talk comfortably of 'the movement' in interviews in that language, reflecting their familiarity with the growing discourse and body of literature on Gülen in the West, but in Turkish they almost always revert back to simply '*Hizmet*'.

Degrees of Affiliation: Core Affiliates

It is impossible to say precisely how many individuals are involved in the Gülen Movement, although an extremely approximate estimation might put the number of close affiliates of Gülen in Turkey somewhere between 500,000 and 2 million people. This ambiguity arises partly because there is no official criteria for belonging; there are no initiation rites and no clear membership status. It is also partly because individuals may be involved in different capacities and with greatly differing degrees of commitment. The movement is characterised by a multi-tiered nexus of engagement, with three degrees of involvement. A broad framework of this kind has previously been identified by Hendrick, who argues for a four-tiered model of affiliation: Gülen and the movement's 'aristocracy' at its core, surrounded at incrementally increasing distance by 'friends', then 'sympathisers' and finally 'unaware consumers'.[34] While the findings of the present research broadly concur with this model, I suggest slightly different terms of categorisation and delineating criteria.

At the heart of the movement is a group comprising dedicated and loyal followers of Gülen, (males only) some of whom may reside with him and receive religious instruction on his ranch in Pennsylvania, but the majority of whom live elsewhere. These individuals are committed disciples and keen consumers of Gülen's teachings, either through personal contact or from a distance through print and digital media. They usually work or study in a Gülen institution of some kind, and are fully dedicated in every aspect of their lives to the furtherance of the movement's vision. These individuals display Muslim piety through their lifestyle, personal conduct and dress. Women adopt the modest, *tesettür* style of clothing that is favoured by conservative, mainly urban women across Turkey, and men often wear smart suits and ties. Interpersonal conduct is regulated by strict codes of Islamic morality, and contact with the opposite sex is usually limited to verbal greetings and minimal interaction.

Individuals within this core group of movement affiliates express a strong commitment to the principle of dialogue, and are consequently generally very open to engagement and conversation with outsiders. The public persona that is projected is extremely affable and helpful. The values of tolerance, hospitality and hard work, which are lauded in the work of Gülen, are scrupulously embodied by the members of this core group, who strive to apply those teachings on a practical level in their daily lives. The motivation for living in this way is described by Zehra,[35] a committed follower of Gülen and a teacher at a Gülen school in Turkey:

> You're not only Muslim when you're praying, you're Muslim when you're living – 24 hours a day. That's why I love him [Fethullah Gülen] so much, and that's why I'm working here in this school. Because it's something related to a sociable life, you know? I want to do something for this society. That's why I'm working here.[36]

This core group of committed individuals like Zehra is surrounded in more peripheral roles by a contingent who might be best described as sympathisers (*onaylayanlar*), who are active yet more casual supporters of the Gülenist vision and the movement's activities. This group includes, significantly, businessmen of a pious disposition who lend critical financial support to the movement's projects. It also includes individuals who might attend, either regularly or sporadically, the events known as *sohbet* (literally, 'conversation'), at which the books and sermons of Fethullah Gülen are studied and expounded by followers in conjunction with the *Risale* of Said Nursi and the Qur'an.[37]

The largest and most peripheral stratum of participation in the broad Gülen project is occupied by those who consume the products and services offered by Gülenist institutions, and who may or may not be cognisant of the connection of those products and services to the movement. These might include readers and viewers of the various print, digital and visual media channels run by the movement, clients in the banking and insurance sector, patients in Gülen-run medical facilities, and parents of children studying at Gülen schools. Within Turkey, it is most likely that these consumers are aware to some extent of the Gülenist origins of these products, but outside the country it is possible that these parents and consumers are not necessarily aware of the existence of Fethullah Gülen or such a thing as the Gülen Movement at all.

Hizmet and *Himmet*

Individuals in the core group generally make up the majority of the staff at the various initiatives and institutions that are connected to the movement – and these include private businesses, media outlets, medical facilities, dialogue platforms and, perhaps most importantly, the movement's network of schools. The teaching profession is afforded very high status by Gülen, who considers it a 'holy vocation' and a central aspect of the wider project of service (*Hizmet*). It is therefore common for core movement affiliates to spend at least a limited period of time during their working lives serving as teachers in one of the movement's schools. The value of offering a contribution to the Gülen educational project is also felt by some alumni, who commonly return to their alma mater to offer private tuition to gifted students in their own field of excellence – usually science or mathematics. The importance of education is therefore very keenly felt across the movement, and making a personal contribution as educators is something that is highly esteemed and encouraged.

Individuals who continue their careers as teachers are typically rotated around different schools on a fairly regular basis; approximately every three to four years. For others, opportunities may be presented for work in other businesses and institutions that are run by fellow-followers of Gülen. This network of patronage and cooperation offers potentially very many opportunities for those within the core group, although the practice of regular rotation of many staff means that the personal preferences of the individual generally remain largely subordinate to the demands and expectations of the larger Gülenist group.

The principle of *Hizmet* shapes and directs the activities of the core group of movement affiliates, and is accompanied by the complementary principle of *himmet*, a Turkish word that in common usage means 'benevolence' but in Gülenist terminology denotes charitable giving. Similarly to *Hizmet*, which requires core group followers to give of their time and energies in the service of the Gülen vision, *himmet* requires the donating of one's own financial resources and assets to the cause. In the case of the core group, it is therefore common for a percentage of one's salary to be regularly siphoned off and re-routed to a Gülen project or institution, although the precise amount that is given appears to vary and is typically rather hard to ascertain.

Himmet represents an interesting reinterpretation of the Islamic practice of almsgiving, which traditionally requires believers to give up to 2.5 per cent of their total worldly assets each year in the service of Islam, and which is generally directed, if not through the State, then through a local mosque or a religious organisation of some kind. In the case of the Gülen Movement, the beneficiaries of tithing, or *himmet*, are rather different. Indeed, Gülen's exhortation to his followers to 'build schools, not mosques' is now well known, and encapsulates the emphasis within the movement on engaging with areas of civil society that are not considered traditionally to be arenas for 'religious', or 'religiously-inspired', activity.

The practice of *himmet* is not limited to the group of core affiliates within the movement, but extends also to those who retain a more distant position from Gülen and are recognisable as 'sympathisers'. Many of the individuals within this group are business entrepreneurs of a pious persuasion who contribute financially to movement projects and activities, either through cash donations or by making assets available for Gülen purposes. For example, a businessperson in possession of a plot of land might lease it free of charge to a group establishing a new Gülen school, or they might equally well contribute towards the financial overheads of establishing and running the institution.

In the same vein, the new generation of Gülen private universities – which have begun to emerge in Turkey and elsewhere since around 2010, and are discussed in detail in Chapter Five – are mostly established and funded in this way; the major investor or investors behind these institutions are not necessarily closely aligned with the movement or members of Gülen's core group of followers. Rather, they tend to be religiously observant individuals who are broadly sympathetic to the Gülen cause of furthering the market share and public visibility of pious Muslim actors in modern Turkish society, and for whom working with others of a similar, socially conservative mindset is an attractive option.

Hidden Hierarchies

One of the defining features of the Gülen Movement at the level of its core affiliates is its hierarchical structure. This is one of the key features that distinguishes the activities of those who are within the core group from those who maintain a more peripheral role. While this hierarchy is generally played down by movement insiders, who typically emphasise the absence of any kind of organised structure linking individual followers of Gülen or initiatives that he inspires, it is nonetheless clearly present.

Responsibility is assumed at different levels by so-called '*abis*' (*ağabey*, literally, 'elder brother') and '*ablas*' (literally, 'elder sister'). These terms are common in daily usage in Turkey, and besides being used in the familial context are also polite but familiar ways of addressing a friend or acquaintance who is senior to oneself in age. In the Gülenist context, these terms denote persons ascribed with a certain degree of responsibility and seniority within the hierarchical framework of the movement. At the lowest level, an *abi* or an *abla* might be charged with leading one of the movement's ubiquitous student houses (*ışıkevi*, literally, 'house of light'), and with the pastoral oversight (generally denoting moral and religious formation) of the small group of students who are resident there. In turn, each *abi* or *abla* is him- or herself under the guidance of a more senior *abi* or *abla*, whose areas of responsibility become incrementally larger as the scale progresses: the faculty of a university, a university itself, a particular neighbourhood or city, a region, and finally an entire country. The *abi/abla* network ensures that there is a system whereby communication can travel down from the highest level – Gülen himself – to individual followers in the movement in Turkey and around the world.

An insight into the functioning of the system was obtained in an interview with an unusually candid junior *abla* named Ayşe on a university campus in Turkey. The following extract reveals that the opaqueness of the movement is not limited to its engagement with outsiders but also characterises its internal dynamics:

CT: *How did you become a house abla (ev ablası)?*

Ayşe: All of my housemates left the house, and they didn't want me to stay alone in the house. I was doing all of the administrative tasks anyway, paying the bills, and so on [...] So they called me and said, 'Congratulations! You've been chosen to be an *abla*'. One of my senior *abla*s (*üst ablası*) called me to tell me. I have two foreign students: one is from Indonesia and the other from Turkmenistan. The other two are Turkish. There are some difficult things of course, but this was the same before I was an *abla*.

CT: *And how were you chosen for the role?*

Ayşe: Actually I don't know the process. I imagine they asked a lot of the senior *abla*s whom they recommended, and they suggested a name. But I wasn't aware of this selection process going on. They just rang me to tell me the news. So I moved my belongings in [...]. This is my sixth house in two years. Hopefully I will stay there, but I think I might be changing my service (*Hizmet*). Actually, being an *abla* isn't really suited to me [...] I can't be strict enough with people. I tell them one time or twice but after that I don't like hurting them. I will know in two weeks what my next job is, but I don't know now. It will be a surprise.[38]

The *abla* interviewed here clearly had very little knowledge of the workings of the movement's internal hierarchy herself. In a subsequent interview carried out two days later, she reported that her role had indeed been changed by her superiors, and she was now responsible for coordinating social events for the female students involved with the movement in her university faculty.

For those within the hierarchical structure characterised by the *abla/abi* system of oversight, life is strictly regulated and commitment to the movement's values and principles is expected to be extremely high. Ayşe elaborated on this in a joint interview with two other students, one of whom (Banu) was affiliated with the movement and another of whom (Melike) had previously been but had since chosen to distance herself. All three students dressed according to the modest *tesettür* style, and projected a pious Islamic image.

CT: *Do you receive support from somewhere to be a house abla (ev ablası)?*

Ayşe: There is always my senior *abla* (*ust ablası*). She is always immediately ready to help, to talk to my students – she will warn them about how they are speaking to me, or how they are behaving [...] Also, financially if there is a need she will help. She is a student too, of literature. You can go wherever and there is an *abla* to help you. I am rather lucky because I really love my *abla*.

Banu: I was in a (Gülen) house too, but I left. I am still attached to the movement though, and really want to join a house again. Actually, I want to join Ayşe's house because she is a really good *abla*.

CT: *Can you request Ayşe's house in particular? Who do you ask?*

Banu: No. You have to ask the senior *abla*, and she will decide. Actually, they don't like students from the same department to live together – because they think if you get on well in the department then keep it that way and don't live together.

CT: *What do you like to do in your free time?*

Melike: I watch soap operas, listen to music, go into town (*geziyorum*), and I like to go to the theatre. I used to act in the theatre when I was in high school, but when I came to university I had to become more serious and so I stopped. Now that I am covered, it is hard...

Ayşe: I don't have free time. Being a house *abla* keeps me busy. I spend my time at school. There is no TV in the house, so I read the newspapers for news.

Banu: I watch TV. I like old soap operas [...] and I read the newspapers.

CT: *What happens when there is an event or a festival* (şenlik) *at the university? Do you come?*

Banu: The *ablas* patrol them to check there are no *Hizmet* girls there. Covered girls should not be dancing and jumping around with boys to music.

Ayşe: You can't always make the right decision yourself. Sometimes you need someone else to tell you what is right and what is wrong. Also, when you join a house you accept its rules, and one of them is not going to *şenliks*. So why would you agree to this and then complain about it afterwards? Dressing modestly (*tesettür*) is not just about what you wear – it is also about how you behave. The individual conscience is very important.[39]

It was clear from this exchange that the maintenance of high standards of personal propriety is highly valued by members of the core group of movement affiliates. The absence of free time, furthermore, was a recurrent theme in conversation with Ayşe, and the conscious absence of a television set in her student house was apparently typical. The priority of core affiliates is generally to spend their time productively, in earnest hard work and study, and this key trait is visible in every area in which the movement is active.

Recruitment and Alumni Networks

The Gülen Movement has its origins in the educational camps of the 1970s in Izmir, and this project, which was aimed at the moral and intellectual formation of students and young people, remains a central component of its vision and activities today. Thus while the *abla/abi* hierarchies pervade the entire movement, they are particularly significant in the school and university context, which is where the majority of new recruits to the movement are made.

Dormitories and student houses (*ışıkevi*), which are subsidized by donations obtained through *himmet*, serve as incubators for the new generation of affiliates and sympathisers with the Gülenist cause.[40] Accommodation is offered at a very reasonable rate in well-equipped and well-funded houses and private dormitories, which often present an attractive alternative to a student's other options on a limited budget. Their attraction is increased in some instances where socially and religiously conservative parents recognise values that they themselves esteem in the lifestyles of Gülen affiliates, and thus feel more comfortable sending their offspring – particularly their daughters – to live in such 'safe' surroundings. While resident in these Gülen houses, students study the teachings of Gülen intensively, and are mentored – as is illustrated by the conversation with Ayşe – by the house *abla* or *abi* in the practice of Islamic piety and the enactment of conservative morality and behavioural norms.

This network of recruitment often begins before the university years, at the high school level. Students who have attended a Gülen school or tutoring centre (*dershane*) often relate the circumstance through which they were directed by an *abla/abi*, most often a teacher, to a Gülen house within the same network in the city where they have gone on to study at university. There is therefore a keen concern with retaining contact with individuals who have been exposed to the movement and to the teachings of Gülen. This contact is facilitated in large part by the unofficial communication that takes place within the *abla/abi* system, but is also demonstrated by more formal and visible Gülen alumni networks. The headmaster of a Gülen high school in Turkey explained the structure and function of alumni associations, which play an important role in nurturing and maintaining connections with graduates from his school:

Headmaster: After our students graduate from the school we continue to stay in touch with them (*takip ediliyor*). We organise different events (*faaliyetler*) though which we bring them together. They might be in America, England, Australia, Africa [...] we have students everywhere. They stay in touch, and tell us for example, oh, I got married, and had a baby, or [...] For example, pray for me – 'May God be my help' and so on [...] Recently, the child of one of our students was taken ill, and so blood was being sought. I was in Ankara at the time, and I rang fifteen of my friends and told them that blood was required by one of our students. Immediately, they gave some. And so in this way we are like a spiritual family [...] they are like my children, so I won't only see them twenty years from now.

CT: *How do you maintain the contact, apart from through Facebook and social media?*

Headmaster: Through the love in our hearts (*gönül sevgisi*). They know that we expend ourselves for them. It's not just words, it's lived out [...] We have associations for graduates (*mezunlar dernekleri*) through which we maintain contact. Every year, these associations organise a shared meal (*pilav günü*).

CT: *Where do these take place? Here, in this city?*

Headmaster: Sometimes here, sometimes in [a different city in Turkey], where I used to work in an association – they can happen everywhere. The students arrange them and they invite us, so we have the opportunity to see them.[41]

There is therefore a comprehensive set of organisational tools whereby individuals are both recruited to as well as retained within the movement. The interpersonal networks that are established as a result create a context for patronage and support that is vital for the movement's operations and the success of its various projects. Affiliation with this broad and amorphous collective is also an important contributing factor in creating a sense of group belonging, and movement insiders often draw parallels with their experiences of close kinship in the context of family to this end.

Conclusion

The Gülen Movement has emerged over the course of the past four decades to become one of the largest and most powerful religious movements in the world. From its beginnings in central Izmir in the 1960s and 1970s, the message preached by Gülen has since attracted a great number of followers and is now global in its scope and application. Individual followers embody a concern with maintaining Muslim piety and rigorous ethical codes while at the same time engaging with and profiting from the opportunities afforded by modern, global society. One of the most significant arenas in which the movement is engaged in this regard is modern scientific education, and its interest in this field as a religious actor is the central concern of this book. Before we move on to explore this topic more fully, however, we turn in the following chapter to a detailed analysis of the broader historical context that frames the emergence of the Gülen Movement. Particularly, we explore the philosophical foundations of the *Risale-i Nur*, which is studied on a regular basis in the context of *sohbet* (reading groups) and which articulates the movement's distinctive modernist Muslim ideology. The *Risale* contains the rationale for the reconciliation of science and Islam, which is the catalyst for the Gülen Movement's interest in science education specifically and its engagement with the modern world more broadly. We move therefore at this juncture to consider the text and its author, Said Nursi.

2

A Nursian Spiritual Framework for Modernity

Said Nursi (d. 1960) is the major religious and intellectual influence on Fethullah Gülen. Known to his followers as Bediüzzaman (literally, 'the wonder of the age'), Nursi is a paradigmatic thinker within modern Turkish Islam and has had a profound influence on the genesis and development of Islamic currents in Turkey over the past century, not least through the influence that he exerts posthumously. Nursian ideology permeates the Gülen Movement, the central text of which is Nursi's seminal work, the *Risale-i Nur* ('Epistle of Light'). This is a focus of regular discussion groups (*sohbet*) run by core affiliates, which form an essential part of the movement's organisational practice. The teachings of Nursi are also disseminated more indirectly through the writings and sermons of Gülen himself, which, while distinctive in themselves, reflect and develop themes that are conceptually Nursian in origin. In order to understand the Gülen Movement and its engagement as a religious actor with modernity in general and modern science in particular, it is therefore necessary to explore the wider Nursian philosophical school to which it belongs.

The Nur (literally, 'Heavenly Light') Movement had its genesis and emergence during Said Nursi's lifetime, gathering momentum in Turkey in the middle decades of the twentieth century.[1] In subsequent years and after the death of its founder, it split into various sub-groups, each of which is distinctive in its own way but all of which continue to emphasise the study of Nursi's *Risale*. The Gülen Movement is the largest, most publicly visible and influential of all Nur-inspired groups by some considerable margin. It is distinctive not just because of its size but also because of the leadership of Gülen, who lends a dynamic kind of entrepreneurship and social activism – a desire to actively change society in order to facilitate the inclusion and material prosperity of religiously devout actors – which complements and expands the Nursian vision of personal spiritual and religious renewal in the modern age.

Historical Context

The distinctive emphases of the Gülen Movement and the wider Nur community, and the teachings of their respective founders, can be interpreted in many ways according to the social, economic and political circumstances that shaped their respective genesis and growth. Said Nursi was born in 1877,[2] during the dying years of the Ottoman Empire, in the village of Nurs in the south-eastern Anatolian province of Bitlis. The span of his life incorporated some of the most transformational years in modern Turkish history. His generation witnessed the collapse, after 500 years, of Ottoman imperial power, and its succession by the assertively modern and secular Republic of Turkey.[3]

Nursi was a prominent figure in Turkish public life from the early decades of the twentieth century. His primary concern throughout his career was the preservation and regeneration of religious faith in Turkish society as it rapidly modernised and secularised. He saw that the prevalence of European Enlightenment ideas – which underpinned the Kemalist project and foregrounded individual autonomy, rationalist thought and the privatisation of religious practice – posed a very real threat to established Islamic tradition and belief. In order to counteract this threat, he sought to construct and disseminate an intellectually coherent way of maintaining literal religious faith and enacting piety in the modern era. To this end, he focused particularly on the practical as well as philosophical challenges posed to religion by scientific rationalism, which constituted a powerful influence on the secularist ideology espoused by Mustafa Kemal Atatürk and the Republican People's Party (CHP). The reconciliation of modern science and Islam thereby constitutes one of the central themes of the *Risale*, Nursi's seminal text.

Nursi's relationship with political power evolved and changed over time, and he had, for a period, a congenial relationship with both the Republican regime and the Committee for Union and Progress (CUP) that preceded it. When the full extent of the Kemalists' hostility to public religiosity became apparent, however, Nursi distanced himself from the political establishment and went on to spend the final decades of his life in internal exile and imprisonment for his 'anti-secular' activities. Besides Nursi himself, many of his followers spent considerable periods of time in detention for their allegiance to him and their commitment to disseminating his teachings. The early Nur Movement was forged, therefore, against a backdrop of state hostility during an era (1920–50) in which it was self-consciously secular in orientation, and when religious voices were closely monitored and controlled. The legacy of this struggle during the Nur Movement's formative years remains strong today in the consciences of its various sub-groups' adherents, including those belonging to the Gülen Movement.

An inherently tense and antagonistic internal dialogue with official Turkish secularism has, accordingly, defined the Nur Movement since its inception. In this sense, although Nursian thought bears the hallmark of the broader school of modernist Muslim reformism that emerged across the wider Muslim world in his time, its contingency upon the very particular historical circumstances of modern Turkey make it distinctive. Contemporaneous thinkers such as Muhammad Abduh (d. 1905), Sayyid Qutb (d. 1966) and Abul A'la Maududi (d. 1979) were similarly concerned with reviving Islam in the modern age, but were largely preoccupied with repudiating the existential threat of Western colonialism in order to do so. Nursi, by contrast, was focused on an internal challenge that had arisen within his own society. Turkey had successfully resisted the imperialist, Westernising threat posed by the European powers throughout its long history. Instead, building on foundations laid by the Tanzimat reforms of the mid-nineteenth century, which introduced sweeping administrative reforms and modernisation processes, it had witnessed a secular revolution of its own making. The threat identified to faith by Said Nursi was therefore one precipitated not so much by direct foreign influences, but rather by the rapid processes of modernisation, industrialisation and secularisation ushered in by the declaration of Ataturk's republic. This internal dialogue with modernity and secularism in Turkey, and its concomitant tensions, continues to permeate the Nur community in general, and the Gülen Movement in particular, today.

Major Phases of Nursi's Life

Said Nursi's life is generally categorised according to three phases, which indicate the extent to which his thinking developed and, in some important ways, changed over the course of his career. The first phase, which Nursi recognised as the 'Old Said' phase, included his childhood and youth and his life as a young man in the years surrounding World War I and its aftermath. It was a period characterised primarily by political and religious activism, during which time Nursi was highly visible in national public life.[4] His writings and speeches during this period focused on social and political topics.[5] After the Second Constitutional Revolution of 1908, he was an open supporter of the Young Turks, a somewhat surprising alliance but one that was likely precipitated by the promise of political freedom that Nursi saw under their regime. His relationship with the Young Turks and with party politics more broadly soured over time, but it is clear that in the period before the 1920s, the solution to the problems facing Turkish society and the Muslim world more widely was, in Nursi's mind, a political one.

This perspective changed radically in middle age and around the year 1922, when Nursi transitioned to what he identified as the 'New Said' phase of his life. While resident in Istanbul under the occupation of the British in the postwar years, Nursi experienced what he described as a spiritual awakening following a period of personal crisis. In the years that followed, he distanced himself quite radically from open political activism, famously claiming from this point on to 'seek refuge in God from Satan and from politics'.[6] Instead, he emphasised the primacy of the Qur'an as the only valid source of knowledge and the only hope for the future of Islam. His focus during this period shifted from the political to the personal, and he began to emphasise the importance of personal piety to a largely rural, Anatolian audience. He wrote most of the *Risale* during this second phase of his life, which he spent largely under house arrest at the behest of the Republican government, and in internal exile in the west and south-west of Turkey. It was during this period that Nursi began to accumulate a significant following, and the Nur Movement emerged and began to expand across Anatolia.

A third and final phase of Nursi's life, less distinctive than the previous two but nonetheless demonstrably different in certain ways, spanned the years from 1950 until his death a decade later, and is sometimes known as the 'Third Said' phase. This period was characterised by a still limited but, nonetheless, higher degree of open political engagement than was apparent during the 'New Said' phase. Perhaps not surprisingly, it coincided with the election of the Democrat Party (DP) to power in the Turkish Republic's first multi-party elections, an event that heralded the beginnings of a gradual re-emergence of religious themes in public life.

Nursi died in his 80s of natural causes in the province of Şanlıurfa. His body was exhumed shortly after burial on the command of the Turkish state, which feared that the site might become a place of veneration for his followers and thus serve to empower the movement that surrounded him. Nursi's remains were therefore exhumed and secretly reinterred in the west of Turkey, at a location somewhere near the city of Isparta. The narrative within the Nur Movement surrounding these events is that Nursi himself had requested burial in an unmarked location precisely to discourage the potential transformation of his tomb into a shrine.[7] In this instance, then, the actions of the authorities are believed to have inadvertently served the purposes of the Nur Movement itself.[8] Today, the exact location of his burial is still unknown to the great majority of his followers.

Nursi and a New Paradigm for Islamic Renewal

The epithet 'Bediüzzaman' was bestowed upon Nursi by his followers,[9] and reflects their belief that he was one of the promised 'renewers' (*mujaddid*) of Islam who are said to be sent every hundred years to purify and revive religious practice.[10] Nursi was profoundly concerned with the issue of renewal, and with this agenda in mind he became an outspoken critic of the long tradition of *taqlid* (imitation) in Islamic thought. He sought rather to encourage in his followers a kind of faith based on reasoning and individual conviction (*tahkiki iman*) rather than blind adherence to the precedent of tradition (*taklidi iman*).[11]

To this end, Nursi was a strong proponent of popular education, delivered in such a way that it would both stimulate religious faith and deliver scientific knowledge. He instigated an ambitious project during his early career to establish a new kind of university, which would model the teaching of the Islamic and the secular sciences in parallel with one another. The intended site for this institution, which was to be called *Medresetü'z-Zehra* (eastern university) was to be the eastern Anatolian city of Van.

Official support was secured from the central government, along with some financial backing, and the foundation stone was laid on the shores of Lake Van in a place called Edremit, in 1912.[12] Following the outbreak of World War I, however, and the later breakdown of Nursi's relationship with the Turkish authorities, the project was never ultimately realised. Nursi's belief nonetheless remained that education would constitute an essential component in reinvigorating the Muslim world in his day. He was reluctant to diminish the role of Islam within the educational project, yet he recognised at the same time that Muslims needed to engage with and understand developments in the modern world, namely in the field of science, in order for their societies to develop and progress. His vision of an integrated system whereby the two streams would both be taught was not realised in his day, but it provides the conceptual framework for the global educational project of the Gülen Movement today.

Nursi's abandonment of political activism in the 1920s coincided with the increasing hegemony of the Kemalists' secularising policies. The vision for Islamic renewal that Nursi espoused during his 'New Said' years was therefore rather expediently based on a different strategy, for which there are few parallels anywhere else in the Muslim world. Nursi turned his back on politics and rejected political Islamism, a doctrine of the modern era that is derived from the belief that Islam constitutes the ideal blueprint for society and which seeks to establish a religious society governed by the only recognised sources of authority, the Qur'an and the Sharia. Rather, Nursi began to argue that individual Muslim piety could legitimately be cultivated under any kind of social or political system. Such piety was a matter for the individual and was built upon the personal conviction of the believer rather than an uncritical adherence to wider societal norms.

Importantly, however, Nursi did not encourage his followers to withdraw from society. Rather, he developed a doctrine known as 'positive action' (*müspet hareket*), which requires pious Muslims actively to contribute through their attitudes and activities to the stability, prosperity and general well-being of society. It is an inherently peaceable doctrine, which rejects not only direct political activism but also violent revolutionary struggle as legitimate channels for the pursuit of the effective transformation of Muslim society. Nursi's priority was always the reinvigoration of Muslim society and the Islamic faith in the modern day. He made it very clear in the *Risale* and his other writings of the 'New Said' period, however, that he did not believe such a project to be immediately realisable at that time through political channels. Rather, Nursi considered that a grass-roots social and religious transformation of the individual was required first, and that broader social transformation would come later on, when the time and circumstances were right.

Although he rejected the traditional demands and mobilising tools of Islamism, Nursi's approach was not essentially apolitical. During the 'Old Said' years, he had been a vocal supporter of constitutionalism and even during his reclusive years during the 'New Said' phase, he encouraged his followers to vote and to remain active participants in the Turkish political process. After the electoral success of the Democrat Party in the 1950 elections he voiced support, albeit muted, for that party in particular. Nursi's actions at this time laid the foundations for the political philosophy of the Gülen Movement, which, in the late 1990s and early 2000s, lent the same kind of unofficial support to the burgeoning AK Party.[13] This alliance, while now firmly over, clearly benefited both parties for a time. It also revealed that, following the Nursian blueprint, the Gülen Movement deliberately yielded some considerable influence in the Turkish political sphere, albeit through indirect channels.

Nursi also turned away from a major institution that has permeated much of Islamic social history: the Sufi brotherhoods. His knowledge of, and engagement with, Sufism was rather complex. Sufi influences featured prominently in his childhood and youth, and, undoubtedly because of this formative experience, certain Sufi themes pervade his later intellectual thought. His father and many other close relatives were active members of the Naqshbandi Order, which dominated the religious landscape of the Bitlis region in the late nineteenth century. In his early years, Nursi himself was educated in the traditional way by a number of Naqshbandi sheikhs as well as sheikhs from the Qadiri order, and yet he chose never to formally enter either of these or, indeed, any other Sufi order himself. Later on in his career, he explicitly forbade his followers from entering orders themselves.

The explanation for this approach lies in his belief that the institutional organisation of Sufi thought and practice made it an unsuitable vehicle for the perpetuation of Islam in the modern age. Nursi believed that the primary imperative on Muslims in his day was to revive the basic tenets of religious faith and praxis, which he saw to be suffering profoundly from neglect and decay. The pursuit of mystical knowledge through the precepts of Sufism was, as he saw it, a luxury that could not be afforded at a time when many Muslims were unsure even of the fundamentals of their religion. He famously declared on this subject that 'A man cannot live without bread, but he can live without fruit. Sufism is like fruit; the truths of the Qur'an are like bread'.[14]

It was particularly the hierarchical structure of the Sufi orders, and their privileging of sheikhly authority, that Nursi consciously sought to counteract, rather than many of the abstract philosophical precepts of Sufi thought. Nursi's belief was that the kind of wholesale submission to a sheikh that is demanded by the Sufi orders was entirely unsuitable in an age which required intellectual engagement with certain existential challenges – namely, scientific positivism – that threatened to undermine belief in God at all. Much of the *Risale* is therefore dedicated to the exposition of what Nursi considered to be 'rational proofs' for the existence of God and the validity of religious faith, in order to stimulate faith based on logic and reason and manifested through independent conviction and personal devotion in the lives of his followers.

The *Risale* as Text

Nursi therefore rejected two major channels for potential societal transformation in the Muslim world: direct political activism and institutional Sufism. In their place, he proposed an entirely new reformist paradigm and system of thought, which he articulated in the *Risale*.[15]

The *Risale* is comprised of 14 volumes, the most important of which are entitled 'The Words', 'The Letters', 'The Flashes' and 'The Rays'. It is often described as a work of *tafsir* (Qur'anic commentary), yet it is not a traditional *tafsir* in any straightforward sense for it does not follow the traditional technique of expounding the text of the Qur'an line by line. Rather, it offers a thematic exposition of the teachings found therein, an exposition which takes the form of parables, stories and letters with advice given by Nursi in response to questions from his disciples. A key thematic concern is the defence of religious faith and its compatibility with rational thought and logic in the modern day. In this vein, the philosophical reconciliation of science with Islam occupies a central position.

More than a mere record of Nursian ideology, the physical text of the *Risale* occupies a highly privileged position within the circles of his close followers. Nursi's critique of the close interpersonal bond between *mürşit* (guide) and *mürit* (disciple) in the context of the Sufi brotherhoods laid the groundwork for the emergence in the Nur community of a new system of religious organisation. Nursi sought to play down his own charismatic importance to his disciples, encouraging them instead to access guidance and knowledge directly and independently in the words of his text. In this sense, the Nur Movement represents a significant break from earlier Muslim traditions of knowledge transmission, wherein learning has historically been passed down through chains of interpersonal relationships. In the case of the *Risale*, the text itself is associated with the charismatic authority that has historically been the preserve of the sheikh.

The special status of the *Risale*, and its inspired nature, was underscored by Nursi himself. In the following extract, he explains his journey from 'Old' to 'New Said' and its spiritual culmination when he understood the *Risale* to have been 'bestowed' upon him by God:

> Sixty years ago, I was searching for a way to reach reality that was appropriate for the present age. That is, I was searching for a short way to obtain firm faith and a complete understanding of Islam that would not be shaken by the attacks of the numerous damaging currents. First I had recourse to the way of the philosophers; I wanted to reach the truth with just the reason. But I reached it only twice with extreme difficulty. Then I looked and saw that even the greatest geniuses of mankind had gone only half the way, and that only one or two had been able to reach the truth by means of the reason alone. So I told myself that a way that even they had been unable to take could not be

made general, and I gave it up [...] Then I had recourse to the way of Sufism and studied it. I saw that it was truly luminous and effulgent, but that it needed the greatest caution. Only the highest of the elite could take that way. So, saying that this cannot be the way for everyone at this time, either, I sought help from the Qur'an. And thanks be to God, the *Risale-i Nur* was bestowed upon me, which is a safe, short way inspired by the Qur'an for the believers of the present time.[16]

The suggestion that his religious insights were inspired rather than learned lends the *Risale* an unusually authoritative status, reflected in the practices of Nursi's followers and their deep commitment to its study. This commitment is evident in the Gülen Movement as much as any other Nur-inspired group. Individual followers of Gülen read the *Risale* on a regular basis and speak of it with great reverence. One fieldwork participant explained her commitment to reading a portion of the *Risale* every day by stating that she could not do without it because 'it feeds/satisfies me' (*beni doyurur*), and another because 'it is completely unlike any other book'.[17]

A frequently overheard criticism of the movement made by pious Muslim outsiders is that the centrality of the Qur'an itself is undermined by its strong emphasis on studying and understanding the *Risale*. The irony of this situation is not hard to see, given Nursi's stated intention that the *Risale* serve as a companion to the text of the Qur'an in order, primarily, to illustrate the latter's supremacy above all things. This observation was substantiated in the same fieldwork interview with a second informant who had recently left the movement. The reason she gave for her decision to leave was as follows: 'The problem with the movement is that they only study Nursi – they do not put the Qur'an at the centre. This was the same at the camps I used to go to.' For this individual, who had previously been highly involved in Gülen-inspired activities, the *Risale* had assumed too exalted a position and she had chosen to distance herself from the movement.

The heavy emphasis on textual analysis in the Nur Movement has the effect of bringing it into line with broadly 'modern' sociological trends. Its emphasis on literacy and the primacy of the written word as valid and authentic channel of knowledge are phenomena directly associated with the modern era. This emphasis, furthermore, opens up the movement to engagement with democratic processes surrounding access to that knowledge. The text is available to all on the same terms, and privileges no elite or aristocratic class. Both of these characteristics are significant to the Nur Movement and to our understanding of its popular appeal in the twentieth and twenty-first centuries. It is in no small part because of the movement's ability and willingness to operate within the parameters of the modern, literate and rationalist world order that it has been able to attract support and expand so convincingly.[18]

Intellectual Themes in the *Risale:* God and Nature

I turn now to the intellectual content of the *Risale*, and particularly to Said Nursi's proposed reconciliation of modern science with religious faith. This endeavour lies at the heart of the Nursian philosophical project. It is framed by a wider conceptual goal, which is to demonstrate the intellectual validity of religious faith – belief in a transcendent God – in an age defined by scientific rationalism. In this sense, Nursi is challenging foundational Enlightenment ideals, which posit that the human being is fundamentally a free and autonomous being whose existence and ultimate purpose might be made sense of without reference to any kind of metaphysical reality. Can humankind make sense of the world without reference to metaphysical concepts, or indeed to a transcendent God? This is the fundamental question at the heart of the *Risale*, and one that Nursi sets out to comprehensively negate.

He attempts this by positing a religious epistemology in which the concept of *reflection* is absolutely central. In the Nursian schematic, the natural world and everything contained within it can only be rightly understood in light of the attributes of God that it reflects.[19] There is a heavy influence from Sufi cosmology on Nursi in this regard, and he draws particularly on the ideas of ibn Arabi (d. 1240), in which God is said to have created the cosmos (and humankind) as a kind of 'mirror' through which his own attributes are seen and manifested back to him. Nursi advances the Sufic idea to propose a distinctive kind of natural theology. He delineates what he sees as two fundamentally different ways of looking at the material world: one that recognises the nominal meaning (*mana-yi ismi*) of material objects, and another that recognises their indicative meaning (*mana-yi harfi*). In the Nursian vision, the world is viewed from the latter perspective.

That is to say, material objects are understood as pointing to, or reflecting, their creator, rather than having any intrinsic meaning of their own. Nursi is highly critical of scientific materialism, which he says adopts the former outlook and therefore approaches questions of reality from a fundamentally mistaken perspective.[20]

At the centre of this Nursian epistemology of nature is the text of the Qur'an. Nursi imagines a close dialectic between nature and text, describing the material universe as 'a macro-Qur'an' that can only be read and understood in the same way as the text of the Qur'an itself. In this way, he follows a long tradition of religious writers who have elaborated on the 'Book of Nature' metaphor, stretching back to early modern scientists such as Galileo Galilei and Francis Bacon[21] and, more recently, incorporating influential thinkers in contemporary debates in the Muslim world such as Seyyed Hossein Nasr.[22]

As is typical of Said Nursi, he makes use of a parable to illustrate his understanding of the 'Book of Nature' concept, in what is one of the most popular and oft-cited passages in the *Risale*. The parable in question tells of a king who makes a copy of the Qur'an whose words are crafted from precious jewels, and then asks for a commentary on his work from two different sources: a 'philosopher' (a term usually synonymous in the *Risale* with scientific positivism and, by implication, unbelief), and a Muslim scholar. The former, being an expert in jewellery but not in Arabic, misses the deeper meaning of the text and offers an analysis of the material properties of the jewels themselves. The latter, recognising that the words are those of the Qur'an, sees that their significance lies in more than their physical appearance and analyses their meaning rather than the material properties of the jewels from which they are crafted. At the end of the parable, Nursi offers the following explanation and critique of the proponents of scientific materialism, whom he refers to as 'philosophers':

> Indeed, the wise Qur'an is the most exalted expounder and a most eloquent translator of this universe (a macro-Qur'an) [...] It looks upon creatures, each a meaningful letter, as bearing the meaning of another (on account of their Maker) and says: 'How beautifully they have been made, how meaningfully they point to the Maker's Beauty and Grace.' Thus it shows the universe's real beauty. Philosophy, focused on the design and decorations

of creation's 'letters', has lost its way. While it ought to look upon this macro-book's letters as bearing the meaning of another (on account of God), it looks upon them as signifying themselves (on account of themselves) and says, 'How beautiful they are', not 'How beautifully they have been made'. Thus philosophers insult creation and cause it to complain of themselves.[23]

This notion of material objects acting primarily as signs and signifiers of a greater reality is the central component of Nursi's philosophy of nature. When 'read' together with the Qur'an, the natural world is effectively 'sanctified', according to this schematic, and imagined as a site for the remembrance of God, the apprehension of his attributes and spiritual encounter.

The concept of reflection also provides a framework for the Nursian vision of the ideal life of the individual believer. In Nursi's estimation, it is the duty of the pious Muslim, as a part of the created order, to live a life that reflects the creator. Accordingly, at the end of a lengthy section detailing nine 'aims of life', he exhorts his reader to see his/her own life, above all, as a mirror with the potential to reflect the attributes of God:

> Your life is an inscribed word, a wisdom-displaying word written by the Pen of Power. Observed and sensed, it points to the Divine Beautiful Names. What gives your life its meaning and specifies its function is that it is a mirror manifesting Divine Oneness and God's being the Eternally Besought One. Through its comprehensiveness as the focal point for all Divine Names manifested in the world, it functions as a mirror that reflects God's being the Eternally Besought One.[24]

Nursi expands on this idea of human life being 'an inscribed word' reflecting the Divine Names with reference to different ways in which those names may be made manifest in the world. Nursi's vision is typically broad and inclusive in this regard. Rather than delineating areas of life which are 'in' and 'out of bounds' to the pious believer (a conceptual framework that is presupposed by the ideology of secularism), he sees the potential for Islamic sanctity everywhere on the grounds that all of life reflects the attributes of the God who created and sustains it.[25]

It is for this reason that Nursi finds religious legitimacy in the pursuit and application of science. He addresses this theme directly in a section of the *Risale* entitled 'Every science speaks of God in its own tongue'. This narrative, which is a response by Nursi to his students who entreat him to 'Tell us about our Creator, for our [school] teachers do not speak of Him', contains five short parables showing the religious and spiritual significance of the practical application of scientific knowledge. The parables – which talk in turn about a pharmacy, a factory, a food store, an army and a city lit by electric lamps – all illustrate how the effective and orderly application of technical science reflects something of the nature of God, who is the creative and sustaining force behind the natural phenomena of the material universe:

> Each science you study continuously speaks of God, the Creator, and makes Him known in its own tongue. So listen to them, not your teachers. For example, a well-equipped, well-designed pharmacy which has many medicines and pills composed of different precisely measured components certainly indicates an extremely skillful and learned pharmacist. In the same way, to the extent that it is bigger and more perfect than this pharmacy, the pharmacy of the earth, which has countless life-giving cures and medicaments implanted within all plant and animal species, shows and makes known even to blind eyes, through the science of medicine, the All-Wise One of Majesty, Who is the Pharmacist of the largest pharmacy on earth.[26]

In this example, through the pursuit and application of medical science, pious believers can imagine their work to offer a reflection of the fuller, more complete virtues of wisdom and healing that are found in God. In this way medicine and, in the parables that follow, engineering, economics and technology are legitimised according to their potential to serve as reflections of divine attributes: the factory owner embodies skilfulness and productivity; the food store proprietor, organisation and provision; the army commander, attentiveness. All of these characteristics are interpreted as reflections of the attributes or work of God, who is described variously as Manufacturer, Owner, Organiser, Administrator, and All-Holy Commander. The illuminated city reflects the stars and planets of the 'city of the universe', a microcosmic depiction of the 'All-Merciful One's guest-house', which are the earth, sun and stars of distant galaxies.

By positing a direct link between the mundane activities of believers on earth to the cosmic purposes and possibilities of God, Nursi effectively sanctifies all manner of practical worldly activity by infusing it with religious meaning and purpose. Indeed, pious Muslims are exhorted to engage in these fields in order to make God known to the 'blind eyes' of unbelievers. It is the concept of reflection, underpinning the entire Nursian schematic of nature, that allows for this distinctive religious epistemology. The familiar Sufic metaphor of the universe serving as a mirror of God, or Reality, is subtly transformed in Nursi's hands into a vehicle for the wholesale sanctification of modern life according to the Qur'anic world-view. In this way, Nursi addresses the same questions faced by his modernist Muslim contemporaries – not merely by providing immediate solutions to pressing problems such as reconciling Islamic piety with modern science and technology (or indeed with democracy and constitutionalism), but rather by comprehensively re-imagining the manifestation of the sacred in domains of worldly life that had been assumed by the Turkish Kemalist project to be profane.

Gülen and the Nursian Legacy

The influence of Said Nursi is clearly very apparent in the work of Fethullah Gülen, and this influence is openly acknowledged. Most importantly for our purposes, Gülen's commitment to science, and to science education, stems from the Islamic philosophical premise outlined in the *Risale*.[27]

There are, nonetheless, areas of the latter's thought in which Gülen departs somewhat from the Nursian precedent. The clearest point of departure is the greater emphasis on *action* in Gülen's teachings, rather than exclusively on the cultivation of the inner life of the believer that was Nursi's major preoccupation. While Nursi was concerned with legitimising worldly engagement on Islamic terms, his priority was fundamentally to revive religious faith in the lives of his followers, and by extension in society at large. Gülen, by contrast, has a much more aggressive vision for the successful integration of pious believers into modern life. His intention is that his followers actively shape modern society, and that they also prosper and benefit from the opportunities it offers. It is therefore important for Gülen that his followers attain to positions of prosperity and influence, and he teaches that this engagement – usually referred to as *Hizmet* – is the religious duty of today's believing Muslims.

The concept of worldly engagement is not wholly absent in Nursi's work; the doctrine of positive action is itself Nursian in origin. It is, however, much more strongly emphasised and developed in Gülen's work, and its outworking is much more visible in the activities of the Gülen Movement than any other Nur-inspired group. Nursi encouraged his followers to remain present in the worldly system and to try to influence it as their faith required, rather than to retreat from it. Gülen's agenda, by contrast, is much more proactive as well as ambitious.

The reasons for this difference can be located in the different social and political circumstances in Turkey within which each man emerged. For Nursi, writing in the period during which the Turkish state was at its most assertively secular, the possibility of religious individuals expressing their faith in public life was small indeed. This was a time when it was most expedient to focus on the maintenance of personal faith rather than a project to openly influence society with an Islamic agenda in mind. For Gülen, however, who rose to prominence during the 1980s and 1990s, Turkish societal conditions were much more amenable to a project based on social activism and the re-enfranchising and targeted empowerment of a Muslim voice. Turgut Özal himself (prime minister and then president between 1983 and 1993) was a religious man, and the transformations in both economic and religious spheres that he oversaw in the aftermath of the 1980 coup were extremely fortuitous for Gülen and the burgeoning movement in his name.

Gülen was, in many ways, ideally placed from the 1980s onwards to take Nursi's philosophical framework and put it into action in a way that the earlier thinker could not have imagined possible. The following section explores the practical application within the Gülen Movement of Said Nursi's framework for reconciling Islam and modernity, investigating particularly the enactment of piety and *Hizmet* in the context of the movement's science-focused schools.

PART TWO
SCIENCE AND EDUCATION

3

The Gülen Movement's Science-focused Schools

At 9.30 on a wet, winter morning in 2013, I stood in the bustling lobby of a Turkish middle school, waiting to meet İrem, a young chemistry teacher and dedicated follower of Fethullah Gülen. I had first met İrem some months before, and now she had invited me to spend the morning with her at school, observing her classes and chatting with her informally during her breaks. The lobby was full of the noise of bells ringing and children streaming into the school building, leaving muddy footprints and trails of rainwater behind them. At 9.35 am, İrem arrived, smiling as she approached me and looking smart in her peach-coloured headscarf, expertly pinned in place around her face, and tucked in at the neck to her long, beige mackintosh. We headed straight up to the female teachers' room on the first floor, and when the door closed behind us the relative peace of an adult-only space descended, along with the immediate sensation of sororal intimacy that is familiar from gender-segregated spaces in Turkey. İrem began chatting casually with me as she hung up her outer coat and adjusted her headscarf in front of a mirror.[1]

İrem was 26 years old, and from a medium-sized town in the north-west of Turkey. She had studied chemistry at a local university, where she had first encountered the teachings of Gülen and the movement that surrounds him. She had gone on to teach science at one of the movement's schools in Istanbul before being reassigned, against her personal wishes, to her present school, which was some considerable distance away in another part of Turkey. I asked her about her choice of profession, and her feelings about living so far from her family:

CT: *Do you like being a science teacher?*
İrem: Yes! I like the kids a lot, and I like my subject – I'm happy. If I wasn't happy then I wouldn't do it, but because I love it I don't notice the hard things. But it is a hard job […]
CT: *Can you tell me about your family?*
İrem: My father was in the military, but he's retired now. My mother did not work – she was a housewife. We are five siblings; my older brother is a businessman, my sisters are housewives and my younger brother is a banker. They're not in *Hizmet* [the Gülen Movement; literally, 'service'] – they serve in different ways!
CT: *Do you plan to get married one day?*
İrem: Yes, of course, if God wills it […]
CT: *A lot of you teachers seem to be married to one another – do you meet at school?*
İrem: There is no dating in Islam, so usually our families introduce us, and we start to see each other after they introduce us.
CT: *And if your family is not here?*
İrem: If our families are not here, we have some very close friends! For example, Aynur hoca! [she laughs, and indicates a slightly older teacher who is listening to us] This is my spiritual family. My mother came and said that she entrusted me to Aynur hoca. There is a verse in the Qur'an that says you get a reward in heaven for raising a good son or daughter […]

For İrem, teaching was clearly more than 'just' a job. She had been willing to accept a redeployment that she had not sought to a position in a new city far from her family. At the same time, her reference to her colleagues as her 'spiritual family', entrusted with the responsibility of arranging her marriage, suggested that these work relationships apparently extended well beyond the norms of professional interaction and that they indeed had connotations of familial intimacy.

As the bell rang for lessons to begin, she ushered me out of the teachers' room towards her classroom, a spacious and well-equipped facility with various modern technologies including a computer and an interactive whiteboard. Twenty-five students greeted her with a standard chorus of *'sağolun'* (thank you) in response to her *'günaydın'* (good morning). She launched into the lesson, a basic revision session in human biology, drawing on high-quality digital resources and pausing regularly in her presentation to check students had understood the point – which they almost invariably had, being very well-versed in the material.

As I watched her teach, I pondered what it was that motivated this evidently pious young woman to leave her family far behind, for the purpose, apparently, of teaching science in a secular middle school. One might expect sacrifice for one's faith in other forms – charitable work, maybe, or even teaching religion – but it seemed unusual for İrem to devote her life as a religious practitioner to teaching chemistry and biology. Furthermore, what was the precise nature of this 'spiritual' school community of which she was a part?

The Gülen Schools in Turkey

Over the past 30 years, the schools run by the Gülen Movement have become widespread in Turkey. Their precise number is unquantifiable as they do not publically affiliate with one another, but one can assume there are well over 500 of them across Turkey. They are found in the large cities of Ankara, Izmir and Istanbul as well as in smaller towns, and while their concentration is rather higher in the west of the country, they are also present in eastern and south-eastern provinces such as Gaziantep, Siirt and Van. Characterised by high levels of academic achievement, particularly in the natural science subjects, they are strong competitors in the Turkish private-education sector. The schools adhere to the secular national curriculum in the classroom context, unofficially reserving explicit moral and religious mentoring and education for extra-curricular time and space.[2] They are predominantly, although not exclusively, favoured by families of a pious religious persuasion who support the conservative values promoted in the schools. They are also, however, able to appeal to a wider and more diverse social demographic on account of their strong academic credentials and reputations for examination success.[3]

The schools are mostly staffed and run by followers of Gülen such as İrem, who are religiously observant and extremely diligent in their professional roles. I could not ascertain what salaries teachers received, but those whom I encountered lived in modest accommodation and showed no aspirations towards improving their material conditions. Anecdotally, I learned that many of them voluntarily channelled a proportion of their salary back into the school at which they worked, meaning that their average take-home earnings were considerably lower than those of their counterparts in non-Gülen schools. This illustrates an important distinction between the lifestyles of Gulenist teachers (and other 'core affiliates' of the movement such as administrative staff) and the generally much wealthier individuals who support and contribute to the movement in other ways.

The Gülen Movement offers educational provision throughout the entire spectrum of childhood and youth. Its portfolio of institutions includes nurseries, primary, middle and high schools[4] as well as, increasingly, a number of foundation universities. In addition, followers of Gülen are amongst Turkey's most prolific contributors to the market for *dershane* education, a central feature of the Turkish educational system whereby additional coaching is provided to schoolchildren at evenings and weekends.[5] *Dershane*s (literally, 'house of lessons, or learning') are operated by independent practitioners and charge fees for their services. Attendance at one is generally considered an essential supplement to a state education if a student is expected to gain a place at university, competition for which is fierce.[6]

Organisation of the Gülen Schools

The schools, *dershane*s and universities run by the Gülen Movement do not publically identify either with Gülen or with one another at a national level, or share any common name or logo. The schools are generally organised in a localised way, with a small group of perhaps four or five Gülen-run primary, middle and high schools being affiliated with one another in a given city. As with every Gülen Movement initiative, it is not immediately obvious that these are Gülen schools, and awareness of this fact is generally obtained through local knowledge rather than any explicit public markers. That is to say, the Gülen schools resemble in many ways their 'secular' competitors in the private-education market, and the features that distinguish them tend to be located in the unofficial realm (namely, the personal piety of their staff and their undocumented, extra-curricular programmes) rather than the information about their educational product that is made explicit on websites and promotional materials.

The absence of an acknowledged centralised structure, or any formal affiliation with Gülen himself, makes it difficult to identify the Gülen schools in Turkey as a coherent group. This feature is entirely typical of the wider movement, which is always at pains to deny the existence of any kind of organisational hierarchy or central coordination of its various interests and activities.[7] Gülen himself has spoken out to deny the existence of a single educational project, or indeed his role as the choreographer of such a project. Both he and his followers prefer to speak of a loose collection of initiatives that are all 'inspired' by his teachings, but which do not constitute a single coordinated entity.

These comments notwithstanding, there exists an elite group of schools within the Gülen network in Turkey, which are the longest-standing and remain amongst the most academically prestigious today, and which are fairly widely known and openly acknowledged to be Gülen institutions. This group of schools was founded by early followers of Gülen in western Turkey in the early 1980s, and includes Yamanlar Koleji in Izmir, Fatih Koleji (recently rebranded as Fatih Okulu) in Istanbul, Samanyolu Lisesi in Ankara and Nilüfer Lisesi in Bursa.[8] Today, each of these schools operates a franchise system and includes a number of affiliated primary, middle and high schools in their city of origin and sometimes, further afield within their region in Turkey. Fatih Koleji, for example, from its central campus on the European side of Istanbul, operates a group of schools across the Marmara region and as far away as Zonguldak on the Black Sea coast.

Reconciling Science and Faith

Education is a central concern in the thought of Fethullah Gülen. In his books and sermons, Gülen speaks of a bifurcation of modern education that has arisen in the modern era, which he sees as inextricably linked to the secularisation of society and the demise of personal faith. He recognises that any *medrese* system of Islamic education, which focuses entirely on the study of Islamic texts and traditions, is unsuited to a modern age that is defined in large part by scientific progress. Equally, he is dissatisfied with a scientific education that is divorced from religious faith and thereby fails, in his view, to instil moral and ethical values in its students and in their scientific world-views. In response to this situation, his vision is a model of education 'that will fuse religious and scientific knowledge together with morality and spirituality, to produce genuinely enlightened people with hearts illumined by religious sciences and spirituality, minds illuminated with positive sciences'.[9]

Following this philosophy, the Gülen schools offer an educational experience that is unique within the Turkish market, spanning the gulf between religious and secular systems that are otherwise sharply polarised. Their ability to bridge this gulf is contingent largely on their willingness to engage with modern scientific education, and their considerable success in doing so, while retaining their ability to proactively project a pious Islamic identity. Judging from the schools' success, for many in Turkey, this is an attractive combination. While there are certainly those who remain suspicious of the Gülen Movement and its ultimate aims and objectives, there are also plenty who are attracted to the combination of moral and religious conservatism along with the very real possibility of competitive success in modern life.

Turkish School Catchments

Within the Turkish education system, the Gülen schools compete with other fee-paying institutions (often known as *kolej*), which are considered elite and are generally entirely secular in orientation. It is not at all common for these schools to be established or staffed by pious individuals. Rather, they tend to cater to a privileged sector of society that is both economically mobile and generally still strongly committed to the principles of Mustafa Kemal Atatürk's secularising project.[10] These establishments provide the same kind of modern scientific education as the Gülen schools do, but without the option of informal, extra-curricular religious education that the latter provide.

The majority of students at Gülen schools in Turkey come from economically mobile families. The schools do, however, offer a significant number of scholarships to academically able students from less financially secure backgrounds – and indeed, this commitment to educating the brightest and the best young people regardless of their financial resources is a crucial aspect of the Gülen educational vision. The schools offer students with strong academic potential a range of full and partial scholarships that cover tuition fees. They also provide such students with full board and lodging in school dormitories free of charge. These facilities are typically very well appointed, and, together with the promise of a high-quality education, make the schools an attractive option for many poorer families with potentially high-achieving children.

For families of children in the much larger Turkish state sector, there are two major routes that their offspring may pursue, and these are differentiated by the amount of official religious education that they offer. The first is the standard state *lise* (high school).[11] These schools were established in the early years of the Turkish Republic, during an era in which the State was self-consciously secular in orientation. They were intended to teach a secular national curriculum and to exclude religious practice from the official school day. State *lise*s have historically provided only two hours of religious instruction per week, under the title *Din Kültürü ve Ahlak Bilgisi* (Religious Education and Ethics). The secularity of the state system has, however, been under an increasing amount of pressure since the AKP (Adalet ve Kalkınma Partisi – Justice and Development Party) government has been in office. Religious influences are resurgent in a variety of ways; most recently (September 2014), the ban on female pupils wearing the headscarf in secular state schools has been lifted and children may now attend school in *hijab* from the age of ten.[12] In a similar vein, religious education classes have recently been made compulsory for state primary-school children in grades 1–3, where previously they were absent until grade 4 and above.[13]

Concurrently, the Department of Education is engaged in a programme to rapidly increase the provision of religiously oriented schools within the state system. These schools, which run alongside the secular *lise* system, are called Imam Hatip *Lise*s and were originally designed to train state imams and employees in the Directorate of Religious Affairs (Diyanet İşleri Başkanlığı). As such, they offer a curriculum heavily weighted towards the Islamic sciences. Students at Imam Hatip schools spend 60 per cent of their time studying non-religious subjects, and 40 per cent studying Islam.[14] Religious practice is also amply accommodated within the Imam Hatip schools; regular prayers are observed throughout the school day, female students cover their heads with regulation scarves, and students are taught in classes or even entire buildings that are gender-segregated. The AKP government has opened a great many new Imam Hatip schools during its time in office, with unofficial estimates suggesting an increase of 215 per cent over the past seven years.[15] President Erdoğan himself is a graduate of an Imam Hatip school, and has spoken out strongly in their favour, defending the merits of the religious education that they provide. Such rhetoric, which is controversial outside the AKP-voting electorate,[16] supports the president's now famously declared intention to nurture the emergence of a 'Golden Age' of religiously educated and piously Islamic Turkish youth.

Imam Hatip schools are thus rapidly becoming more integrated into the mainstream of the Turkish education system. Until very recently (2012), however, graduates from these schools were effectively prevented from gaining admission to study any subject at university besides theology.[17] Thus there was a high price to pay for parents wishing their children to study within a religious environment, as it was near impossible for Imam Hatip graduates to secure a competitive university degree and entrance into the Turkish job market.[18] The Gülen schools were, for a time, a major beneficiary of this situation. Many families of a pious persuasion opted to send their children to Gülen schools where – alongside studying a secular, scientific curriculum, and thereby potentially qualifying for university entrance – they could expect to receive additional instruction in religion from their teachers. Such families further appreciated the assurance that high standards of Islamic morality (generally articulated in Turkey as refraining from smoking, drinking and close interaction with the opposite sex – as well as, for women, covering one's hair) would be maintained in the school environment, modelled to their offspring through the example of the religious piety and conservative lifestyles of their teachers.

The law was changed by the AKP government in 2012, meaning that it is now possible for Imam Hatip graduates to qualify on merit for university entrance along with their peers from the secular state-school system.[19] It is not yet clear what the immediate impact of these changes will be on the Gülen schools, but it is to be expected that the religious constituency from which they attract a percentage of their students is set to shrink to some degree.

Studying the Gülen Schools in Turkey

The success of the Gülen schools is demonstrated by the strong position that they have carved out for themselves in the Turkish education market. Central to their brand appeal is the emphasis that they place on science, and their apparently high levels of success in this area, which can lead to success in university entrance examinations. School websites typically display lists of student achievements in the science subjects, particularly in international competitions called the 'Science Olympiads', which are independent of the Gülen Movement. The schools' engagement in these competitions, which will be explored in some detail below, is an important vehicle through which their proficiency in teaching science is displayed.

The ability of Gülenist educators to teach modern science apparently so successfully, while retaining at the same time a strong Islamic religious identity, sets them apart from their competitiors in Turkey. This situation raises a number of questions, and is something that requires closer scrutiny. How, for example, do the religious convictions of Gülenist educators tangibly shape their work during the course of the school day? How is science taught within a secular educational curriculum while being informally framed by a Said Nursi-inspired Islamic philosophical discourse? And how do the Gülen schools achieve such apparently high rates of student success, not only in Turkish university entrance exams but also in rigorous, internationally recognised science competitions?

In order to explore these questions, I carried out fieldwork at two Gülen school communities in Turkey between March and December 2013.[20] Each community was located in a different large city in the west of Turkey, and each comprised a locally affiliated group of schools. I refer here to the first school community (at which İrem, the young chemistry teacher, worked) as Kelebek, and the second as Yunus. Each establishment was composed of a majority-girls' high school, a majority-boys' high school, and various mixed-gender primary-to-middle schools. I conducted research at all three school levels and at both gender-specific schools at Kelebek, and at the majority-boys' high school at Yunus.

Full gender segregation in high school is not permitted by Turkish law, which has required since the 1980s that high schools be mixed. The Gülen schools studied met this legal requirement by including a very small number of girls in a majority-boys' high school, and vice versa. The teaching staff was generally, although not exclusively, male at the majority-boys' schools and female at the majority-girls'. The preference for single-sex education was explained in pedagogical rather than religious terms; that is, young people were widely known and proven to attain greater academic success when educated in single-sex environments. However, the de facto gender segregation in the Gülen schools also played a crucial role in facilitating their distinctive educational culture. This culture was characterised, at least in part, by the following two features: first, a pious religious ethic and conservative conception of Islamic morality (which *demanded* gender segregation); second, close interpersonal relationships, in informal social networks incorporating teachers, students and parents (which was *facilitated by* gender segregation).

The schools observed displayed two distinctive features, each of which offers an insight into their ability to teach science to such an apparently high level while operating all the time within a self-consciously Islamic frame of reference. The first observation concerns the unusually high levels of commitment demonstrated by the teachers, something that was referred to internally as *fedakarlık* (self-sacrifice), and which facilitated the schools' thriving extra-curricular cultures. The second observation concerns the sense of rigorous competition that framed the schools' approach to science teaching, and this was made most clearly manifest in the intensive preparations for students' entry into the international Science Olympiads. These two areas will be explored in turn below.

Religious Motivation and Pedagogy

In the girls' high school at Kelebek, the great majority of teachers were religiously observant and projected a pious Islamic identity. This piety was expressed in various ways – namely their choice of a strict *tesettür* style of clothing,[21] their regular visits to the designated prayer room to perform *namaz* (ritual prayer) throughout the course of the school day, and the preference for teaching in an all-female environment because they were 'more comfortable' without the presence of men. Gender segregation was practised rigorously, with, for example, the few male staff eating in a separate area of the school canteen and meticulously avoiding interaction, or even eye contact, with their female counterparts. The piety of the staff was generally more uniform than that of the students. That is to say, not all of the girls adopted the *tesettür* dress code outside of school, and not all performed regular prayers.

A major distinguishing feature of the school was the exceptional degree of commitment that the teachers demonstrated to their vocation. They drew a clear distinction between the role of a 'teacher', which was limited in their definition to someone who 'simply' transmits knowledge to students, and the role of an 'educator', which was much broader and connoted responsibility for the personal, ethical and possibly religious development of the student. Hatice, a 37-year old English teacher at Kelebek, explained this distinction in the following terms:

> I don't see teaching as only English teaching. That is actually quite a small part of education. In fact we are educators – we are trying to educate these children. If it was just a question of teaching then it would not require a great deal of self-sacrifice (*fedakarlık*). You go into your classroom, you teach your lesson and then you leave. That's it. But when you're an educator, [...] you take inspiration from others and model how to behave to the students. This is not just in class, but also in the breaks and sometimes after school in the evenings [...] we spend time together with our students then too. I have a group of eight students who are very young and sometimes they behave very badly. They can be disrespectful and use bad language, for example. I find this really hard. Trying to show them a better way to behave is a great act of self-sacrifice. I don't know how successful I am, but I am trying to be.[22]

Hatice prioritised the personal and ethical dimension of the pedagogic endeavour as much as the academic one. That is to say, she sought to personally model (*temsil etmek*), and thus transmit to her students, the moral principles that directed her life as a pious Muslim believer. She went on to explain the rationale for her commitment to this heavily expanded role of teacher/educator in more detail:

CT: *Where do you find the inspiration for such self-sacrifice?*
Hatice: First from the Prophet Muhammad, who was himself a teacher (*öğretmen*) [...] and then from Hocaefendi [Fethullah Gülen], who is a great living example. Also, we have an understanding of the natural world which means that we can learn from it. So the world, and school, and my family are all my workshop (*atölyem*). I am trying to be a good person. While I am educating these children, I am also educating myself and becoming a better person. My work is like an examination (*imtihan*) for me. We must be prepared for when we go to the other world.[23]

It was clear that Hatice derived religious meaning from her professional role, despite the fact that her official responsibility was to teach English rather than religion. She was deeply immersed in the thought of Fethullah Gülen, whom she professed to read or listen to on at least a weekly basis, and thus directly reflected his ideas on the subject.

Gülen regards teaching as a kind of sacred duty, an act of religious piety in the service of God.[24] Whilst the pursuit of religious knowledge has long had a sacred function in the Islamic tradition,[25] Gülen reinterprets this tradition to 'sanctify' and legitimise the teaching and learning of non-sacred subjects in a secular environment. In this way, he encourages his followers to teach as a kind of religious service (*Hizmet*) or vocation, stating that:

> Education through learning and a commendable way of life is a sublime duty that manifests the Divine name *Rabb* (Upbringer and Sustainer). By fulfilling it, we attain the rank of true humanity and become a beneficial element of society. [...] In essence, a school is a kind of place of worship whose 'holy people' are teachers.[26]

Teachers such as Hatice are therefore highly motivated to carry out their duties as diligently as possible, seeing their professional role as having sacred connotations. A further conversation with İrem at Kelebek revealed the same expectation of religious reward attached to her professional role:

CT: *Why do you invest so much time and energy in your work, in your students?*

İrem: It's like this: we can't receive the reward for everything that we do in this world (*dünyada*) – only to a limited extent. But the good works that we do as extra, we will find reward for in the afterlife (*ahirette*). So if we give our students extra time and help them with their lessons, then we will be rewarded in part for this now and in part for it in the afterlife. We leave some of the reward for the afterlife. We like helping our students, and as you know, Allah will not leave anything unrewarded (*karşılıksız*).

CT: *You think very often about the afterlife?*

İrem: Yes, I believe this: a Muslim must live in the awareness of the afterlife. It should inform everything that we do as Muslims. A human being can live to some extent for the things that are in the world, but really it is necessary to think beyond that. This is how we try to live.[27]

İrem was expressing the commonly held Islamic belief in the importance of carrying out good deeds (*sevap*) in this life, in order to be rewarded on the Day of Judgement. For Gülenist educators, the *sevap* tradition is re-imagined in a way that foregrounds the merits of education and learning, and thus provides an Islamic context for the teaching vocation. This was explained to me by a movement insider who worked as a university academic in the city in which Kelebek was located:

> There is a teaching that you get a share of the *sevap* from those who continue to be affected by you after your death. While you are waiting for Judgement Day, you can still be accruing *sevap*. Therefore if you teach, and the person whom you teach goes on to teach, then knowledge is being passed on down future generations and you are steadily accruing more and more *sevap* for your part in it.[28]

İrem and Hatice did not express interest in career progression, in financial reward or indeed in any personal benefits available to them because of their work. Rather, they ascribed meaning to their roles as educators from their understanding of Islamic eschatology, and maintained a perspective on their work that was rooted as much in the spiritual world as it was in the material.

Extra-curricular Input

The practical outworking of this distinctive Islamic philosophy of education took various different forms. First and foremost, it manifested itself in the unusually long hours that teachers worked. These extended well beyond the end of the official school day, and teachers were typically available to provide additional, one-to-one tutoring for their students until around 7.00 pm. They were also dedicated to the cultivation of strong personal relationships with their students, and would visit students' homes on a regular basis in the evenings and at weekends. This high level of teacher–student commitment was greatly valued by students, as was exemplified in this conversation with a group of ninth grade (15-year-old) students at Kelebek:

CT: *Are you happy with this school?*
Girls: Yes, very happy.
CT: *What do you like about it most?*
Girls: Our teachers. They are very concerned with us (*çok ilgileniyorlar*) and give us a lot of help with our lessons. They're so much better than at state schools. In state schools, they just watch for the clock to strike four so that they can leave [...]
CT: *Do you see your teacher outside of the school?*
Girls: Yes, often! We visit [our class teacher] at her home. She often invites us over for breakfast at the weekend. In Ramadan, we even went once for *sahur* [...][29]

The way in which students interacted with the teaching staff at Kelebek was, indeed, often more familial than professional, with teachers having an attitude in some ways more reminiscent of a 'big sister' (*abla*) than a distant authority figure. Besides reciprocal home visits, this intimacy was cultivated through teachers accompanying the students on social excursions such as trips to the cinema or a local shopping mall. It was clearly shown at an organised school picnic during the course of the present research, where teachers and students mingled freely together socially. Teachers sat with their students, chatting and joking along with them, ate their meals with them and even joined in playing certain games, such as skipping. Furthermore, it was clear that religious instruction was taking place here informally, with groups of students and teachers engaged intermittently in Qur'an reading together, and others performing *namaz* throughout the course of the afternoon, on mats laid out in the shade of some trees.

Religious Mentoring and Instilling Islamic Ethics

There was no mandatory religious instruction at the schools studied besides that required by the Turkish state. Students who chose to, however, could take part in *sohbet* groups led by their teachers outside of school hours. These groups were usually convened in the school dormitories, which were located, at Kelebek, about a half-hour drive from the main school campus. I was unable to attend such a *sohbet*, but was informed anecdotally that (as is typical of *sohbet*s in the wider movement) the students were instructed in the *Risale* and the Qur'an, and that they also studied the books of Fethullah Gülen.

In the girls' high school, this kind of explicit religious mentoring was kept self-consciously separate, in both time and physical space, from the main activities of the school day. On occasion during the school day, teachers enquired of certain students whether they had yet performed their *namaz* and, on replying in the negative, they were invited to accompany the teacher to the designated prayer room to do so. The invitation was not, however, issued to all students but only those who were personally selected by a given teacher.

The project to instil in the students ethical behaviour derived from a conservative conception of Islamic morality was, however, a regular feature of all teacher–student interaction. Students were forbidden from wearing make-up or jewellery, or from wearing their hair loose, and were frequently warned of the dangers of interacting with the opposite sex. This warning was made explicit in a ninth grade (14–15 years) religious culture and ethics class, in which the teacher used the Qur'anic story of Joseph and Zuheyla to elaborate in detail on the importance of chastity (*iffet*) for Muslim women. The heavy emphasis on the female students' sexual purity was also illustrated during an excursion to the beach, when teachers became very agitated to see a group of their students walking close to some young men whom they suspected had been drinking alcohol. Two teachers hurried to divert them, and bring them back to the group, and the girls were subsequently reprimanded for their behaviour which was seen as 'dangerous'.

Teachers' Community

Besides devoting considerable time and energy to both the personal formation of their students in Islamic ethics and to their academic development, teachers also invested heavily in the teacher community at the school. They attended weekly *sohbet* (discussion) groups, where the *Risale* of Said Nursi and the works of Fethullah Gülen were studied intensively, and also assembled every Tuesday evening to listen together to Gülen's regular sermon, broadcast through a video link on his website, www.herkul.org. There were occasional additional seminars at the school, in which an individual (referred to as an *abi*) from Gülen's inner circle of disciples who reside with him on his ranch in Pennsylvania, would visit in order to provide local followers with theological instruction and oversight.

In addition to these regular weekly commitments, teachers participated in a rigorous schedule of additional activities over their holidays and in the summer months. Hatice described her continued close involvement with the school community outside of term time:

Hatice: Our school is a bit like a family. We have so many common interests (*ortak noktalar*) of course. In the summer, we have one month off school, although the spiritual community (*manevi birliktelik*) continues. We meet for *sohbet*s in one anothers' houses. But we usually visit our families, for example my mother and mother-in-law, as this is the tradition (*sünnet*) of the Prophet, it's what he did. He showed that it is important to honour our families […] we also have a few days or a week on holiday, when we take the children to the beach.

CT: *I have heard that there are 'camps' during the holidays […]?*

Hatice: Yes – this is what I meant when I referred to our spiritual community continuing. We meet together for 'camps' […] it might be for educational training or it might be for spiritual conversation. For example, in February we have a two-week break, but

>   we always take five or six days before we go on holiday to come together spiritually. We read a lot, we listen to talks […] we read the Qur'an. These are for our teacher friends, and they usually take place here at school.
>
> CT: *Do students or parents or other people attend as well?*
>
> Hatice: No. We don't do much work of a spiritual nature with parents, but if they want to have *sohbet*s then we arrange them for them separately.[30]

Most Turkish schools allow three months' holiday over the summer, so the reduction to just one month is significant. It was apparent, therefore, that the lives of teachers such as Hatice were tightly regulated, both in term time and for most of the holiday period. In the same way, the teachers viewed the education of their students in holistic terms; their own lives and careers as educators were similarly lacking in clearly defined boundaries between 'personal' and 'professional'. This blurring of boundaries was further facilitated by the fact that a significant majority of teachers were married to fellow-teachers employed within the same group of locally affiliated Gülen schools. Thus their personal and familial lives were able to intersect with their professional lives as educators on a variety of different levels.

Classroom Pedagogy

Hatice's mention of 'educational training' that took place outside of term time is indicative of the fact that, while input into the personal lives and behavioural patterns of the students was clearly sought, at the same time, excellence in classroom pedagogy was also prioritised. This was clearly reflected in high-school lessons observed, in which standards of teaching and learning were high and student engagement was very good. Student resources were of a high quality, and the classrooms were well equipped with interactive whiteboards and other modern technological teaching aids. The teachers were generally well qualified for their roles, holding university degrees in their specialist subjects along with a number of years of relevant teaching experience.

In addition to these standard indicators of good pedagogical practice, the Gülen schools had certain additional techniques for the assurance of high standards of teaching, one of which was the strategic pooling of knowledge and resources. This practice was explained to me by the university academic mentioned above:

> The schools use meetings very effectively to share experience. The teachers don't compete with one another inside the movement. In the schools and *dershane*s, for example, teachers are grouped together according to subject specialisms, and one teacher with the most experience leads the group (*zümre*) in order to pass on his or her knowledge. This means that the quality of teaching in the *Hizmet* schools is more homogeneous than [it is in] normal schools.[31]

Religious Themes in the Science Classroom

In the high schools observed, there was no mention of religious themes in the classroom context, apart from in the hours that the national curriculum demands be reserved for religious culture and ethics. Science classes resembled those in any secular school, and as such there was no discussion of Islamic philosophical ideas in conjunction with the material being studied.

This segregation was not, however, so apparent lower down the school system, and there was considerably more blurring of boundaries between religious and scientific ontologies in the context of the middle-school classroom. For example, in a seventh grade (12–13 years) science lesson entitled 'Systems of the Body', the teacher offered an Islamic framework for her explanations for natural phenomena on more than one occasion. Explaining the anatomy of the human eye, she posed the following rhetorical question: 'If you didn't have eyes, you wouldn't be able to see the beauty of nature. Why would you not give thanks for having two eyes?' Explaining the anatomy of human skin, and drawing on an example of an extreme medical skin condition, she provided her students with the following interpretation:

> This disease has been given to this person because this life, as you know, is a test (*sınav*). This person's test is a skin disease, and look – he's not asking 'why me?', or complaining about it. We need to give thanks (*çok sükür etmemiz lazım*) that we don't have a skin disease like this.[32]

It is significant that the teacher did not refute or discredit the scientific explanation for the disease in question, but rather superimposed an ethical Islamic framework upon it. In this way, she was able to accept the scientific information and interpret it in a way that was not incompatible with religious meaning. Aynur, a 35-year-old physics teacher at Kelebek middle school, explained that there was a place for religious commentary and interpretation such as this within the science classroom:[33]

CT: *Is there anything different in the way that you teach science in these schools?*
Aynur: No, there's no difference. However, our aim is also to show how great God is.
CT: *How do you do that?*
Aynur: We do a lot of teaching through stories in the classroom. The kids respond to this better than, 'right then – where did we get to in the text book?' We use stories to engage the students, and then we draw links between the scientific facts and the proofs of God.[34]

There was therefore a marked difference between approaches to teaching science at the lower levels of Kelebek and at its girls' high school, where religious inferences appeared to be entirely absent from the classroom. It is of course true that the Gülen schools present themselves as secular institutions, something which would seem to preclude the inclusion of Islamic ontologies in the science classroom. Yet it is perhaps equally true that, in a largely religious society such as Turkey, the mention of God in such a context is not as remarkable as it might be in an equivalent classroom in Western Europe. Further, comparative research with other non-Gülen schools in Turkey would be necessary in order to explore this question further, and to establish how uniformly references to God are excluded from middle-school science classrooms around the country.

It was clear, however, that there was a commitment to rigorous standards in science education, and an absence of religious explanations for natural phenomena in the classroom context, at the *high school level* in the schools studied. Here, the physical presence of the teacher herself served as an implicit emblem of Islamic piety, for her students knew her personally and understood her to be a pious practitioner of the faith herself, and yet religious discourses were not made explicit here but rather saved for explication in extra-curricular time and space.

The high-school classroom was devoid of fixed religious symbols, and religious and Qur'anic references were absent. Nursian ideas from the *Risale* about the compatibility of science and faith, which constitute the philosophical foundation of the schools' pedagogic ethos, were not discussed in this context. The sole distinguishing feature of the science lessons in the high schools studied that channelled a religious influence into the teaching of science was the embodied personal faith of the teacher him- or herself. It was the teachers, practising Islam as private individuals yet conveying scientific knowledge to their students, who therefore served, in the classroom context, as a material illustration of the reconciliation of science and religion.

The 'Science Olympiads'

If the schools studied were characterised on the one hand by the extraordinary commitment of the teachers to their vocation, then they were equally characterised on the other hand by a strongly competitive academic culture, which surrounded the teaching of science in particular. This was particularly evident in the heavy investment made by the schools into prestigious international competitions called the 'Science Olympiads'.[35]

The Gülen schools have been competing at the Science Olympiads since the early 1990s, and their success in these competitions forms an important part of the schools' identity. Olympiads take place on a national and international level, with the national events providing the selection ground for the team that represents Turkey at the more prestigious International Olympiads. Turkey has regularly sent teams to compete in each of the five different International Olympiads (mathematics, physics, chemistry, biology and computer science) since 1993,[36] before which time they received relatively little domestic interest. The increase in interest in the Science Olympiads in Turkey in the early 1990s was concurrent with the emergence of the first Gülen schools, and whilst the selection and training of the national team is overseen each year by TÜBİTAK,[37] high numbers of Gülen-school students are selected and participate every year.[38]

Accordingly, a popular internal narrative of the movement, voiced especially by the school science teachers, is that the Gülen schools have contributed to an overall improvement in standards of science education and public engagement with science in Turkey over the past 20 years.

While this narrative is very much in line with the movement's broader aspiration to demonstrate its successful engagement with modern science within an Islamic framework, it is nonetheless in need of further investigation. A major motivation behind the Gülen schools' success in the Science Olympiads appears to be their highly competitive ethos and intensive work ethic. The Olympiads are attractive because of the prestigious rewards and incentives within the Turkish education system that are offered to winning students. Furthermore, a high degree of competitiveness characterises the rigorous student selection process and intensive tutoring methods used in the Gülen system to train Olympiad candidates. Accordingly, it seems that their desire to successfully *compete* is an essential component to understanding the Gülen schools' interest in the Olympiads, and their engagement in the field of science more broadly.

There are both financial rewards and new academic opportunities offered to students who win a medal at the International Science Olympiads. Besides receiving a cash prize from TÜBİTAK, each medal winner has his or her chance of acceptance to a prestigious university (private or state) in Turkey greatly enhanced by the automatic addition of points to their score in the LYS (Lisans Yerleştirme Sınavı – Degree Placement Exam) exam: 30 extra points are added for winning a bronze medal, 40 for a silver and 50 for a gold. Medal winners are, furthermore, granted automatic admission to a degree programme in the department of their subject specialism at any state university in Turkey. If they choose to accept this opportunity, they are also awarded a full state scholarship for the duration of their undergraduate studies. Success in the Science Olympiads therefore offers gifted students an alternative way of directly negotiating a place for themselves at Turkey's top universities, for which competition is extremely high. Schools that are able to boast of medal-winning alumni also benefit from the associated prestige, and frequently reference their successes in order to boost their competitiveness in the private-education market.[39]

Strategies for Success

The success of the Gülen schools in general, and at the Science Olympiads in particular, is due at least in part to their high academic entrance requirements and their strategy of targeted recruitment. The schools' focus on recruiting able students is especially notable with regard to their early selection of potential Olympiad candidates. Starting in the last year of primary school, the schools target students who have demonstrated academic potential and the ability to perform well in exams. Capable students are then offered scholarships and tutored intensively throughout middle school for entrance in the national junior Mathematics Olympiad, which is administered by TÜBİTAK.[40] Medal winners subsequently progress (again, with scholarships) to a high school that is affiliated to the same local Gülen group as their primary and middle schools. The teacher responsible for coordinating the Science Olympiads at the boys' high school at Kelebek described the process of targeted recruitment of students with the potential to win medals:

> There is a national exam every year, which fifth graders sit before they start middle school. We give the top sixty students in our city medals (gold, silver and bronze), and we invite them to come for lessons at our school for one month over the summer. We select the students we want to take, a decision based not just on their academic ability but also on their character, and we offer them scholarships. We also check the exam results for the primary schools across the province, and travel to different schools to offer the best students scholarships. So these are the two ways in which we find our students.
>
> Then, in the sixth and seventh grades, we teach these students the high-school mathematics curriculum, and in the eighth grade we start teaching them how to answer National Mathematics Olympiad questions. If they are good, we teach them material from the International Mathematics Olympiad. TÜBİTAK organises the National Mathematics Olympiad for eighth graders, and we enter our students. Then, we accept the top thirty [of them] into our high school without requiring them to sit the entrance exam. So you see, this is how our primary school supports our high school.[41]

It is clear from this process that the school not only pursues a very proactive policy of attracting the best students, but it also trains them in competition skills from an early stage. The culture of medal winning is introduced in the fifth grade, and remains a constant motivation thereafter for students studying for the Olympiads.

As the curriculum diversifies at the start of high school, after the 8th grade students choose which branch of the sciences they will focus their Olympiad preparations on. Different schools are stronger in different branches – for example, Yamanlar in Izmir has a reputation for success in Physics whilst Samanyolu in Ankara is particularly successful in biology. Of the schools studied, the boys' school at Kelebek had a mathematics and chemistry focus, and the boys' school of Yunus a computer science and chemistry focus. The girls' school at Kelebek had yet to establish any specialisms, as this was their first year entering any students in the Science Olympiads.[42] Student specialisms are dependent in large part on the expertise of the science staff at their school, and the latters' ability to tutor students at a high level. The demands of the Olympiad exams are much greater than those of the standard science curriculum, and the teachers consulted considered the level of study to be more commensurate with university undergraduate level.

Both student and teacher commitment were extremely high in preparation for the Olympiads. Students were required to work for ten hours every day in preparation for the competition, whilst also keeping up with the rest of their classes. At Yunus, Olympiad students were encouraged to board in school dormitories even if their families lived locally, to enable them to focus on their studies more intensively and with fewer distractions. Dormitory accommodation was offered free of charge by the school to these students. Students were also required to attend intensive study camps in the winter mid-semester break and in the long summer holiday, thus forfeiting the normal holidays that non-Olympiad students enjoy. The dedication of the Gülen-school teachers was a vital prerequisite of these camps, which they convened and taught in their own holiday time as unpaid volunteers.

As a further motivation, recent school alumni who have won medals previously may return to the school or attend the summer camps in order to offer their services as tutors.[43] These alumni were often now studying at prestigious universities, and provided a powerful source of encouragement and inspiration to the younger students who sought to replicate their success. This was evident in the following extract from a conversation with Burak, a tenth grade Olympiad student at Yunus:

Burak: I'm an Olympiad student and I'm preparing for computer science. It is hard work and we study without breaks, but of course I want to win a medal. I want to study computer engineering at [a prestigious private university in the same city].
CT: *Why do you want to go to that university especially?*
Burak: A student who came to this school won a bronze medal at the Olympiads, in computer science, and he is now studying in the computer engineering department at [the same university]. He comes and helps us at the camps, and gives us advice on how to study.[44]

The older student's success was clearly an important motivation for Burak, who was eager also to win a medal and a place at the same prestigious university department. Burak had not merely heard second-hand reports of the older student's success, but had benefited from a personal tutoring and mentoring relationship with him. In this way, the Gülen schools harness the successes of their alumni very effectively and maximise their potential to inspire the next generation of Olympiad competitors.

The Gülen schools therefore have a comprehensive strategy for succeeding in the Science Olympiads, and invest a considerable amount of time, money and human resources to this end. For students entering the Olympiads from the state sector, and even from other private schools, comparable specialist training and support is not available. The high intensity of the Gülen schools' Olympiad training is facilitated primarily by the willingness of the teachers to spend considerable extra time tutoring their students outside of school hours and in the school holidays – an investment that goes far beyond their normal professional duties. This is another instance of the outworking of *fedakarlık* in Gülen pedagogy mentioned above. State-school teachers can attend a two-week summer training course run by TÜBİTAK, qualifying them to tutor students for the Olympiads. Beyond this brief training, however, their preparation of candidates takes place within the framework of an only slightly extended school day.[45] By comparison, the Gülen school system ensures that its students' chances of selection for the national team, and thereby their qualification for the International Olympiads, are greatly improved not only by requiring them to work more intensively but also by a litany of other strategies (ranging from targeted recruitment to the effective utilisation of peer role models) designed to maximise their competitive edge.

Conclusion

Followers of Fethullah Gülen in Turkey have developed a model of education that has proved, in recent decades, both popular and successful. In an educational landscape that is otherwise sharply polarised between 'religious' and 'secular' schools, the Gülen schools offer high standards in modern scientific learning within an informal milieu that is characterised by Islamic piety and a conservative interpretation of Islamic ethics. Teaching staff frame their commitment to the teaching vocation in religious terms, and derive an extraordinary work ethic from an expectation of reward for their efforts in the life to come. Accordingly, they are willing to provide extra-curricular support to their students in order to best facilitate their chances of academic success while at the same time schooling them in Islamic ethics in order to shape them into pious religious practitioners themselves.

The sustained interest of the schools in the international Science Olympiads reveals a heavily competitive ethos surrounding their engagement with science. This ethos should be understood in light of the broader interests and priorities of the Gülen Movement, which has sought to challenge the hegemony of secularist voices in Turkish society and to reintegrate a Muslim constituency seeking participation in public life and prosperity in the modern world. Science education serves as an effective vehicle through which the movement has challenged the status quo, and through which it appears to have proven the ability of Islamic actors to engage successfully with a critical aspect of modernity.

4

Islamic Creationism in Gülenist Thought

Hakan, an assistant professor of nuclear physics at a state university in the west of Turkey, was a committed follower of Fethullah Gülen. Married and in his late thirties, he had been a regular attendee of the movement's *sohbet*s since his days as an undergraduate student in the 1990s. I met him one autumn afternoon at his office on the main university campus. Hakan was unusually casually dressed for a follower of Gülen, and, also unusually, he offered me his hand to shake on arrival, an action that contravened normal gender etiquette within the movement's core group. He spoke very openly with me, but reacted nervously when I mentioned Gülen's name. Conscious that our conversation might be overheard by his mainly secularist colleagues at the university, he closed the door and spoke thereafter in a low voice. I began by asking him some questions about his work as a scientist and its relationship with his religious faith:

CT: *How would you describe your philosophy of science?*
Hakan: Modern science was initially propagated by ignorant or irreligious people [*cahiller*]. A separation occurred, so there was no longer any shared ground between philosophy and physics. The movement is trying to change this, but it is up to the individual to be interested [...] Our understanding of Creation is that it is a

book, and science is the act of reading that book. But science is a vehicle, not a belief system in itself.

The purpose of life is to explore the world – humankind is a mirror of God and therefore we are meant to pursue and understand things, and to do new things. We have a conscience, and we can make choices ourselves. After you accept that God exists, you start to ask questions – science answers the 'how?' questions, but it does not answer the 'why?' question. Asking questions is a good thing for a Muslim, but when finding our answers we must not look to ourselves. You can ask however much you like, or are able to, but some things have an answer in religion and not in science.

CT: *Do you believe in miracles?*
Hakan: When you believe in a religion, you have to believe it all. You can't just believe this but not that – if you do then you are not a Muslim. Believing is believing [...]
CT: *Do you accept evolution?*
Hakan: God could have created the world however He wanted, but the important thing is that we believe we were *created*. The Qur'an says that we are descended from Adam, and therefore we do not accept evolution. There are problems with evolutionary theory in the West – we accept micro-evolution, but not human evolution.[1]

It was clear from listening to Hakan that he was deeply immersed in the thought of Fethullah Gülen. His ideas reflected Gülen's very closely, not just his reference to the so-called 'secularisation' of science but also, more specifically, his rejection of the theory of human biological evolution. Anti-evolutionism is a major feature of Fethullah Gülen's religious thought, and indeed of Gülen ideology more broadly. Often conflated in Gülen discourse with 'Darwinism', the rejection of evolution is a feature of the movement that is well known in Turkey. While Gülen, and the movement that he inspires, are willing to engage as pious Muslim actors with various challenges to faith posed by secular modernity, evolution appears to be one subject on which they are firmly unwilling to negotiate.

The movement is, however, as we have seen, defined in large part by its proactive embrace of modern science, and dedicates a good proportion of its energies and resources to high-quality science teaching. It maintains a philosophical discourse, alluded to by Hakan, within which modern science and Islamic piety are seen as compatible entities rather than ontological enemies. The rejection of human evolution by Gülen and his followers therefore raises important questions related to the movement's activities in science and science education. In light of its apparently serious commitment to the scientific project, how and why is biological evolution – widely accepted as constituting the lynchpin of modern scientific and medical knowledge – so firmly excluded?

Fethullah Gülen on Evolution: Sources

The most explicit summary of Gülen's teachings on evolution is accessible in Turkish in his short book *Yaratılış Gerçeği ve Evrim* (Evolution and the Truth about Creation).[2] Published in 2003, it is a summary of Gülen's ideas on the subject, which, as he states in the foreword, he first began teaching in the 1960s. Unlike most of his work, this book has not been translated into English.

Gülen's teachings on evolution are therefore more accessible to his Turkish-speaking audience than his English-speaking one. There is only one long article of note on the subject available on the English section of his official website, besides various scattered references elsewhere.[3] The various teachings of Gülen have been translated and published as books in multiple languages. In addition, his official website offers online resources in 32 different language options from which the visitor may choose.[4] The content of each site is not, however, uniform, and different works are selected for dissemination amongst particular national and linguistic audiences. In this instance, it seems that his work on the subject of evolution is aimed more at his domestic than his international audience. The tailoring of its materials and activities to suit different audiences at different times is a tactic by which the Gülen Movement is identifiable, and will be further explored in the discussion below.

In addition to pieces written directly by Gülen himself, the monthly science-focused periodical *Sızıntı* (published in Izmir, Turkey) and its

English-language counterpart, the *Fountain* (published in New Jersey, USA), regularly publish articles on creationism and evolutionary theory by writers and scientists sympathetic to the movement.[5] Gülen writes the regular editorial for *Sızıntı*, (this is in fact the only place where he has written regularly since the 1970s),[6] and it can be assumed by and large that the views expressed in these publications reflect his own opinions.

'Darwinism' in Gülen Thought

The underlying reason for Gülen's rejection of evolutionary theory is that he views it as an atheistic ideology and thereby a threat to religion. This is immediately clear in the introduction to *Yaratılış Gerçeği ve Evrim*, in which he begins by bemoaning the lack of religiously observant scientists who might challenge the hegemonic and 'materialist' assumptions of what he refers to as 'Darwinism':

> In our day, we are not in a position to question this mistaken perspective or to research the causes of this distortion. It is helpful to stress certain things: starting from a particular time in history, our laboratories have become sterile. We have been tied to such a trajectory that unfortunately, the proponents of scientism (I use the term idiomatically in place of the term 'scholar') at many laboratories and research centres immediately ask the question 'how?' but are distracted from then asking the question 'why?' Until today, how many world quality thinkers or scientists have we been able to produce from generations raised in an education system which does not even teach one to think about or search for an answer to the question of 'how?' in its lessons and laboratories, let alone questions of 'why?' or 'who?'
>
> How many scientists have we managed to produce who have challenged the mistakes of Western scientists? How many have exposed the limitations, mistakes and distortions of 'Darwinism' and renewed the idea of humankind as a 'creature of honour'? How many have shown the courage to debate the theory as other theories are debated? [...] Science, especially when confronted with religion, has become a taboo subject and has been sacrificed to ideology, unable to escape from the limits of crude, nineteenth-century positivism and materialism.

> [...] Today, unfortunately, biology is like a fantasy established upon unproven theories. It is entirely clear that the theory of evolution is the foremost of these fantasy theories. It is not the task of an individual like myself, who is occupied with other matters, to write and speak about evolution. However, until a geneticist, a biochemist, a palaeontologist and a religious scholar who can engage with the subject from a religious perspective, can come together as experts and discuss this matter – which has long been discussed in scientific circles – in Turkey and indeed around the world, people like me will continue to hold the right to talk about it.[7]

This passage contains an indication of the key themes that Gülen returns to throughout his work in defence of Islamic creationism. One of these is his synonymous use of the terms 'Darwinism' and 'evolution'. While it is true that Charles Darwin (1809–82) first put forward the theory of the evolution of species through *natural selection*, the broader subject of evolution had been discussed by many of his predecessors and was not in itself original to Darwin. Furthermore, the science of evolution has developed considerably since Darwin's lifetime, and what we know today as modern evolutionary theory has been heavily influenced by more recent scientific discoveries, specifically those in the field of genetics with the discovery of DNA in the 1950s. This discovery marked the emergence of the Modern Synthesis, also refered to as 'neo-Darwinism', which is generally accepted as paradigmatic within evolutionary science as we know it today.[8]

These facts notwithstanding, Gülen gives scant attention to the details of either pre- or post-Darwinian evolutionary theories in his broad rejection of evolution. Rather, it is apparent that it is primarily the *materialist ideology* that Gülen associates with Darwin (i.e. what he calls 'Darwinism') that is the target of his hostility:

> At the roots of evolution lies the proposition that existence came into being of its own accord and by chance. Lamarck, who was the father of evolutionists and who came before Darwin, attributed evolution to Allah and saw the ability of Allah to have created nature and the material world. Contrary to this, Darwin attributed the creative spirit to the material world and to atoms. In a sense, he was a monist or a believer in the unity of

existence. Those who came after Darwin chose to ascribe existence entirely to materialism, and diverged into absolute denial, worldliness and materialism and used evolution as the basis for their denial of Allah.

Today, those who subscribe to Darwinism are [those from] a materialist world who embrace it in order to deny him [Allah]. They are those who believe in the eternity of matter. What terrifying ignorance that, in the name of science, they have denied the author of life [and chosen] this kind of knowledge, freedom and power [over] the eternal knowledge, freedom and power which creation requires. Without even being able to describe it or understanding it [fully], they have raised matter to the level of creator – matter, which is lifeless, conscienceless, unenlightened, weak and powerless but is shaped by the hand of humankind.[9]

Elsewhere, he states in a similar vein that:

Darwinism will never be a theory belonging to one individual person, be it either Lamarck or Darwin. Apart from those who propounded it in earlier centuries, in our generation there are neo-Darwinists. [These neo-Darwinists], in order to supposedly prove evolution – to confirm Darwin's theories and support him – they develop other theories and when one of these proves false, they pursue another one.[10]

Gülen sees 'Darwinism' as a disguise for atheism and, concomitantly, for an agressively atheist agenda. Evolutionary theory is therefore seen primarily as a tool within an anti-religious ideology that must be challenged, rather than as a neutral scientific field that stands apart from the claims of religious faith. Evolutionary theory can, of course, pose a number of challenges to religious creation narratives, and has implications on wider theologies of human meaning and purpose – all of which are debated variously in religious as well as some scientific circles.[11] In Gülen's work, however, these debates are not entered into in any discursive way. Rather, evolution is a primary arena for contesting atheism, and his response to it is shaped first and foremost by his concern with battling unbelief. By utilising the term 'Darwinism' in his refutation of evolutionary theory, Gülen makes a powerful discursive association with nineteenth-century positivism, the intellectual foundations of which he seeks to counteract.

The Turkish Context

The association of Darwin and *human* evolutionary theory with atheism is not an unusual position to hold in contemporary Turkey – or indeed much of the wider Muslim world, where the theory is widely rejected.[12] In Turkey, the subject is complicated by its association with the aggressively secularising policies of the early twentieth-century Kemalists; Mustafa Kemal Atatürk was a keen advocate of evolutionary science, and embraced it along with other aspects of Western culture and civilisation as part of his radical programme of social and educational reform in the 1920s and 1930s.

The theory of biological evolution, which was gathering pace in Europe at the time, thus served as a mainstay of Kemalist ideology, and Atatürk himself wrote parts of the new school curriculum that taught Darwinian ideas to Turkish schoolchildren for the first time.[13] The inclusion of evolution in the national Biology curriculum has ebbed and flowed over the course of the past century, depending on the religious sensitivities of particular governments. Today, it is included only in passing and schoolchildren are not required to learn it in any detail. Nonetheless, for Gülen and his followers, the subject of evolution is still negatively located in a nexus of assocation with Kemalist secularism and atheism. The struggle with these forces has defined the movement (as it has the broader Nur Movement) throughout its history, and continues to do so today.

Homo Sapiens as Vicegerent

There are certain key thematic concerns that underpin Gülen's creationist teachings. One of these is the defence of the notion of homo sapiens as a 'creature of honour' (*eşref-i mahlûkât*), something which he finds to be incompatible with the implied randomness and indignity of our biological descent from other species. Significantly, while Gülen is willing to accept the scientific evidence for micro-evolution (changes within species), it is macro-evolution (changes between species) that he strongly refutes – largely because of his fundamental aversion to the idea of human and animal origins being one and the same.

The concept of humankind as 'vicegerent' (*khalifa*) of God is at the heart of the Islamic understanding of the human condition, and stems from the Qur'an. The special status of humans is underlined in the Qur'anic creation narrative, in which the angels are commanded to prostrate themselves before Adam and Eve in recognition of their unique position at the pinnacle of the created order – something that Iblis (Satan) refuses to do, which consequently leads to his fall from grace.[14] For Gülen, the unique and God-given status of humankind, a central Qur'anic motif and the mainstay of the anthropocentric Islamic religious worldview, is entirely at odds with the claims of evolutionist science.

This position was defended unanimously by those of his followers who were interviewed in Turkey – a group primarily comprising schoolchildren, teachers and university students. A common rationale for the rejection of the theory of human evolution was that so noble a creature as the human being 'could not possibly have descended from monkeys'. The same view was also expressed by a focus group of professional research scientists – including Hakan, the nuclear physicist mentioned above – who were active within the Gülen Movement and were personal subscribers to Gülenist thought. Another member of the group, the head of the mechanical engineering department at a private university, explained to me his reasons for rejecting evolutionary science, which were also rooted in an understanding of humankind having special status as the created vicegerent of God:

> Without a metaphysical side, science makes no sense. In addition, atheism has no rational or scientific foundation, in my opinion. For example, [British physicist] John Barrow in his book *Impossibility*[15] talks about our explorations in space today, and argues that our explorations are derived not from our desire to obtain knowledge but from our ancient ancestors' impulses to survive. So for him, science is a side-product of evolution. But the holy texts say that man was made as vicegerent. Our purpose is to take materials and make a world in which we can live – to build aeroplanes and houses and so on. Our brains were given to us for a reason [...] we are not just a developed

version of a caveman, driven by base impulses like surviving hunger and cold. The role given to man is much more special, much more complex than that. Barrow is over-simplifying our reason for existence.[16]

For this follower of Gülen who was himself a practising scientist, it was essential to maintain the doctrine of creationism in order to defend the vicegerency of humankind according to the Islamic canon. It was ironic that his reading of John Barrow led him to assume that he was 'a Darwinist and an atheist', when in fact Barrow, while accepting evolutionary theory, is well known as a popular science writer for attempting to reconcile modern science with questions posed by religious belief.[17] For the engineering professor interviewed, it was inconceivable that an eminent modern physicist and defender of evolutionary principles such as Barrow might also be a person of faith, the two being assumed to be mutually exclusive categories.

Evolutionary Theory as Conspiracy

Gülen defends his position on evolution by contending that the theory is a hoax. Evolutionary science is discredited in his eyes, on the grounds that it relies on poor or incomplete scientific data. One of Gülen's major areas of criticism is the fossil record, which he believes is both incomplete and replete with instances of fraudulent interpretation:

> From times past and in the foreseeable future, however rigorously they defend it in certain scientific communities and in the books of certain scientists, there has been [and will be] no solid basis or sound evidence for the theory of evolution. No fossils have been discovered which link humankind with monkeys. Some fossils have been faked, others have been collected from different places [than suggested], and the rest have been assembled according to [these scientists'] dreams.[18]

The subject of fraudulent interpretation of the fossil record comes up specifically with reference to transitional forms, popularly referred to as 'missing links', in the evolutionary process. Mirroring creationist thought in the USA,[19] the existence of such transitional forms is denied in Gülenist thought, and is seen as further evidence of the falsity (and even deliberate falsification) of the evidence supporting evolutionary theory:

> Some allegedly extinct intermediate transitional forms have turned out to exemplify only the temptations of forgery and distortion in the service of falsehood into which some scientists have allowed themselves to fall [...] Although the evolutionists are embarrassed on scientific platforms, they do not have a hard time deceiving the ordinary person in the street, because the theory is so well-packaged. You draw an imaginary schema representing transition from water from land, you invent Latin words for the animal in water, and for its descendant on land, and you draw sketches of both (both wholly imaginary constructs), and the package is completed or, as we should rather say, fabricated.[20]

In addition, famous evolutionary hoaxes such as the Piltdown Man receive substantial attention in the Gülen materials, and are showcased as proof of the scientific unreliability of evolutionary science; they are used, furthermore, to endorse the view that there is a dishonest and subversive anti-religious agenda at its heart.

Evolution as 'Bad Science'

The Gülenist refutation of evolution relies on the contention that it is 'only a theory', and one which is allegedly not even fully accepted by scientists themselves. This point was raised repeatedly by followers of Gülen in Turkey, who confidently rejected evolution on account, they explained, of its questionable status as a 'theory'. Their interpretation of this term led them to conclude that evolution could just as easily be deconstructed on scientific terms as it could constructed, and that neither persepective was scientifically definitive.

This idea appears not to be limited to the Gülen case, but to have considerable currency in the wider Muslim world also. In his recent book on Islam and modern science, Nidhal Guessoum reports that 62 per cent of his informants in the Gulf state of Sharjah rejected Darwin's theory of evolution on the grounds that it is 'only an unproven theory and I don't believe in it'. He goes on to comment on the problems inherent in this stance, which derive from a wrong understanding of what is meant by the scientific term 'theory':

[this] idea is totally erroneous, as I will show in this chapter; it stems from the following double ignorance: (a) of the known facts about species in the past and in the present; and (b) of the meaning of the term 'theory', which *contrary to popular understanding signifies a largely confirmed general description of some part of nature* (like planetary orbits or geological plate tectonics etc.).[21]

This critique seems equally applicable to the Gülenist discourse. It has implications on approaches to the teaching of evolution as 'only a theory' in Gülen schools, a point to which I shall return below.

Many of the arguments that Gülen employs to refute human evolution are familiar from creationist debates in the largely Christian context of the USA. The consistency of the fossil record is similarly contested by American creationists, who argue in the same vein as Gülen that 'missing links' undermine the theory of macro-evolution. Indeed, there is some overlapping of ideas and resources to this end – the work of some American creationist scientists on this, and other topics, features in the *Fountain* and, in translation, *Sızıntı* magazines from time to time.

Yet there are also some important differences between debates in the Christian context and the Gülenist Islamic discourse. Besides highlighting areas of perceived tension related to the science of evolution, Christian debates tend also to focus in significant detail on the scriptures of that tradition, which contain a creation narrative that (when read as a literal account of a six-day creation period that took place only 6,000 to 10,000 years ago) clashes with the findings of evolutionary biology which posit a much older earth. In contrast, in the Gülen case, the text of the Qur'an is not a major area of discussion, and the conversation engages only in a limited way with Qur'anic hermeneutics.[22] Rather, it is first and foremost on the grounds of *science* rather than *theology* that Gülen refutes the theory of evolution.[23] That is to say, the major objection that he voices to evolution relates to its reliance on perceived poor scientific data rather than its necessary incompatibility with the religious texts of Islam.

The fact that attention is directed away from the Qur'an and Hadith, and toward modern science, in Gülen's evolutionist discourse is one of its most interesting aspects. There is arguably no *a priori* reason why Gülen and his followers, as pious Muslim practitioners, must necessarily refute the theory of human evolution based on their reading of the Qur'an.[24] Unlike the Bible, the Qur'anic creation story is vague about timescale and allows that the world as we know it might have come into being very slowly and over a long period of time. While the Qur'an refers to a six-day creation narrative, no mention is made of 'evening' or 'morning', and it qualifies this time-frame by asserting that the length of a day may take different forms. For example: 'a Day [...] will measure a thousand years in your reckoning'.[25] There is therefore no theological defence in the Islamic tradition of the notion of a 'young earth', something which dominates the Christian debates on this subject and makes it much harder to reconcile a literal reading of the Bible with acceptance of evolution.

The Qur'an states a number of times that Adam was created by God out of clay, or dirt (Arabic: *turab*).[26] Interpretations of the meaning of this assertion vary, with some commentators – including Gülen – concluding that God created Adam directly and instantaneously from a clay mould, and that humankind did not emerge through a long and complex process of biological evolution. Others, however, have pointed to the fact that the Qur'an goes on to refer to *all* human beings (accepted as biological descendents of Adam)[27] having been created from clay in the same way. This implies a metaphorical meaning, whereby 'clay' or 'earth' refer to the general matter of creation from which humankind emerged and not the actual matter from which the person of Adam was created.[28]

While the latter interpretation has been developed and defended by some Muslim writers in recent years as part of a broader project to legitimise evolution according to Islamic sources, they are a small minority and the general trend in the Muslim world seems to favour the former explanation, which precludes human biological evolution.[29] Therefore, although it appears *technically possible* to condone a reading of the Qur'an in light of evolutionary theory, this nonetheless appears to be an unattractive option for many Muslims today, including for Fethullah Gülen and his followers.

Historical Trajectories

In order to understand the reasons for this position, it is helpful to explore the historical background to the rise of anti-evolutionary sentiment, which reveals that the situation has not always been thus. Indeed, anti-evolutionism in Turkey is a relatively recent phenomenon with little precedent before the late twentieth century. Rather, it has been concurrent with the Islamic revival of relatively recent years.

During the early years of the secular republic, various Islamic scholars in Turkey presented readings of the Qur'an that showed it – quite contrarily to Gülen's position – to be compatible with Darwinian biological evolution. Official religious influences were minimal at this time, yet the self-consciously secular state nonetheless established the Directorate for Religious Affairs (Diyanet İşleri Başkanlığı) in 1924 in order to regulate and oversee the public practice of Islam. Two of the early heads of this department, Ahmet Hamdi Akseki and Süleyman Ateş, wrote religious commentaries that deliberately sought to show how not just evolutionary theory in general, but even human evolution in particular, could be successfully reconciled with the Qur'anic text and Islamic world view.[30]

Veysel Kaya, who has analysed the work of these two scholars, reports that Akseki, in order to do this, stressed the differences between the Qur'anic creation narrative and those of the Judeo–Christian scriptures. Akseki showed how exactly the absence of a specific timeframe in the former – referred to above – made it more amenable to the theory of evolution (and, by implication, more credible as a religious text) than the Jewish or Christian Bible. He even discussed the possibility that 'previous Adams' had existed before Adam the progenitor of the human race.[31] Ateş employed similar arguments to Akseki related to the Qur'anic basis for an 'old earth', and also developed the notion of evolution as a fundamentally 'Islamic' principle, seeing no *a priori* incompatibility between the work of God in the creative act and the processes of natural selection.

The perspectives of Akseki and Ateş in the early twentieth century seem to be profoundly at odds with the teachings of Fethullah Gülen today. Their approach reflects the demands and preoccupations of a different age, when religious influences in Turkey (and in the world more widely) were largely subsumed within the project to create a secular state, bolstered by new discoveries in science and the concomitant self-confidence of modernism. Official Qur'anic interpretation in Turkey at that time was in many ways subordinate to the findings of modern science, and was undertaken by the religious officials of the Turkish state with the intention, primarily, of defending its legitimacy as a religious text in the modern age.

Yet Akseki and Ateş were also following in a much older tradition within Islam that was comfortable with proto-Darwinian ideas. Classical scholars such as Ibn Miskawayh (d. 1030), Ibn Khaldun (d. 1406) and even the Persian poet Jalal al-din Rumi (d. 1273) all discussed ideas to do with the progressive impetus of creation, which included the transmutation of plant life and the evolution of species.[32] There is no suggestion that any of these thinkers developed a clear theory of biological evolution such as was put forward by Darwin; rather, they reflected a similar, pre-modern, understanding to the ancient Greek philosophers regarding the progressive processes governing the natural world.[33] Nevertheless, the willingness of classical scholars to countenance prototypical ideas of human evolution is significant, revealing that the sensitivities associated with it in the Muslim world today are clearly rather recent in origin.

The Rise of Islamic Creationism in Turkey: Harun Yahya

In Turkey, the emergence of a popular movement opposing Darwinian evolution can be traced specifically to the 1980s, the decade during which Islam became publically resurgent. The genesis of popular hostility towards the idea of human evolution was therefore broadly concurrent with religious revival and the rise of political Islam, which was consolidated under the prime ministership and later the presidency of Turgut Özal between 1983 and 1993. This was the era in which Fethullah Gülen rose to prominence and a popular movement surrounding his teachings emerged. It was also the decade in which his fellow-Turk Adnan Oktar, the foremost anti-evolution voice in the modern Muslim world, began to garner a following.[34] A comparison between Gülen and Oktar throws into sharp relief one of the most salient features of the Gülen Movement. Both men promote a similar doctrine of Islamic creationism. For Oktar, though, this doctrine forms the centrepiece of a lavish multinational, multimedia enterprise, and is the issue by which he and his circle of followers are defined. For Gülen, by contrast, anti-evolutionism is a relatively understated aspect of his public teachings, especially in the international setting, and it is not something that he chooses to promote aggressively. In this sense, the movement is reluctant to be openly confrontational or controversial, and is willing to work *within* the status quo in order to achieve its aims, rather than to publically challenge it.

Adnan Oktar writes, undoubtedly along with many other contributors, under the pen-name of Harun Yahya. He is a Turkish entrepreneur and the founding president of the country's Scientific Research Foundation (Bilim Araştırma Vakfı – BAV), an institution that was established in 1990 for the promulgation of creationist ideas. Today, he is a household name in Turkey and across much of the Muslim world, where he is well known for his anti-evolution stance. This stance commands broad support among the Turkish populace and, apparently, in wider Muslim societies and European diaspora communities.[35] Oktar is a contentious figure in his home country, where his flamboyant personal style has been the source of controversy, and questionable financial dealings have seen him serve time in prison.[36]

Under Oktar's direction, Harun Yahya and the BAV distribute materials seeking to refute evolutionary theory. These are of dubious scientific merit yet are produced to a high standard, indicating that significant (although unidentified) financial resources are available to their project. In 1999, Harun Yahya published *The Evolution Deceit: The Scientific Collapse of Darwinism and Its Ideological Background*.[37] In 2007, he produced *The Atlas of Creation*, an elaborate, full-colour work seeking to refute evolutionary theory, which was distributed, unsolicited and free of charge, to university libraries across Europe and North America.[38]

While the refutation of Evolutionary Biology constitutes the focus of the Harun Yahya group, Oktar's own background is not in science at all but rather in the arts. He studied Fine Art at Mimar Sinan University in Istanbul in the early 1980s, followed by philosophy at Istanbul University. It should come as little surprise, then, that his concerns surrounding biological evolution are largely ideological rather than scientific or even theological. Oktar's rejection of evolutionary theory is based on a conspirative and anti-Semitic world view, which sees Social Darwinism and materialist atheism (sometimes represented by Communism) as the major threats of modern times. He seeks to challenge these perceived dangers by dismantling the theory of biological evolution, which is emblematic in his mind of a broader existential threat:

> For some people the theory of evolution or Darwinism has only scientific connotations, with seemingly no direct implication in their daily lives. This is, of course, a common misunderstanding. Far beyond just being an issue within the framework of the biological sciences, the theory of evolution constitutes the underpinning of a deceptive philosophy that has held sway over a large number of people: Materialism.
>
> [...] Modern scientific discoveries reveal over and over again that the popular belief associating Darwinism with science is false. Scientific evidence refutes Darwinism comprehensively and reveals that the origin of our existence is not evolution but creation. Allah has created the universe, all living things and man.[39]

Oktar's ideas must be understood according to the circumstances of his time. He rose to prominence and began to attract a following in the 1980s, a decade of modern Turkish history that was defined by the 1980 coup and the fight against left-wing ideas situated against the global backdrop of the Cold War. He emerged as a public figure during an era in which religion established itself as a primary identity marker in Turkey, in the context of an ideological civil war in which Soviet communism was felt by many to be a great threat, both externally and internally. His anti-materialist and anti-Marxist ideas therefore held considerable currency in religious circles at that time, and have continued to do so since.

Harun Yahya and the Gülen Movement

The societal changes that Turkey underwent in the 1980s, which facilitated Otkar's early success, were the same ones that favoured Gülen and the burgeoning movement in his name. The relationship between Harun Yahya and the Gülen Movement is nonetheless rather complex. They share a number of key concerns, not least an ostensible preoccupation with combatting atheism and restoring religious sentiment to a place of prominence in the modern world. In this battle, the dismantling of evolutionary theory is seen as a major arena for intellectual challenge and confrontation, and both groups adopt a similar tactic for doing so; like Gülen, Harun Yahya generally criticises evolution on pseudo-scientific grounds, arguing that it is a hoax. Both groups are similarly adept at publishing and disseminating their materials through high-quality print media as well as digital means, although Harun Yahya has a much larger and more public presence than the Gülen Movement in this area. The two groups have some history of collaboration, with Gülen-run newspapers and TV channels having promoted certain Harun Yahya materials in the past.

Amongst followers of Gülen in Turkey, Harun Yahya was, however, met with rather a mixed reception. His books were available in the libraries of the high schools studied, and some teachers confirmed that their students were encouraged to read them. The same books were also on sale in the bookshops of universities affiliated to the movement. Yet when asked directly for their opinions on Harun Yahya, most respondents indicated strong disapproval of his methods and style, and stated that they considered his behaviour inappropriate for a Muslim and unbecoming to Islam. Particularly, they commented on the rather flamboyant nature of his TV chat show, which regularly features very heavily made-up, provocatively dressed and surgically enhanced women who smile and offer traditional Islamic responses (*inşallah*, *maşallah*, etc.) to his discursive monologue.[40]

The Harun Yahya TV shows are indeed eccentric; the appearance and attire of these young women contravene many of the norms of conservative Muslim conduct, as does their flirtatious interaction with Oktar. For this reason, the shows have offended, as well as amused, different audiences in Turkey.[41] In the Gülen Movement, female modesty is a highly prized value and a key marker of pious Islamic identity. Female followers of Gülen generally dress very conservatively (adopting the smart but very modest *tesettür* style of dress and headscarf), and avoid interaction with males as much as they possibly can. There is therefore an inevitable degree of discomfort with the ostentatious and sexualised style of the Harun Yahya group. The two communities share the same anti-evolution, pro-Islamic stance, and their motivations and discursive strategies for refuting evolution have much in common, yet they maintain very different styles and ways of presenting themselves to the wider world.

Teaching Evolution in the Gülen Schools

Islamic creationism plays an important part in the teachings of Fethullah Gülen, and finds almost unanimous support amongst his followers. During my fieldwork in different Gülen communities in Turkey, I only met one individual follower who indicated that s/he was sympathetic to the theory of human biological evolution.[42] All of my other interlocutors, including schoolteachers and pupils, firmly rejected it. Given that many of these individuals were educators, many of them science teachers, how was evolution dealt with in the classroom context, and how were pupils prepared for exam success in subjects including biology?

Gülen himself makes it clear that he opposes the inclusion of evolutionary theory in the school curriculum, in his principle text on the subject, which was written in the late 1960s:

> How unfortunate that this unproven theory, which is in fact impossible to prove, is taught in all kinds of schools and educational institutions from middle schools and high schools as far as the final year of university courses, as though it were a proven scientific fact. Here, although it does not directly relate to the topic, I would like to express a wish and make a request of the most transcendent God. If He wills, the celebrated generations of the future will not occupy themselves with theories such as this which are impossible to prove. [God willing they will] thoroughly expose this subject, as they will every subject, whether it be in [the context of] school courses or in scientific forums.[43]

As has already been mentioned, the emphasis on evolution in Turkish school curricula has fluctuated throughout the twentieth century, depending largely on the public religiosity of successive governments. Evolution has been included in some shape or form since Atatürk first introduced it in the 1920s, but in the mid-1980s, bolstered by new Turkish translations of creationist materials produced by the Institute for Creation Research in America, creationism was also included on the biology curriculum for the first time.[44] Since then, creationism has been taught to high-school children alongside evolution as a viable explanation for human origins. Therefore, while it is a requirement for high-school biology teachers to cover evolution, it is not a requirement that they present it as scientifically authoritative. Rather, they can teach it as a 'theory' (a term that has connotations of 'an opinion', as discussed above with reference to Guessoum's comments), and teach Islamic creationism alongside it as a viable alternative.

In the case of the Gülen schools studied, this was how teachers described their approach to the subject, reporting that both they and students found the theory so ridiculous as to be amusing. I was not able to observe a lesson on evolution, there not being any classes that were at the appropriate stage of the curriculum during the period of my fieldwork. It was not difficult, however, to imagine how the topic was presented, as my informal conversations with both students and science teachers indicated that it was the subject of ridicule rather than serious academic attention. One middle-school physics teacher explained the situation in the following terms:

CT: *How do you teach evolution to your students?*
Teacher: We reject the theory of evolution. We do not have to cover it much in class anyway [...] It's not like the 1980s when it was included for ideological reasons. The students laugh when we talk about evolution![45]

Teachers were, however, willing to take evolution more seriously and teach it in some detail in order to prepare their most able students for entry into the international 'Science Olympiads'. Biology is one of five subjects in which students may compete (the others being physics, chemistry, mathematics and computer science) and evolutionary theory is amongst the material on which entrants' knowledge is tested.[46] While those students at Gülen schools who are academically able enough to be put forward for the competitions may choose their preferred subject, they are constrained somewhat by the specialist tutoring offered by their school. Biology was a subject specialism at one of the schools that I studied, and the teacher responsible for Olympiads coaching there explained to me that chosen students studied evolutionary theory in considerably more detail than their classmates, in order to achieve competition success. In this instance, the importance placed on competition success (discussed in Chapter 3) apparently superceded the misgivings that are prevalent in the movement about evolution. Although biological evolution was still not presented as a valid scientific theory, it was nonetheless taken much more seriously when opportunities for competitive success were at stake, and students demonstrated a keen familiarity with the material even though they remained sceptical of its ultimate veracity.

Concluding Remarks

My field research in different Gülen communities in Turkey revealed unanimity amongst Gülen's followers on the subject of evolution. My interlocuters all shared the same Islamic creationist perspective, regardless of their age, level of education or professional status – schoolchildren and teachers, university students and professional research scientists were all of the same opinion that human biological evolution was, first and foremost, scientifically unproven and, furthermore, that of necessity it contradicted the basic requirements of religious faith.

It was striking, however, that the subject of evolution was rarely raised in conversation by my interlocuters themselves.[47] Rather, it was me, as the researcher, who brought it into conversations, and opinions were offered in response to my questions. Similarly, evolution was not discussed in the science lessons that I observed, and nor was it mentioned by teachers outside class time apart from at my instigation. This seems to suggest that, while anti-evolutionism is undoubtedly an important (and established) element of Gülen thought, it is not an issue that is publically emphasised by the movement today to a significant degree.

The lack of availability of Gülen's teachings on the subject in English is significant in this regard. While a great number of his books are available in English (and other) translations, and the movement operates publishing houses in the USA[48] dedicated to the dissemination of his teachings to an international audience, Gülen's work on evolution is conspicuously absent from the English-medium collection. The priorities of the movement have certainly shifted since its early days in Turkey, when it was focused exclusively on a Turkish domestic audience. To such an audience, especially in the domestic climate of the 1970s and 1980s in Turkey, anti-evolutionary sentiment was becoming widespread and was already shared by the majority of pious believers who were Gülen's early constituents. Since Gülen's move to the USA in 1999, however, the movement has shifted its discourse to suit its new international surroundings, primarily emphasising its commitment to interfaith and intercultural dialogue.[49] Creationism, while remaining deeply embedded in Gülenist ideology, has not transferred to the international arena in the same way, and it does not appear to occupy as prominent a position in the movement's wider agenda today as it did in its formative years.

The Gülenist position on evolution, and willingness to hold onto it in some ways as a secondary issue, reveals something of the pragmatism and adaptability that has defined the movement since its inception. This pragmatism has allowed the movement to incrementally expand and prosper since the early 1980s, and in recent years has faciliated its successful globalisation. Today, the movement clearly retains Gülen's early doctrine of Islamic creationism, which is partially available to a global audience while being tailored primarily for a Turkish one. A high-profile and controversial public project of anti-evolutionism, however, along the lines of the one offered by Harun Yahya, is clearly not at the pinnacle of the movement's agenda in the twenty-first century. Rather, the subject of evolution remains largely implicit rather than explicit within the Gülenist discourse, and it seems to have little appetite for extended public confrontation on this issue.

5

Higher Education, Networking and Careers in Science

Since their inception in the 1970s, the Gülen schools have proved successful in attaining high standards in secular education, with a particular focus on the natural-science subjects. The combination of the Muslim piety of their staff and the schools' commitment to modern science education is, in large part, what makes them distinctive. Yet while it is apparent that the schools are adept at training their students for exam success in science, it is not immediately clear what the impact of this training is on students' longer-term career paths. Do they go on to pursue their studies in science at university level, and if so in what capacity?

This question is important, because it addresses the potential significance of the Gülen model of religiously-inspired science education vis-à-vis the wider Muslim context. While many Muslim-majority societies have become voracious consumers of modern technology in the twentieth and twenty-first centuries, they have not, generally speaking, kept pace with non-Muslim counterparts in the fields of scientific discovery and innovation.[1] Levels of investment in research and development are structurally lower in Muslim nations, and the number of scientists and scientific outputs per capita is generally far lower. There are clearly many reasons for this situation, and a complex web of economic, social and historical factors all play a part. Nonetheless, the Gülen model of science education, both intellectually successful and located within a self-consciously Islamic frame of reference, has potentially much to offer. If it were to show evidence of stimulating enduring interest in experimental science in its graduates, and potentially invigorating the 'culture of science' in a Muslim context, then it would be a development of note and, potentially, of wider regional application.

The movement's interest in science education has been focused since its inception in the late 1970s on the primary and secondary sector as well as the *dershane* market. In recent years, followers of Gülen have expanded their interests into the tertiary sector, and today they run a number of private universities in Turkey and abroad. In many ways, the expansion of the movement into higher education opens up new avenues for the investigation of its interest and objectives in science pedagogy. So what characterises these new Gülen universities, and what kind of careers are the movement preparing the next generation for? With regard to its interest in science specifically, is there any evidence to suggest that a new generation of Muslim research scientists might be poised to emerge from the Gülen Movement?

Irfan University[2]

Arif, Majid and Rustam were students from Indonesia, Afghanistan and Tajikistan respectively, studying at Irfan, a new university in the west of Turkey, which was established by followers of Gülen in 2012. They spoke to me on a sunny November day in 2013, in a plush boardroom at the university's administrative block, under the watchful eye of İbrahim, a senior university administrator. All three students had attended a Gülen high school in their home country, where their strong academic performances had secured them scholarships to study at this new university. They explained to me some of the details of their respective journeys to Turkey:[3]

    CT: *Arif, how did you hear about Irfan?*
    Arif: One of the teachers from Irfan came to my school in Indonesia and gave the opportunity for one student to come here with scholarship [sic]. The teacher chose me and [...] yeah, I accepted [...]

	because I heard that in [this city] they have a good university – especially they said that this university was one of the best [...]
CT:	Did anyone else from your school come to Turkey to study?
Arif:	From that school that year we were four students, but in different cities. In this city, it is just me.
CT:	What about you, Rustam?
Rustam:	It was the same for me. I was studying in the Turkish [Gülen] high school before I came here. There are too many [sic] Turkish high schools all over the world and some of them are in Tajikistan. I was there and they came to advertise this university – my plan was to come and study in Turkey because I was studying in the Turkish high school. He came and introduced the university and this was the only international university in Turkey and that was great for me – that is why I wanted to come [...] because I'm interested in different cultures and that's why I came. This was a great opportunity for me to get acquainted with different cultures.
Majid:	My story is a little bit different. I went to the Turkish high school but I started university there in my home country [Afghanistan], according to the general exam that we have. So I started studying civil engineering. Then, I was in my second year, third semester, and one day my teacher called me and said 'I want to talk to you'. He was one of my teachers in Turkish high school, and you know my relation[ship] with this teacher was very close. He called me and said that this university had just given a scholarship, and they selected one student from the whole country according to the grades of the general exam and also according to the high school grades. So they told me, 'If you are interested in it, you can come and take the scholarship'.

The three students were studying for degrees in international relations, computer engineering, and electronic and electrical engineering. They all intended to continue their education to master's level, and ultimately to return to their home countries to find profitable employment. Their connection to Turkey had begun years before, during their time at Gülen high schools in Indonesia, Tajikistan and Afghanistan. I asked them about their interest in Turkish culture, and their experience of being connected to Turkey:

CT: *What do you know about Turkish culture?*
Arif: Many things! They have a good culture, and also it is not so different from Indonesian culture.
CT: *In what way?*
Arif: How we behave – it is the same. And also, Turkey and Indonesia are Islamic countries – so we don't have a very different culture. Almost the same.
CT: *Did you learn about Turkish culture at high school?*
Arif: Yes, I learned [...] because when I was a senior in high school, I took the Turkish Olympiad. And I learned about *Hakkari yöresi*, a Turkish dance, so I can dance that dance [...]
Rustam: In the summers, some students went abroad with their teachers, so there was an opportunity to see the world – the USA, England, Turkey [...] I didn't come but every year more than ten classmates would come to Turkey with their teachers.
CT: *Is Turkey somewhere that people in your country want to visit?*
Rustam: In our country, Turkey and Tajikistan are probably the best at doing business with one another. The economy is dependable [...]
CT: *What do you all hope to do after you finish university? What do you plan to do for work?*
Majid: For me, it's not sure and maybe I'm going to stay here but most probably I'm going to go back to my home country and work there. And of course it's going to be in my own branch, my own department [electrical and electronic engineering] [...] I'm thinking about getting my Masters, but I want to study in the USA or a European country. It's not only about getting an education, it's also about different cultures and speaking different languages.
CT: *Do you have much exposure to the culture here?*
Majid: Yes, yes. My country and Turkey are also Islamic countries, so when I came here – the first year – it was not so difficult for me to live here. Most of the things were kind of the same [...] the way of talking and behaving and being and sitting, these things

were the same as our own country and so I just continued with the same things and I didn't find any difficulty.

The university in question had become fully operational in the autumn of 2013, only a few months before this interview took place, and these students were amongst its first undergraduate cohort. It was located about a half hour drive outside the city on an extensive campus, the construction of which was still only partially completed. The main administrative building, a lavish and impressive neo-Seljuk structure heavily decorated in geometric tiling, was complete, along with one large faculty building built in a similar style and a male-only student dormitory (female students were housed some considerable distance away, in university-run accommodation in the city centre). Plans were under way for the construction – within five years – of seven more faculty buildings, a large library and an extensive sports facility including a football stadium.

When I had first approached the university a few months earlier, in the spring of that year, I was directed to İbrahim, the senior administrator responsible for the university's public relations. İbrahim, a committed follower of Fethullah Gülen, was affable, welcoming and very willing to talk with me and answer my questions fully. He gave me permission to talk freely with students and staff,[4] while at the same time facilitating the kind of 'official' presentation that became a familiar feature of my interaction with the movement in Turkey.

In order to do this, on a spring day in 2013, İbrahim hosted me for lunch in the university's luxurious VIP dining room, a facility equivalent to the restaurant of a five-star hotel. He also invited the head of the English preparatory school, a man called Ahmet who had pioneered the early Gülen schools in Kazakhstan in the early 1990s and had gone on to teach in Poland and, latterly, back in Turkey. During the course of our conversation, İbrahim explained to me the university's vision to be an international institution attracting students to Turkey from all over the world, apparently appealing particularly to students from Muslim backgrounds:

İbrahim: The university currently has students from 51 different countries [...] they are mostly from Central Asia – Tajikistan and Kazakhstan and so on. Next year, we are planning to increase the number of countries to 75. We have 300 students now, and 130 of them are foreign. We aim to keep the percentage between 30 and 50 per cent. Scholarships are available from 100 per cent down. The language of instruction is English – it is forbidden to speak Turkish on the campus in the faculty area.

CT: *Why did you choose this location for the university?*

İbrahim: Because this is a very accessible city internationally [...]

CT: *Most of the foreign students appear to be Muslim. Roughly how many would you estimate are from Muslim countries?*

İbrahim: Yes, approximately 60 per cent are Muslim students. After they have graduated, there will be international networks established between students with contacts in over 50 countries.

The Gülen Movement and Higher Education: New Initiatives

Irfan University is one of a new generation of Gülen higher-educational institutions that have opened in recent years, both in Turkey and abroad. As with the schools, it is difficult to quantify their precise numbers – İbrahim estimated that there were (at the time of speaking) approximately ten Gülen-run universities either recently opened or close to opening in Turkey.[5] In addition, similar universities have opened in recent years in Albania, Bosnia, Georgia, northern Iraq, Romania and Turkmenistan.[6]

Irfan was established with the financial support of a group of investors who make up the board of trustees, principal amongst whom was an extremely wealthy Turkish businessman and owner of a large chain of luxury hotels. This individual was not a member of the Gülen Movement's core group – that is to say, he was not, like İbrahim or Ahmet, one of the loyal and dedicated followers of Gülen and was not accountable to the movement's internal hierarchy. Mustafa, a professor in the university's economics department explained to me that 'the board members are not organically connected, but they are sympathetic to the movement. That is to say, they are not in networks like the *dershane* staff and the university's administrative staff.'[7] As practising Muslims with a socially conservative outlook, these board members were 'sympathisers' or 'approvers' (*onaylayanlar*) of the broad Gülenist project. It is individuals such as this who provide the necessary financial backing to the various Gülenist initiatives, and who constitute a secondary tier of allegiance to the movement.[8]

In funding a new foundation (*vakıf*)[9] university, this group of investors is following a strong contemporary trend in Turkey, whereby the market for private higher education has expanded exponentially in the past decade.[10] This trend reflects wider global movements in higher education, especially in developing and middle-income countries where state provision is increasingly supplemented by degree courses offered by fee-paying private universities.[11] In Turkey, expansion in higher education has received strong support from the AKP government, which has legislated for the establishment of more state universities across the country while simultaneously facilitating the creation of many more private universities. Between 2006 and 2011, 50 new state universities and 36 new private universities were founded.[12]

The Gülen Movement's involvement in the university sector has intensified of late, but it stretches back to 1996 and the founding of Fatih University in Istanbul. Fatih is widely known in Turkey to be a Gülen institution. It was established in the pre-AKP era, and was preferred for many years by religiously conservative members of society when they felt themselves to experience considerably more marginalisation from the State than they do today. Fatih continues to function from its main campus on the outskirts of European Istanbul, and still attracts a generally more conservative student demographic than many of its competitor institutions. Despite its relative longevity in Turkish terms, it does not rank amongst the most academically successful private universities and has a reputation for its socially and religiously conservative ethos rather than its intellectual prestige.

The new Gülen-run universities such as Irfan, however, represent a very different – and much more intellectually ambitious – direction in the movement's strategy for higher education. Unlike Fatih, which is viewed as an asset within the movement primarily because it succeeded in functioning in the 1990s within an education system that was hostile to religious influences, the new universities are aiming to become research-led and academically competitive. Central to this strategic vision is the recruitment of high-quality faculty staff. At Irfan, the great majority of professors were Turkish citizens with doctoral qualifications from foreign universities – most of them American and some of them Ivy League. Mustafa, the economics professor who had obtained his PhD from a world top-100 university in the United States, explained his own relationship with the movement as well as his impressions of working at Irfan:

> Mustafa: I am not organically connected with [the Gülen Movement], but I won't listen to bad things being said about them.
> CT: *Why do you choose not to be organically connected?*
> Mustafa: Maybe because I am more independent in my thinking. But working at [Irfan] is like working in the USA. All the professors are educated in the US or abroad, and therefore they are open to new ideas and new people [...] University education in the movement is new. They are trying to compete with Sabancı and Koç and Bilkent, which have been established for 20 years. It is hard to attract the top students. We have some from the top one thousand, though, mainly through scholarships and the attraction of being a small community of excellent scholars.[13]

It is not essential to the movement that all of the faculty staff be core affiliates of Gülen.[14] Many of them, like Mustafa, were broadly sympathetic to the movement but preferred to maintain a distance from the strict hierarchy of its internal organisation. Rather, the salient feature of the faculty staff at Irfan was their strong academic credentials, and the promise of research-led excellence and intellectual prestige that they brought with them. This feature underscored the university's extremely ambitious vision which was, according to İbrahim, to rank as the top university in Turkey, and amongst the top 100 universities in the world, within the next ten years.

Administrative Structure

Metin, a doctoral student and research assistant in the political science department who, like Mustafa, was not a core member of the Gülen community, shared with me his impressions of the university, including its academic and administrative structure:

> The administrative staff are almost all in *Hizmet*. They can be moved around at intervals, like every four years or so. But the

academic staff, only around 30 per cent are *Hizmet* people. It is different from Fatih – academic standards are much higher here […] professors are hired for their prestigious PhDs and for their good research profiles.[15]

In most of the institutions and initiatives run by the movement, the connection to Fethullah Gülen himself is played down and is not publically acknowledged. At Irfan, this was especially apparent. Metin estimated that 70 per cent of the faculty staff were not movement insiders, but it was to be assumed that – if they were Turkish – they were at least aware of the movement and the university's connection with it. The same may not, however, be true of foreign academic staff. A casual encounter with a Canadian business studies professor in the canteen revealed that he was not only unaware of the university's religious or ideological associations, but furthermore he had never even heard the name Fethullah Gülen.

Such an encounter caused me to question in what ways Irfan could accurately be defined as a 'Gülen university', if members of its core academic staff were either ambivalent about the movement or even entirely unaware of its existence.[16] The structure of the university's administration, however, made this clear. Members of administrative staff such as İbrahim were all dedicated followers of Gülen, and core members of the Gülen community. As Metin indicated, these individuals could be rotated to a new post on a regular basis – either to a new administrative position within the university network or to one in the broader portfolio of Gülen projects. Their commitment was primarily to the Gülen cause rather than to their own personal well-being or professional progression – and as such they shared much in common with the teachers at the primary and secondary schools, who were also rotated between posts on a regular basis. Academic personnel, on the other hand, were recruited primarily on the strength of their professional achievements, and their personal allegiance to Gülen was not an essential requirement.

The commitment and professionalism of the administrative cadre is a strength of the Gülen Movement in the many areas in which it is operational. At Irfan, it was apparent that this was the contribution made by the core affiliates of Gülen to the operation of the university. As one of my interlocutors put it, 'the board of trustees *allows Hizmet* to operate within the university', apparently in return for its administrative efficiency and pool of dedicated staff.

Patronage, Networking and Recruitment

Individuals who are core affiliates of Gülen demonstrate extraordinary commitment to the Gülenist vision, and dedicate time, personal resources and finances to it. It is not apparent that these individuals see any immediate financial benefit from their commitment – indeed, the teachers at the schools where I carried out research mainly lived in very simple accommodation and received a lower salary than their state-sector counterparts.[17] Similarly frugal lifestyles were observed in individuals working for the movement's other initiatives in Turkey, such as its dialogue platforms. Yet individuals in the movement's second tier of affiliation, a group that I have identified as 'sympathisers', appear to benefit directly from a wide range of personal economic opportunities and privileges derived from their membership of a powerful Gülenist patronage network.

At Irfan, for example, the brightest and most ambitious students were to be offered employment on graduation in the various businesses of the university's benefactors. The student named Rustam, who was mentioned above, and İbrahim the administrator both stated this directly; Rustam recalled his decision to study at this institution because '[it] was new and international, and they promised us many things – many good things – like [...] great opportunities to get jobs and things', while İbrahim informed me that 'the best students can meet [the individual who funded the university] directly, and job opportunities with him after graduation are good'.

For a student such as Rustam, involvement with the Gülen Movement had begun in his native country of Tajikistan, where his parents had enrolled him at a Gülen school. Demonstrating academic potential as well as an openness to religious devotion, and specifically the teachings of Gülen, had made him an eligible candidate for his university scholarship in Turkey. He was now in a position to engage with and benefit from the extensive patronage systems that are operational within the movement, and it was likely that upon graduation he would secure a bright future for himself by way of these internal Gülenist networks. In this way, the movement's networks extend internationally, all the while positioning Turkey as the cultural centre of its expansive vision for training and equipping a new generation of religiously observant, global youth.

Many students at Irfan had been 'fed' through the Gülen school network, whether in Turkey or abroad. One such student, Bahar from Istanbul, spoke with me at length about her journey all the way from a Gülen kindergarten to this Gülen university. Bahar had progressed through the full spectrum of Gülen education by way of academic scholarships, and was now a full-scholarship student at Irfan. She had been born into a nominally Sunni Muslim family in a working-class neighbourhood in Istanbul, and had encountered some resistance from her family on account of her involvement with the Gülen Movement. She had a twin sister, Betül, who had left the Gülen system after primary school in order to attend a state high school, and was now studying at a private university in Istanbul. Bahar was a keen supporter of Gülen and was resident in one of the student houses (*ışıkevi*) attached to the university. That is to say, she was a willing participant in the activities of the movement and was accountable to an *abla* and, by association, to a wider internal hierarchy of authority. Her story reveals much about the movement's recruitment strategies, its targeted promotion of talented students and the rewards that are available to those who choose to participate in the Gülen system.

When I interviewed her in May 2013, Bahar was just about to complete her first year at Irfan, during which time she had been studying in the English preparatory department. The following autumn, she would begin her undergraduate degree in law. Bahar was bright and outgoing, dressed casually in jeans and a tee shirt with her long, brown hair uncovered. She spoke very quickly and with great animation. After about half an hour, the conversation moved on to the subject of her choice to pursue the opportunities given her by the Gülen Movement, and her family's reception of that choice:

CT: *Are your family religiously observant?*
Bahar: They only fast in Ramadan – apart from my aunts, who don't fast. They believe, but they are the kind of people who say that it is enough to have a clean heart – they aren't very active in terms of practising their religion.
CT: *But they're not opposed to you?*
Bahar: No, they're not opposed [...] but it would be wrong to say that I haven't had problems! Sometimes I have trouble, especially with my aunts [*yenge*]. They're completely opposed to some things [...] for example, they say 'ok, go to school, study, eat your meals and so on, but don't get mixed up in other things – definitely don't

	become an *abla* (for example)'. But it's because they don't know – they have just heard negative things from the outside, this is why. I don't argue about it – I don't want to get into a discussion, so I just say ok!
CT:	*Why don't they want you to get involved, do you think?*
Bahar:	Why? Because they think it will be bad for me.
CT:	*How?*
Bahar:	Well, exactly! I say to them, 'how can it be bad to be praying and studying and fasting? What is wrong with worshipping God?' But they say, 'Oh, they're going to use you for their own purposes, and send you away somewhere, and you won't be able to live your own life'. But I'm happy doing these things, and this is what I want! They're always thinking about the future – 'maybe in the future you'll be unhappy, or you'll want to leave' – but I'm happy now, doing what I'm doing.
CT:	*Did they also think like this when you were at high school, because that was also a Hizmet school?*
Bahar:	Yes, and I went to Anafen[18] as well! But since I was young I've won scholarships – I got a tuition reduction at FEM[19] *dershane* and from there I got one to the *kolej* [private high school]. We couldn't have afforded it, and the *kolej* offered much better opportunities. I got cover for my tuition, for food, for accommodation, for everything. And of course because it was a *kolej* there was much more personal input from the teachers. If you go to a normal [state] Anadolu high school you don't get that degree of input. And once I was there at the *kolej*, I decided to come here!
CT:	*What does your twin sister, Betül, think about it all?*
Bahar:	She went to Anafen as well, but she thinks a little differently [...] She's the kind of person who likes to help people, but our characters are quite different. For example, I'm always working to get somewhere, to achieve something – she's not so tenacious, so she didn't get a fee-reduction at the *dershane*, for example. She didn't want to go – she was quite affected by her friends at her [state] high school [...] of course it's a personal thing, it depends on what the individual wants, but I really wanted it, and now I'm here and she's somewhere else. We both started at Anafen together, but

now we're in different places. There was no pressure on either of us, thank God. She's living in a normal house, not a *Hizmet* house – she lives with some of her friends.[20]

Bahar was evidently a bright and ambitious student. It was clear from talking to her that she had recognised the educational opportunities available to her from the Gülen Movement, and that she had enthusiastically embraced them. Her twin sister had chosen not to pursue those same opportunities, either because she lacked Bahar's academic talent or because she was – like her wider family – more ambivalent about engaging directly with the movement.

Bahar's interest in religion had developed because of her involvement with teachers who were followers of Gülen at the *kolej* that she had attended in Istanbul. She had first been introduced to Gülen's teachings while living in a student dormitory attached to the school, and this is where she had begun to actively practise her Islamic faith:

> I have learnt so much. For example, I learnt to do *namaz* at my school, not from my parents. I've only recently learnt how to read the Qur'an, at home. I didn't know anything at all! But I've learnt. There is the opportunity to learn, and so I have learnt. If I want to do this then I can do it, but I don't have to – it's up to me. And my family let me make my own decisions. And because I see how beneficial it is, I want to be a part of it and I want to help others too.[21]

For Bahar, the introduction to Islamic piety had come along with opportunities for personal advancement. She had attended high-quality educational institutions, and was now well positioned to ultimately establish for herself a successful career in law. Her intention was to pursue postgraduate studies and become a university academic at Irfan itself, 'because [I] really love this school, and there are many opportunities here'. Her admiration for Gülen and his followers was clearly genuine, and her decision to embrace Islam in a more proactive way than her family had chosen to do was very clearly her own. This was partially evidenced by Betül's decision, equally of her own making, to the contrary. For Bahar, though, the convergence of religious piety with the promise of personal opportunity and reward through her membership of a network of Gülen affiliates was both attractive and logical. Such are the possibilities for individuals who choose to participate within a Gülenist system which, potentially, has very much to offer.

Science in Higher Education

Along with Bahar who was studying law, Arif, Majid and Rustam were enrolled for degrees in international relations, computer engineering, and electronic and electrical engineering. These various subjects reflect the academic focus of Irfan. The university has five faculties: business, engineering, law, tourism and architecture. There are no plans to open a faculty for natural science, or for the humanities.[22] In this way Irfan is typical of the new generation of *vakıf* universities in Turkey, which mostly offer courses in applied sciences (namely engineering and medicine) and social sciences (law, sociology, psychology, politics, economics), demand for which is high amongst the student population.[23]

The country's state universities, which were either established or overhauled from their earlier Ottoman manifestations in the middle of the twentieth century, all include a broad sweep of academic provision, and all include faculties of natural science. The same is true of *vakıf* universities such as Bilkent in Ankara, and Sabancı and Koç in Istanbul, which were established in the 1980s and 1990s. At the time of their foundation, these universities were legally required to include Fen-Edebiyat (science and literature) faculties, within which the natural science subjects are generally accommodated in the Turkish system. A change in the law in 2008 gave new universities autonomy in relaxing the law to require only that they open a minimum of three faculties, and a Fen-Edebiyat faculty is no longer a mandatory component. The choice of its faculty focus is up to the university to decide. Post-2008 institutions may therefore choose their academic structure themselves, and orient their provision according to specific disciplinary interests. As a result, very few, if any, of this new generation of universities offer degree courses in physics, chemistry or biology, preferring to concentrate their science provision on more marketable (and profitable) courses in engineering and medical science.[24]

The Gülen Movement is clearly following a national trend in terms of the disciplinary bent of its involvement in the Turkish higher-education sector.

This fact comes as no great surprise, but it does throw into sharp relief the influence of market forces on the movement's interest in science and science education. The movement's schools have developed a successful model of education, in which the natural science subjects are taught to a high standard, yet it is far from clear that the movement has an agenda for the promotion of natural science in any serious or sustained way at a professional level. Students are competently trained in physics, chemistry and biology at school, and the brightest of them are intensively coached for success in the Science Olympiads. Nonetheless, its does not appear that the movement's Nursian philosophical discourse on science and Islam is leading to sustained interest in scientific research, or indeed that it is facilitating the imminent emergence of a new generation of Muslim research scientists.[25] This was apparent not only from the structual exclusion of the natural sciences from the new Gülen universities, but also from my one-to-one encounters with high-achieving science students at the high schools where I conducted research.

At the schools that I studied, only a very small number of students who excelled in science chose to study for a university degree in the pure sciences. Rather, the overwhelming preference was for acceptance into university engineering departments, with a very few interested in pursuing medicine. At the school named Yunus, the Olympiad coordinator estimated that as many as 90 per cent of his competition students applied for engineering, and 10 per cent for medicine. An interview with a group of eight mathematics and chemistry Olympiad students at the boys' school of the school named Kelebek revealed a similar statistic, showing that six of them wanted to study a branch of engineering at university, and two of them medicine.[26] The Olympiad coordinator at the same school reported that this was quite typical, and explained the situation as follows:

Teacher: If they are strong at sciences (*fen bilgisi*) then they choose engineering [...] or sometimes medicine.
CT: *Do they ever prefer to study for a degree in their own field of science, for example, chemistry?*
Teacher: No. If they choose that route then the only career choice open to them when they graduate will be teaching. If you become an engineer or a doctor then you know you will find a good job. These are more successful professions, with better salaries.

CT: *So none of these students pursue careers in scientific research?*
Teacher: Well, a few do [...] we had a very successful chemistry student [...] he went to Germany to work for a pharmaceutical company. And another student went to the USA to do a Master's degree in physics. He's still studying, maybe doing a doctorate [...][27]

It was clear from this conversation with the Olympiad coordinator that the priority for his science graduates was entry into professions that would guarantee job stability, earning power and social prestige, which are all encompassed in Turkey by engineering and medicine. The aspirations of high-achieving Gülen-school science graduates were, therefore, no different from high-achieving students all over Turkey, for whom acceptance to study engineering or medical science at one of the top universities represented the 'Holy Grail' of higher education. For that minority of students who did desire to pursue studies in natural science subjects, their futures lay abroad at universities in Europe or the USA.

Science in the Muslim world: A New Direction?

The emergence of the new Gülen universities in recent years underscores a question that is anyway precipitated by the movement's broader interest in education: given that religiously motivated Gülen educators are committed to, and apparently excellent at, teaching science at secondary level, *to what end* is this endeavour being undertaken? That is to say, what are the fruits of the Gülenist pedagogical project vis-à-vis science in the modern Muslim context?

One of the central components identified as essential to the development of a strong scientific culture in the Muslim world is the fostering of critical, independent thought. This observation has been made in an editorial to a special issue on science and Islam in *Nature*: 'What are the critical components necessary for any Muslim nation with serious ambitions in science? A minimal requirement is an education system that embraces science as well as a critical approach.'[28] With respect to the Gülen schools, it is not clear that this critical approach is being adopted, or that this aspect of Gülen pedagogy differs in any substantive way from the rote-style of teaching that prevails in both the state and private branches of Turkish education.

Students whom I encountered spoke often of the extraordinary commitment that their teachers showed to their work, and the value of this extra support in preparing them for competitive exams such as the YGS (Examination for Entrance to Higher Education) and the LYS (Degree Placement Exam). Both of these exams are, however, composed entirely of multiple-choice questions, and they do not assess students on their critical analytical skills.

It does not appear at this stage that the Gülen schools have devised a new or innovative way of teaching science in the Muslim context. Rather, they seem to have developed a model that is extremely *successful* according to prevailing pedagogical and societal norms. The same pattern is discernible in the movement's new ventures in the field of higher education. It is primarily the desire to prosper by excelling in modern life that drives the Gülenist educational project, both at secondary and tertiary levels, and in turn its engagement with the field of science. A few very talented science graduates of Gülen schools may pursue a career in research, but, following the wider national as well as regional trend, they will generally do so abroad. In turn, the new universities themselves are equipped, in the field of science and technology, to train technicians (engineers and medics) rather than to push the boundaries of scientific knowledge or to cultivate anything resembling a 'renaissance' in Muslim science.[29]

It would therefore be mistaken, or at least premature at this stage, to assume that the Gülen Movement's commitment to science education is connected to a serious interest in invigorating the relationship between modern science and Islam. Rather, science education provides a valuable milieu through which the movement recruits, influences and equips the next generation of pious Muslims for successful engagement in a rationalist and technological world order. The new generation of Gülen universities illustrate this point well, being characterised by the ambition to become prestigious, research-led institutions and leaders in the Turkish higher-education market, but clearly avoiding the inclusion of natural science in their intellectual agendas. The movement has a variety of strategies, besides science and education, through which it seeks to exert influence as a conservative Muslim group in the modern world. The chapters that follow explore these strategies further, and in so doing set the Gülenist project in science and education in its wider national and transnational context.

PART THREE
THE WIDER CONTEXT

6

Intercultural Dialogue

The Journalists and Writers Foundation (*Gazeteciler ve Yazarlar Vakfı*, GYV)[1] is a civic initiative that purports to 'look for ways to [...] build a common living space based on reconciliation and mutual respect'. Since its foundation in 1994, it has spearheaded a number of civic, interfaith and intercultural dialogue initiatives. The GYV is one of the main public mouthpieces of the Gülen Movement in Turkey.[2] Gülen himself serves as its honorary chairman, making it the only movement initiative in Turkey with which he is officially affiliated. The fact that he does so reveals something of the centrality of dialogue activities to the movement at large.[3]

The headquarters of the GYV are housed in a smart, glass-fronted office building in Altunizade, a prosperous and bustling business district on the Asian side of Istanbul. Further down the hill, staff run an associated research centre in the luxurious surroundings of an Ottoman-era mansion nestled on the banks of the Bosphorus. From here, a panorama of Istanbul stretching from Topkapı Palace to the Bosphorus Bridge opens up, and the faded glory of the nineteenth-century Dolmabahçe Palace is visible across the water. I paid a visit in the spring of 2013, and met with the centre's director, an extremely affable and engaging man called Uğur. Like many of the individuals operating at a relatively high level within the movement in Turkey, Uğur was happy to talk with me and answer my questions,[4] and he did so for the most part in impeccable, American-accented English.

I spent a few hours drinking tea with Uğur in the comfort of the building's main reception room, newly renovated and lavishly decorated in the Ottoman style. Our conversation covered many themes, including a major conference being planned by the centre, entitled 'Philanthropy and Peacebuilding'. This was an event intended to attract academics, businesspeople and other intellectuals in order to fulfil the GYV's mandate to 'organise events promoting love, tolerance and dialogue'. Uğur also kindly invited me to another forthcoming event being organised by the foundation, which would feature a performance of sung poetry from the Turkish mystical tradition (*tasavvuf*) and to which members of the Alevi community in Turkey had been invited.[5]

I was intrigued that over the course of our quite lengthy conversation about dialogue between faiths and cultures, Uğur made no explicit reference to Islam or to his own Muslim faith. This in spite of the fact that the atmosphere in the waterside mansion was heavily imbued with Ottoman-Islamic influences, which were visible everywhere from its external architecture to its soft furnishings and the artwork adorning the walls. The staff at the centre, Uğur included, all projected a pious Islamic identity both through their dress (the women were all dressed in the *tesettür* style) as well as in their conservative personal comportment, namely the conspicuous distance maintained between men and women on an interpersonal level. Clearly, Islam was an important motivator in the lives of the centre's staff, yet it did not feature in our discussion of the foundation's work. I left the mansion that afternoon wondering why this should be so, and wondering furthermore what connected Islam and dialogue in the Gülen Movement.

A Brief History of Gülen Dialogue

The rationale for dialogue in Fethullah Gülen's thought is derived, like most of his ideas, from the work of Said Nursi. Nursi was deeply interested in interfaith issues, primarily in the specific context of Christian–Muslim relations. He was keenly aware of what he perceived as the rising tide of secularism and atheism in his day, and he was amenable to finding areas of commonality with the Christian world if it might, in broad terms, strengthen the intellectual case for religious faith. Nursi's interest in Christianity was also underpinned to some extent by his admiration for the scientific progress achieved by Western societies in recent times. His exhortation to his Muslim followers to engage with Christian civilisations was based at least partially on the premise that they should learn certain lessons from the West and, in so doing, that they might prosper and flourish themselves.

The *Risale-i Nur* is in essence a Qur'anic commentary, a thematically arranged work of exegesis, and it is replete with criticisms of Christanity and Christian doctrine – particularly, of the incarnation and the notion of a Trinitarian God. The refutation of these concepts is an important feature of the Qur'an and of Islamic theology more broadly, and it is no surprise that Nursi also refutes them.[6] There are also, however, sections of the *Risale* which indicate a certain tolerance in Nursi's approach to other monotheistic faiths. In one passage for example, he highlights the famous Qur'anic injunction to 'come to a common word' with the People of the Book (Muslims, Christians and Jews):

> With all its strength and freshness, the Qur'an makes the whole world resound with its call: *Say, 'O People of the Book! Come to a common world between us and you, that we worship none but God, and that we associate none as partner with Him, and that none of us take others for Lords, apart from God.'* (3.64)[7]

Elsewhere, he admits to the possibility that some Christians might find their way to Paradise in the afterlife:

> my opinion [is] that in our century there are many who, since the truths of Islam have not been conveyed to them, may be regarded as similar to people of the 'interregnum'. Especially if these people are religious Christians who are victims of war, they may be saved in the Hereafter and regarded as martyrs of sorts.[8]

In the grammar of interfaith dialogue, this extract gives grounds for locating Nursi in the 'inclusivist' school. That is to say, while it is clear to him that Islam is the ideal religion and the only sure guarantee of salvation in the afterlife, he appears to admit that other religions (namely, Christianity) contain elements of the truth within them, and that salvific opportunities might extend beyond the realm of Islam.

Nursi is clearly not a pluralist in the sense defined by the theologian John Hick.[9] That is to say, he does not admit that all religious traditions are equally valid in their own right, and that none has a greater monopoly on the truth than any other. Rather, in the words of Ian Markham, a leading expositor of Said Nursi's theology of interfaith dialogue, Nursi is 'committed to the truth of Islam as disclosed in the Qur'an and the life of the prophet Muhammad. Yet he acknowledges that other traditions have a partial insight into the truth.'[10] This position has a strong Qur'anic precedent, as Islam generally presents itself as the correction to Judaism and Christianity and as the final and conclusive word on divine revelation. Nursi's decision to emphasise the value of the previous traditions is, however, what sets him apart from other Muslim scholars and exegetes, many of whom have chosen historically to overlook this in their defence of Islam as the final revelation of God.

Following the Nursian precendent, Fethullah Gülen has written about and participated in dialogue activities for much of his career, beginning in earnest in the 1990s. In 1998, four years after the foundation of the GYV, he famously travelled to Rome to meet Pope John Paul II. The image of the two men shaking hands has been widely circulated since, and is perceived as emblematic of the movement's commitment to pursuing dialogue with the Christian world. A few years before, in 1996, Gülen had held public meetings in Istanbul with the Greek Orthodox Patriarch Bartholomew and the Chief Rabbi of Turkey, David Aseo.

The movement's interest in dialogue spiked after Gülen's move to the USA in 1999, and it has been a consistent area of growth since that time. Coinciding directly with Gülen's arrival in Pennsylvania in 1999, his followers established the Rumi Forum in Washington, DC.[11] Today, the Rumi Forum is the largest and most publically prominent Gülenist dialogue initiative in the USA, running an extensive programme of conferences and public lectures, often with an emphasis on Turkish culture and current affairs. Drawing inspiration from the thirteenth-century Sufi mystic from whom it takes its name, the forum seeks 'to facilitate dialogue by promoting love to transform hate, understanding to prevent misinterpretation, flexibility against rigidity, and, above all, tolerance to overcome bigotry'. As with the GYV in Istanbul, Gülen serves as its honorary president.

In 2002, three years after the foundation of the Rumi Forum, the movement founded the Dialogue Institute Southwest (previously the Institute of Interfaith Dialogue).[12] Headquartered in Texas, the institute has branch offices in five different US states. Its staff contributed to the establishment in 2007 of a prestigious new venture in Gülenist dialogue, the Gülen Institute at the University of Houston. This is an academic research centre dedicated to 'the promotion of peace and civic welfare' and underpinned by 'the belief that by bringing people of diverse ethnic, religious, and cultural backgrounds together, we can advance mutual understanding, respect, and cooperation'.[13] In Texas as in Washington, DC, where the Rumi Forum has collaborated with the Center for Muslim–Christian Understanding at Georgetown University, the movement garners the tacit as well as vocal support of American academics – some of them very influential – in its peacebuilding, interfaith agenda.[14]

There are now, in addition to the Gülen Institute at Houston, a number of academic chairs dedicated to the study of interfaith issues around the world. These include: the Gülen Chair for Intercultural Studies at the Catholic University of Leuven in the Netherlands; the Fethullah Gülen Chair in the Study of Islam and Muslim–Catholic Relations at the Australian Catholic University in Melbourne, Australia; the Nursi Chair in Islamic Studies at John Carroll University in Ohio; and the Fethullah Gülen Chair at Syarif Hidayetullah Islam University, Indonesia.

As well as these academic initiatives, the movement runs numerous smaller dialogue organisations across the USA and around the world. It is reasonable to suggest that in every country in which the movement is active today, there are some form of local, grass-roots, dialogue-focused activities taking place. The Gülen Movement began in the 1960s with a mandate for education, and it continues to invest a great deal of time, resources and personnel in that sector today. Over the past decade and a half, however, dialogue has emerged alongside education as perhaps the defining characteristic of the now, global, movement as it moves into the twenty-first century.

Gülen's Philosophy for Dialogue

The movement's approach to dialogue has evolved and changed over the course of the past 30 years. In its earliest incarnation, Gülenist dialogue appeared to focus primarily on interfaith issues – namely those facing the three monotheistic religions – as evidenced by the meetings between Gülen and various high-level Christian and Jewish leaders in the 1990s. This is confirmed by Gülen in his article entitled 'Dialogue with the People of the Book', which he wrote in 1995:

> The attitude of believers is determined according to the degree of their faith. I believe that if the message is put across properly, then an environment conducive to dialogue will be able to emerge in our country and throughout the world. Thus, as in every subject, we should approach this issue as indicated in the Qur'an and by the Prophet, peace and blessings be upon him. God says in the Qur'an:
> *This is the Book; in it is sure guidance, without doubt, to those who are God-conscious, pious.* (Al-Baqara 2.2)
> [...] Using a very gentle and slightly oblique style the Qur'an calls people to accept the former prophets and their books. The fact that such a condition has been placed at the very beginning of the Qur'an seems to be very significant to me when it comes to talking about the establishment of a dialogue with Jews and Christians. In another verse God commands:
> *And argue not with the People of the Book unless it be in (a way) that is better.* (Al-Ankabut 29.46).[15]

It has become clear over time, however, that Gülen's vision of interfaith dialogue between Muslims, Christians and Jews is not one that foregrounds an engaged discussion of the thorny historical and theological issues that separate the three traditions. In this sense, it is arguably not actually 'interfaith dialogue', with its usual associations of deep theological wrestling and hermeneutical analysis, in which he is interested. Gülen does not attempt to engage a Christian or Jewish audience on such subjects as the Trinitarian God, the incarnation and resurrection of Jesus, the prophethood of Muhammad or the purposes of God in Jewish history. Rather, he steers entirely clear of these major sticking points and emphasises instead the areas of *commonality* that are shared between Jews, Christians and Muslims as co-participators in a shared humanity:

> In Islamic thought, every individual is a manifestation of the same essence; we are different facets of the divinely bestowed reality. Indeed, all who gather into a community, whether united under one God or one land, resemble the 'limbs of a body' of which the Prophet spoke. The hand does not compete with the foot, the tongue does not reproach the lips, the eye does not reprehend the ears, and the heart does not struggle against the mind. If we are complementary parts of the same body, why should this union be seen as discrepancy? Why should we disrupt the unity among us? It is in unity that we can make this world like a paradise, and through unity that we can attain Paradise. When will we remove from our souls the thoughts and feelings that alienate us from each other?[16]

The tenor of this extract is typical of Gülen's later writings, within which the notion of shared human existence, and a commitment to attaining peace between peoples on earth, are frequently stressed. The emphasis in Gülenist thought on stressing unity over difference begins, perhaps, to explain why my interlocutors' Muslim faith was not made explicit to me on my initial visit to the GYV research centre. Uncomfortable with making our differences explicit, Uğur and his colleagues chose instead to talk about areas of mutual interest and concern, such as the value of philanthropy and the need for better social cohesion in Turkey.

Such a strategy for attaining 'universal peace' clearly steers away from open disagreement on an intellectual or philosophical level. This feature of the movement's approach to dialogue was made very clear to me during a conversation with Erin, an American teacher of English working at a Gülen school in Turkey. Erin was a Christian, and was interested in discussing issues to do with religious belief with her Muslim colleagues. She was rather disappointed that theological discussions were not easily forthcoming:

> One day, I brought up the subject of Abraham, and who he is in Christianity compared to in Islam. We were in the staff room and just starting to talk about it, and I had my Bible out and [my colleague] had her Qur'an open in front of her. At that point,

> Neslihan the religious studies teacher overheard us speaking and she got extremely upset [...] she said that we should only talk about areas of commonality and not of difference, as that that was what Fethullah Gülen taught. She got really upset about it.[17]

Gülen's vision for dialogue is clearly not one predicated on direct engagement with the religious texts, along the lines that Erin was wanting to initiate here. This therefore begs the question: if not theological or textual encounter then what, exactly, characterises Gülen inter-religious and intercultural dialogue, and why, furthermore, is it so important to the movement?

Functions of Dialogue in the Gülen Movement: Interpersonal Encounter and Networking

There are, I suggest, multiple ways in which dialogue activities serve the movement's interests and support its broader agenda, many of which overlap and interact with one another. Primarily, dialogue provides a forum for interpersonal encounter and networking, something on which the movement relies very heavily and at which it is adept. Accordingly, it is less interested in the intellectual details of interfaith debate than it is in the lived realities of encounters between people of different cultures and backgrounds.[18]

This fact is reflected very clearly in the preference for the term 'intercultural dialogue' over 'interfaith dialogue' in Gülen circles. The former is considerably more nebulous than the latter and allows for a much broader agenda that is not limited to the specifics of theological discussion. It is also considerably less sensitive a term in Turkey, something which was pointed out to me by a senior employee of the GYV when I enquired:

> CT: *How does inter-cultural dialogue differ from inter-faith dialogue?*
>
> GYV employee: For us in Turkey it means the same thing, but when we established the foundation platform, we used culture because it was more expedient. Some Muslim scholars say there cannot

be any dialogue as Islam is the right religion and the others are wrong. Secondly, the government is sensitive about non-Muslims. In Urfa (when we had the first meeting),[19] they put a bomb in front of my office and also in the churches of the Greek Orthodox and the Armenians. So we put the name culture, not religion, but it means the same thing.[20]

Besides offering an effective forum for face-to-face encounter and networking, dialogue initiatives also provide the movement with various other secondary opportunities. The ones that I choose to focus and expand on below are as follows: first, they offer a chance to present Islam in a positive light, a need that is keenly felt by many Muslims living in the West in the post 9/11 era; second, they offer an effective vehicle for the promotion of Turkey and Turkish culture, a value that lies at the very core of the global Gülen project.

In 1998, the Gülen Movement facilitated a meeting of public intellectuals, academics and businessmen to discuss a range of policy-related issues pertaining to Turkish affairs. The group met in the town of Abant near Istanbul. The meeting spawned the so-called Abant Platform,[21] and has since become an annual event held in different locations across Turkey as well as internationally. The Abant Platform is the most prominent such initiative of the movement in Turkey, but there are many others operating at a local level. Such meetings bring together influential individuals for interpersonal networking and an exchange of ideas with the intention, ultimately, of influencing society through civic and non-political channels. They fall under the broad rubric of 'dialogue' activities in the movement's terminology.

In the spring of 2013, I attended two related events at the Marriott and Sheraton hotels in Ankara, at the invitation of the then-director of the GYV's Ankara branch. The events featured a lecture entitled 'Islam and Democracy: The Arab Countries, Turkey and the USA', to be delivered by a Turkish professor of politics, himself sympathetic to Gülen, working at a large, public university in the USA. The lecture was delivered in Turkish at the first event, for which the audience comprised local university academics, and in English for the second event, for which the audience comprised diplomatic staff from the various foreign missions represented in the capital. Ankara, it is often said, is a city of politicians and students. The city is home to the Turkish parliament as well as a great number of universities, and the guest list for the two events reflected this demographic very clearly.

Despite the highly relevant and potentially controversial nature of the lecture subject, the organisers steered clear of difficult issues and were clearly keen to avoid confrontation. In this sense, the events mirrored the experience of Erin the American teacher, who had found her interlocutor in the schoolteachers' room to be uneasy about discussing areas of potential discord or disagreement – on that occasion the subject had been theology; on this occasion it was politics, but a similar principle seemed to be at work on both.

For the Turkish audience, a dinner was held in a private function room in the Marriott, an elite hotel in the centre of Ankara's affluent Çukurambar district. I was greeted by my contact at the GYV and escorted to my seat in a room rapidly filling up with men, smartly dressed in suits and ties. Of 50 guests there in total, there were only three other women at the event. Shortly after I sat down, a young woman in very smart *tesettür* dress arrived and sat down next to me. She was shy and embarrassed at first that she spoke no English, a hindrance that we overcame by switching to Turkish. It was clear that she had been sent to accompany me as a lone female in a room almost entirely full of men, in order to avoid the uncomfortable situation whereby nobody approached or spoke to me on account of my gender. This was one of my earliest encounters with the movement and I was somewhat surprised by the rigidity of the gender segregation, but it was a thoughtful gesture with clearly hospitable intentions behind it.

The atmosphere was very different at the English-language event, where, not only was the gender distribution much more equal but the question-and-answer session was also considerably more vibrant and challenging. During the discussion time afterwards, some of the foreign diplomatic staff raised some particular thorny questions pertaining to Turkish political Islam and the AKP. The event took place in April 2013, shortly before the nationwide riots that errupted from protests in Istanbul's Gezi Park and before the erruption of the AKP corruption probe later that year. The question of (then) Prime Minister Erdoğan's ultimate aspirations concerning the integration of Islam into politics was nonetheless a very pressing one, which commentators on Turkey had long been discussing. Following the events of the so-called Arab Spring, Turkey was still being touted by many as a potential 'model' or 'inspiration' to its neighbours – a suggestion that has long since been dropped, partly because of the turn of events in Turkey itself (where the relationship between Islam, politics and secularism is being re-negotiated) and partly because of the subsequent descent into chaos of many of the Arab states. The speaker refused, however, to be drawn on these potentially difficult issues, preferring to keep the discussion at the level of abstract intellectual models and firmly avoiding entering into territory that might be controversial or politically sensitive.

The primary draw of the events, it seemed, was not the engaging nature of the debate or the immediate application of ideas on Islam and democracy to the Turkish political situation. Certainly, the professor gave a fine lecture on these broad principles, but these were not applied to current affairs apart from in the (largely unanswered) questions raised by a number of the foreign diplomats. Its purpose, rather, was to provide a forum bringing together academics and diplomats with the goal of networking, interpersonal conversation and the cultivation of one-to-one relationships. This kind of networking characterises the Gülen Movement on every level at which it is operational, and is the highly effective vehicle through which it accrues and exercises its influence in the civil realm.[22]

Local Variations

Events such as this one, catering for the diplomatic and academic communities, take place on a regular basis in Ankara. It is a strength of the movement at large that it understands local demographics very well, and to some extent tailors its activities to suit them. This is true on an international level, where the movement differs slightly from country to country, but it is also the case domestically. The movement is far from uniform across the whole of Turkey, but rather diplays notable regional variations.

In the southern coastal city of Antalya, for example, the movement runs a dialogue initiative called AKDİM (Antalya Kültürlerarası Diyalog Merkezi, Antalya Inter-Cultural Dialogue Centre).[23] Antalya is a city with a high proportion of foreign-national residents, a great number of them of Russian and German origin. It is not a serious intellectual city like Ankara, but rather a vacation spot. The movement's dialogue activities in Antalya reflect this fact very well: its director, a man in his mid thirties named Halil, explained to me when I visited in late 2013 that the aim of the centre was, first and foremost, to be a place of support and friendship for foreigners living in the city. Accordingly, its different projects were arranged under the headings of 'language', 'living together', 'sport', 'women' and 'culture'. Both Halil and a female colleague who was responsible for the women's activities spoke fluent German, having lived and studied in that country, although neither of them spoke English. They were well positioned to work with the sizeable German-speaking community in Antalya, and their programme was tailored to meet the specific needs of that particular community.

The contrast between the movement's dialogue-related initiatives in Ankara and Antalya is revealing. Rather than promoting a single, cohesive agenda or even model for dialogue in both locations, the movement adapts its activities in light of local tastes and proclivities. Its priority, it appears, is to bring people together around themes that interest them, and to cultivate interpersonal encounters at a local level. Its strength in doing this is related at once to its willingness to adapt to local circumstances, and its ability to understand and engage with the interests of local populations.

Defending Islam in a Post-9/11 World

The movement's interest in dialogue has increased substantially since Gülen relocated to the USA in 1999, a move that precipitated the spread of its activities in the United States as well as elsewhere in the world. Gülen had already been speaking about the importance of interfaith dialogue, and its intrinsically Islamic value, since the 1980s, well before the 9/11 attacks. Dialogue is, however, a theme that he and his followers have strongly emphasised in the years since 2001 – an epoch that has been defined by the threat of Al Qaeda and international terrorism, and the concomitant rise of anti-Islamic sentiment in many Western nations. The need for positive representations of Islam in the West in order to counteract this widespread negativity is felt accutely by many Muslims, and Gülen's dialogue initiatives seem designed in many ways to meet this need.

The Gülen Movement is still a Turkish organisation at its core, which is to say that the vast majority of Gülen's committed followers are Turkish citizens, wherever they may reside in the world. Nonetheless, the importance of the USA to the movement, and its evolution since 1999, cannot be overestimated. Gülen himself is resident in Pennsylvania, meaning that the physical centre of the movement's activities is located in the United States, and many senior members of the Gülen hierarchy pass through on a regular basis to visit him there. Although Gülen himself lives a reclusive life on a private ranch, rarely – if ever – venturing out in public, his followers have made themselves very much at home in the US and are engaged in all manner of activities there. They have capitalised on the freedoms afforded them in that country both to initiate enterprise in business and education and also to establish forums for dialogue, political lobbying and civil-society engagement.

In turn, the cultural markers of twenty-first-century America have shaped and influenced the evolution of the movement itself, and this is nowhere more apparent than in its interest in speaking up as a positive and peace-seeking voice for Islam. I have been unable to visit the movement in the USA, but have investigated aspects of its manifestation in the UK, where this is also a major concern.

The British Gülen Movement is considerably smaller in scale than its American counterpart and is mostly concentrated in London.[24] It is also smaller in scope than its equivalents in various countries on the European continent, namely Germany and the Netherlands, which have larger and more prominent Turkish diasporas.[25] The primary vehicle for the movement's activities in the UK is a charitable foundation called the Dialogue Society (established 1999), which operates from offices in Tottenham, a district in the north of London close to the city's largest Turkish and Kurdish communities. The society is staffed predominantly – but not exclusively – by Muslim individuals of Turkish background, who are inspired by the teachings of Fethullah Gülen. It is active on a number of different levels: first, the society facilitates regular grass-roots engagement events, at which people from different ethnic and religious backgrounds are brought together in face-to-face interactions, such as discussion forums and shared social events; second, it provides academic training in dialogue studies, running an MA in that subject in conjunction with Keele University in Staffordshire, central England; finally, it hosts lectures by high-profile speakers from the British political and religious spheres and from civil society, and publishes academic material on themes such as multiculturalism and religious radicalisation.

In November 2014, the society hosted a premiere of a new documentary film about the Gülen Movement that had been made by an American filmmaker, entitled *Love is a Verb*,[26] which I was invited to attend. I went with great interest, curious primarily to explore more of the movement in its British manifestation in order to draw some comparisons with its activities in Turkey, with which I was more familiar.

The venue for the screening was a cinema on Leicester Square, the most prestigious, and presumably expensive, location for such an event in the country. A large crowd of invited guests (including some elected members of the British parliament) attended a smart drinks reception beforehand, hosted by individuals from the Dialogue Society. Professional photographers captured conversations on camera for later dissemination on the society's website. The showing of the film itself was followed by a question-and-answer session with its director, who had flown in from the USA for the event.

Love is a Verb was a glossy and well-researched production, featuring some fascinating video and photographic footage of Fethullah Gülen's early career as an imam and public preacher in Turkey. For this reason alone, the screening was well worth attending. It was obvious, however, that the film had been made for a foreign audience that was largely unfamiliar with the intricacies of Turkish Islam and its relationship with the State, rather than a domestic one that would be accutely aware of those intricacies. Accordingly, the film's narrative was extremely idealistic. It told the story of an army of selfless volunteers, inspired by a Sufic interpretation of Islam and motivated by the altruistic requirements of their Muslim faith to bring education and healthcare to poor and war-ridden societies such as Bosnia-Herzegovina, Somalia and Iraq. There were some very veiled references to the political situation in Turkey, the tensions surrounding the role of religion in public life and, indeed, to the controversies surrounding the amount of power and influence that is yielded by Gülen and his followers there, but these issues were not explored in any depth. When asked at the end whether there were any plans to show the film in Turkey, the Dialogue Society host responded in the negative, indicating that the film had been made for an international audience and that the information contained within it would already be 'obvious' to many Turkish viewers.

It was very apparent to me on leaving Leicester Square that evening that the movement operates rather differently, and with different priorities, in the UK than it does in Turkey. The motivation behind showing *Love is a Verb* to an audience of invited guests, some of them quite influential in various spheres of British politics and civil society, seemed to be primarily to present a positive image of Islam in order to counteract the negative stereotypes that prevail in that country. The image that was offered, and was warmly welcomed by many in the audience, was of a peaceable Muslim movement characterised by charity, hard work and heroic self-sacrifice. Certainly these are important aspects of Gülen activity both in Turkey and around the world, but the movement is surely rather more complex – and certainly more wealthy and powerful – than this somewhat one-dimensional narrative seemed to suggest. A Turkish audience, whatever its particular stance on the movement, would have realised this immediately.

The point I wish to make is not that the movement willingly promotes misleading material about itself, but rather that it very effectively selects the most appropriate material for a given audience and a given agenda. In this instance, the motivation behind the showing of *Love is a Verb* to an influential group of invited guests in the British capital seemed to be to promote a side of Islam which, inspired by a Sufic notion of love, is peace-loving and altruistic. In this sense, the movement succeeded in presenting a Muslim counter-narrative to a select Western audience, challenging popular perceptions of Islam that are often dominated by Salafi ideology and fears of violent extremism. This is a role that the movement is well placed to carry out, and one to which it appears to attach a high value.

Promoting Turkish Culture

A further important and ubiquitous feature of the Gülen dialogue project is its commitment to the promotion of Turkish culture. This is a central conceit that runs through Gülen Movement activities like a leitmotif; indeed, the concept of Turkishness is absolutely foundational to the

Gülen discourse. In the context of dialogue particularly, Turkey is usually promoted, and engagement with its culture, language and peoples is encouraged. The Rumi Forum, for example, offers regular Turkish language courses and facilitates visits to Turkey 'with the mission of exploring social, economic, cultural, security and political issues in Turkey and the wider region'.[27] Turkey itself is also an important component of the movement's international schools, where Turkish is taught as a second language, along with key aspects of the country's culture. The promotion of Turkishness in this way through the global Gülen Movement has accrued a great deal of soft power for Turkey in recent years, not only in regions where it has historically been involved (Central Asia, Eastern Europe) but also those where it has not (sub-Saharan Africa, the USA).[28]

Perhaps the clearest example of this desire to teach Turkishness to a global audience is the annual events called 'Turkish Olympiads' (*Türkçe Olimpiyatları*).[29] These competitions bring together children from different countries and cultures all around the world in what is packaged as a celebration of intercultural engagement and understanding. Specifically, the Olympiads test children studying at Gülen schools around the world in their knowledge of Turkish language, music and folk dance, and they culminate in finals for which qualifying students travel to Turkey in the summer. The finals are huge events held in sports stadia and attracting crowds in the tens of thousands. Having begun in 2003 with 62 participants from 17 countries, the Olympiads have grown exponentially, and, in 2013, approximately 2,000 students from 140 countries participated in the finals in Turkey.[30]

Following the row with the government that erupted in December 2013, President Erdoğan declared an end to the Turkish Olympiads in March 2014, stating that the necessary premises would no longer be made available to their organisers in Turkey. In light of this situation, the movement held the finals of the events that year in Germany instead.[31] In June 2013, however, shortly before relations had soured, I was able to attend the opening ceremony of the Olympiads in Ankara. Interestingly, on the evening that I was present, the Gezi Park riots were in their first week and were just gaining momentum.[32] Riot police were tackling protestors all over Ankara, and many roads were closed or filled with tear gas on my approach to 19 Mayıs Stadium. Inside, the venue was full to capacity, mostly with conservative Muslim families and their children. The atmosphere was a carnival one, with vendors selling a wide variety of food and drink, and families who had failed to gain admission eating picnics in overflow carparks and watching events inside on large screens. The slogan for the event, which was projected all around the venue – rather ironically, given the violent protests taking place just outside – was the familiar strapline from the GYV, *'Evrensel Barışa Doğru'* (Towards Universal Peace).

The evening was hosted by a young Turkish man dressed in a modern suit and tie, and a woman of Central Asian nationality dressed in her own national costume. It began with the entrance into the arena of children from 140 different countries, who paraded in wearing their national dress, holding the flags of their respective countries aloft. They then launched into a confident performance in Turkish of a poem by Fethullah Gülen, which had been set to music and which extolled the virtues of pursuing the path of peace.[33]

On the night I was present, entrants recited poetry, sang folksongs (*türkü*) and performed some folk dances and dramatic sketches. The events also featured sections for Turkish grammar, essay writing and general knowledge, which I did not witness.[34] The primary purpose of the event was to promote the vision of Turkish becoming an international language. This was underscored by one of the many visiting dignitaries from the AKP, former minister for the interior Muammer Güler, who told the following anecdote in an opening speech:

> One day recently, I was in Paris, walking down the Champs Elysees. Someone stopped me and asked me for directions, and so I gave them. Then I asked him why he had spoken to me in Turkish, and he told me that he didn't know any other language in which to ask. One day, all over the world, God willing, it will be normal to speak Turkish as a common language![35]

In bringing children from all over the world together in Turkey for the event, the geographical centrality of the Turkish nation to the Gülen project was also further underscored. Other cultures were included and celebrated as well, namely through the diverse range of national costumes that was on display. Yet while the emphasis was on dialogue between cultures and a shared humanity, the linchpin of the entire project was, very clearly, Turkey itself.

Pluralism in Gülenist Dialogue: Shi'is and Alevis

Dialogue performs a number of interrelated functions in the Gülen Movement, and supports the wider purposes of the movement, as well as its organisational structure. But how is the Gülen rationale for dialogue applied in situations that are inescapably challenging? The question I wish to raise in closing concerns some of the thornier issues related to pluralism and coexistence that stem from the movement's commitment to intercultural and inter-religious dialogue.

The greatest challenges to the Gülen discourse on this subject come from very close to home, on one level from within Turkey itself and on another from the wider Muslim world. While Gülen writes extensively about the need for tolerance and engagement across religious and cultural borders, he almost always refers to Christianity and Judaism and remains silent on the subject of sectarian differences within Islam itself. Outside Turkey and the Turkic world, he does not appear to attract a significant following amongst fellow-Sunni Muslims, who are perhaps troubled by the heavily Turkish nationalistic tenor of his writing, and the movement is notably less active in the Arab Middle East than in many other regions of the world. Perhaps more significantly, as a Sunni scholar he does not apply the same pluralistic rationale in his perspective on the Muslim Shi'i minority. Gülen's views on Shi'i-majority Iran, particularly, reflect centuries of hostility between the Ottoman and Safavid Empires, and he shows no inclination to reach out across historical sectarian or political divisions. Despite being a direct neighbour to Turkey, Iran is one of the few countries in which the Gülen Movement is not, and has never been, active in any capacity.

The number of Shi'i Muslims in Turkey itself is all but negligible, but a similar challenge to Gülen's commitment to dialogue and pluralism is presented instead by the Alevi community, which numbers somewhere in the region of 15–25 million people.[36] Although the great majority of Alevis in Turkey identify themselves as Muslims, their intepretation of Islam is not recognised by the Sunni-run Directorate of Religious Affairs and they receive no official acknowledgement as a non-Sunni Muslim group.

Between 2002 and 2007, however, the AKP instigated a series of workshops – an initiative known as the *Alevi Açılımı*, or Alevi Opening – aimed at understanding Alevism and identifying the major demands of Alevi citizens.[37] The project was welcomed by many sections of the Alevi community at the time, but was ultimately perceived as a failure as it did not deliver on any of its major demands.[38]

High on the list of demands was that Alevi places of worship (*cemevi*s, literally, 'houses of meeting') should be afforded official, legal status. Some Alevis may occasionally pray in mosques, but praying five times a day is not a requirement of Alevism and many Alevis prefer to maintain their distance from the religious apparatus of Sunni Islam. The fact that *cemevi*s do not currently have legal status means that they receive none of the state utility subsidies that mosques, churches and synagogues do. More significantly, their non-recognition is seen as a major snub by Turkish Alevi citizens.

Gülen and his followers were supporters of the Alevi Opening, which was largely to be expected as it took place at a time when the movement was still an important ally of the AKP government. Perhaps more signficantly though, in recent years, Gülen has spoken out specifically on the *cemevi* subject. Together with an influential leader from the Alevi community, İzzettin Doğan from the Cem Vakfı, he instigated a joint *cemevi*–mosque construction project whereby Sunni and Alevi Muslims would come together in congregation to worship side by side.[39] Such a project had not been undertaken in Turkey before – in part because *cemevi*s are mostly recent phenomena that have only been a major feature of Alevism since it experienced an urban revival in the late twentieth century. The idea was, however, loaded with potential controversy on many counts: not only do the Alevis feel marginalised and threatened by an increasingly hegemonic Sunni mainstream in Turkey today, but in addition, the legacy of their past persecution (in Ottoman as well as Republican times) continues to loom large. Even though the idea was supported by Doğan and his colleagues at the Cem Vakfı, bringing the *cemevi* into alliance with the mosque – a symbol of Sunni dominance to many Alevis – was always going to be a step riven with tension.

Nonetheless, a series of joint *cemevi*–mosque projects were planned across Turkey, and construction began on the first one in Tuzluçayır in the Mamak district of Ankara in 2013, with the implicit support of the local government authority. However, following the rapid deterioration in AKP–Gülen relations later on that year, the project ground to a halt, and at the time of writing the site is under demolition on the orders of the AKP-run Mamak district council.

Gülen's interest in reaching out to the Alevi community through the joint construction projects can be read in different ways. On the one hand, the gesture is a positive one that appears to indicate a willingness to recognise Alevism and engage with it in the public sphere. On the other hand, the kind of engagement that was offered was in fact perceived as profoundly threatening by many Alevis in Turkey, who saw in it not a relationship of equals but rather an implicit subjugation to the dominant Sunni majority. The Gülen Movement's familiar discourse focusing on the virtues of 'harmony' and 'peaceful co-existence' did not sit well with an embattled Alevi community that is conscious, above all else, that it has neither legal recognition nor equality of status with its Sunni counterpart in Turkey. The *cemevi*–mosque projects were therefore controversial with those Alevis who, already deeply sensitive to the threat of assimilation, resented the perceived 'Sunnification' of their religious tradition.

Conclusion

The Gülen Movement invests a huge amount of time and resources into a wide variety of intercultural dialogue initiatives, and dialogue has clearly been one of its major priorities in the twenty-first century thus far. Perhaps the defining feature of Gülenist dialogue is its emphasis on stressing areas of common interest and concern rather than facing up to confrontation on areas of difference. The movement is not interested in voicing disagreement or discord on any level, and, I have argued, its dialogue activities are characterised by conflict-avoidance and grassroots networking above all else. Gülenist dialogue activities are characterised by their positive representation of Islam in the West, and by their transmission of Turkish language and culture around the world. At the same time, they tend to be tailored to suit particular local circumstances. In this way, the movement's dialogue initiatives reflect one of its core strengths, which is its ability to understand given social and cultural demographics, and to adapt itself accordingly. These dialogue projects seem, however, to be largely designed with a non-Muslim audience in mind, and have, as yet, achieved limited success in the sphere of intra-faith relations within the Muslim world itself.

7

Globalisation of the Movement, and Gülen in the USA

One of the great idiosyncrasies of the Gülen Movement, which is Turkish and Muslim at its heart, is the permanent residence of Gülen himself, along with a good number of his followers, in the United States of America. Gülen left Turkey in 1999 amid allegations of illegal Islamist activity, although he claimed at the time – and has done so ever since – that his poor health and access to superior medical facilities in the USA were the reasons for his emigration. A number of his followers were already present and active in the US when he arrived in 1999. With some schools and other interests already established on the East Coast, he chose a private estate in Pennsylvania as his home – close to the Turkish communities in Boston and New York, and within easy distance of the political powerhouse of Washington, DC. His proximity to the US capital has proven to be of great strategic importance to the movement. It has gone on to establish its most influential organisations there, promoting Turkish culture and providing forums for the discussion of Turkish current affairs.[1]

Gülen's private estate, called the 'Golden Generation Worship and Retreat Center', is located in a sleepy backwater near to the town of Saylorsburg in the Pocono Mountains. It is closed to visitors and unremarkable to the passer-by. Gülen himself maintains a low profile and admits outsiders and journalists to the compound only very rarely, meaning that the centre and its activities are shrouded in a certain degree of mystery.[2] While most of the movement's dialogue foundations and other initiatives are generally open to visitors – in most cases, actively encouraging them – the compound in Pennsylvania is the exception, and no public activities take place there. Despite his best efforts to keep the estate out of the headlines, however, Gülen's presence on it is well known. In the recent row that has erupted with President Erdoğan, the president has repeatedly referred to his new foe as 'the man in Pennsylvania' (*Pennsylvania'daki adam*), a term that is intended to cast aspersions on Gülen's residence overseas and particularly his ambiguous relationship with US political power. In turn, 'Pennsylvania' has become a word entirely synonymous with Fethullah Gülen in current Turkish parlance.

The issue of Gülen's residence in the USA provides fertile ground for conspiracy theories in both Turkey and the US. These theories question the willing accommodation of Gülen and his followers by the US authorities, as well as the alleged connections that exist between Gülen and the CIA. A brief internet search will reveal dozens of journalists and bloggers keen to expose shady links between the two.[3] One of the most regularly touted pieces of evidence on the subject concerns Gülen's application for green card status, which he was awarded in 2008 after a protracted seven-year legal case.[4] The court's original rejection of his application, submitted as an 'alien of extraordinary ability in education', was overturned after personal references were provided by senior members of the US diplomatic and intelligence community. The most high-ranking and controversial of Gülen's referees was Graham Fuller, ex-CIA agent and vice-chairman of the National Intelligence Council. It remains unclear how Gülen was able to secure the cooperation of such a senior member of the US Secret Service, and this is not something that his followers have been willing to discuss in any detail.

Fascinating though this subject is, it is not my intention here to probe the evidence for Gülen being an illicit ally of the United States, or to explore in any depth the question of whether the US government is knowingly sheltering him. Readers may find prolific material both supporting and refuting these assertions elsewhere. Rather, I am interested in exploring the ways in which Gülen's residence in the USA since 1999, whatever the reasons that led to and sustain it, has gone on in the intervening years to shape the evolution of the movement that surrounds him. Furthermore, I propose to investigate the internal structure of the movement wherein a nexus of exchange exists between its spiritual homeland of Turkey, its administrative centre in the USA and the various other countries around the world in which it is operational.

The Movement in America: Education and Controversy

Second only to Turkey itself, the USA is the country in which the movement is most active. The close association with the USA has its origins in Said Nursi's rather unusual willingness to open up to the Christian West for the purposes of interfaith dialogue and understanding. For this reason, the Gülen Movement is distinct from any other Turkish Islamist group, none of which sustain the same degree of openness to Western ideas and influences. Gülen's decision to pursue particularly close ties with the United States rather than any other Western nation with Christian heritage was likely informed by his admiration for the country's specific interpretation of secularism, and the relatively prominent role that its constitution allows for religion in public life. Gülen's followers speak openly of their admiration for the freedom with which the individual may practise religion in the US (and to a lesser extent, the UK), and they often draw an unfavourable contrast with the stricter application of *laïcité* in France as well as, more significantly, with the Kemalist tradition in Turkey.

The USA is also the country in which, besides Turkey, the movement has attracted perhaps the greatest degree of public controversy. A major focus of its activities in America is education, and it runs well over 100 schools in approximately 25 states. The highest concentration of Gülen schools may be found in Texas, where the Harmony chain, operating from its headquarters in Houston, runs 45 schools in which, according to its website, a total of 28,500 students are enrolled.[5] Other states in which Gülen schools are particularly prolific are California, where it runs 14 schools in the Magnolia chain, and Ohio, where it runs 19 schools in the Horizon chain. The movement also runs a number of smaller, locally-affiliated groups of schools in various other states.

Unlike their counterparts in other countries, most of the Gülen schools in the USA are publically funded rather than private institutions. Under the US system, private groups and organisations may bid for and run so-called 'charter schools', which are offered as an alternative to mainstream state schools. Charter schools are funded by public taxes, yet resemble private schools in that they are required to be competitive in order to attract their students. The Gülen charter schools, particularly, boast high standards in mathematics and science and, as is the case elsewhere, they have generally strong academic reputations. Many of them have been awarded prizes for their achievements, and appear amongst the top public schools in official state rankings.[6]

Because of the charter-school system, the student demographics of the US Gülen institutions are rather different from those in other countries. In Turkey and elsewhere around the world, the movement's schools are generally elite, fee-paying institutions that attract the children of an economically and socially mobile class. In areas where there are significant Turkish diaspora communities, such as Germany and the Netherlands, they also attract disproportionately high numbers of Turkish students. In the United States, with the exception of a few private institutions, this is not the case. Unable to rely in most areas on sizeable Turkish diasporas for their intake, and operating anyway within a public rather than private school system, the Gülen schools in the USA attract students from a wide ethno-linguistic, social and economic catchment. Some of them are located in areas of economic deprivation, and, crucially, they are also required to accept students of all academic abilities, which is not the case elsewhere.

Despite these more demanding circumstances, however, the schools in the USA still tend to achieve high academic standards, especially in Mathematics and Science. The reasons for their success, like the schools in Turkey, seem to be related to the extraordinary commitment of the teachers and their provision of extra-curricular tutoring and additional student support. The schools are governed and run predominantly by Turkish followers of Gülen (the great majority of whom appear to be male), and they employ a large number of teachers of Turkish origin (also followers of Gülen) – especially for mathematics and science. They also, however, employ non-Turkish staff for their teaching provision in other areas.

In common with their counterparts in other countries, none of the schools in the USA publically acknowledge their connection to Fethullah Gülen. As may be the case elsewhere, many students and their parents are apparently entirely unaware of who Gülen is, or of the existence of a movement in his name. In the USA, this realisation, when it has dawned, has caused some consternation in recent years.[7] This has led to a certain amount of public outcry, with critics protesting about the use of public money – and, in some cases, its alleged misuse – to support a Turkish Muslim organisation whose very secrecy raises alarm bells for many parents and onlookers in the American context.[8] A number of court cases have been brought against the schools amid allegations of financial mismanagement, mostly involving the allocation of contracts to businesses linked to the Gülen Movement. There have also been FBI-led investigations into some of the schools' preference for hiring and promoting of Turkish nationals over qualified US teachers, and their associated abuse of the foreign-worker visa (H-1B) application system. Most of these cases have thus far been settled out of court, but they have nonetheless led to a degree of public controversy surrounding the movement's activities in education in the USA, which has had a negative effect on its public relations in that country.

Promoting Turkey in the USA

While education continues to form the backbone of Gülenist activities in the USA as it does elsewhere, the movement is also deeply invested in other areas – namely, in constructing channels for public engagement, informal networking and political lobbying, and, crucially, for the promotion of Turkey and Turkish culture. These initiatives, which fall under the rubric of 'dialogue' in the movement's terminology, are not linked in any obvious way with the schools. They do not, therefore, appear to have suffered any negative consequences as a result of the controversy that some of the schools have courted.

The oldest and most significant organisation run by Gülenists in the United States is the Rumi Forum (established 1999), which is based in Washington, DC and which operates chapters in five states. The forum hosts regular seminars, conferences and round-table discussions on a wide range of cultural, religious and political issues related to Turkey and the Middle East in particular, as well as global current affairs more widely. It cultivates relationships with a host of influential figures ranging from ex-US president Bill Clinton, who has spoken out in its support, to UK-based Muslim intellectual Tariq Ramadan, who has been a visiting speaker. The Rumi Forum casts its net wide and seeks to appeal to a broad range of individuals and interest groups in the DC area. A major focus is, however, the promotion of Turkish interests and culture. To this end, it organises regular, funded trips to Turkey for invited guests including journalists, academics, businesspeople and local public officials.[9] These tours typically include visits to major historical sites as well as to selected Gülenist dialogue platforms and educational institutions. Their purpose is to promote Turkey and the movement in equal measure.

A recently established Gülenist organisation in Washington that has a more singular political focus is the Rethink Institute. This is a think tank providing political analysis of, amongst other things, domestic affairs in Turkey from the perspective of Fethullah Gülen. Recent incidents that have targeted Gülen and his followers' assets in Turkey have featured in the institute's analysis of the 'persecution' facing the movement in its homeland. These include the incident surrounding Bank Asya, a Gülen-affiliated bank headquartered in Istanbul, which was forcibly taken over by the State in early 2015 – ostensibly in order to prevent it from failing, but probably more realistically as a deliberate move to downsize Gülen assets in Turkey. They also include the arrests in December 2014 of senior management figures at Gülen media outlets in Istanbul, including *Zaman* newspaper and the Samanyolu media group.[10] The analysis provided by the Rethink Institute unequivocally defends the movement's position and provides a Gülenist perspective on these events.

Through the Rethink Institute, the Rumi Forum and other initiatives in Washington, DC, the Gülen Movement has established a highly influential audience for itself in a global centre of power. Access to this audience will strengthen its hand, and prove of great worth, in the battle in which it is currently engaged with President Erdoğan. While the movement's major assets and media platforms in Turkey may be under threat, it is nonetheless remarkably well equipped today to defend itself in the international arena. The platform that it has established for itself in the US capital is likely to be of great significance as regards the struggle for legitimacy in Turkey and, by association, the future directions of the movement.

Gülen in Pennsylvania: A Reclusive Persona

The private estate in the Poconos where Gülen has resided since 1999 is a relatively short distance from Washington. Despite his proximity to the capital, however, Gülen himself lives a reclusive life reputedly characterised by religious asceticism. He is said to inhabit only one small, modestly furnished bedroom on the extensive property, where he devotes himself to Qur'anic study and prayer. Unusually within Islam, he has never married, something which his followers interpret as a sign of his extraordinary devotion to God. To his followers, his public persona (which, needless to say, needs a considerable amount of unpacking) is of a saintly individual who, living in voluntary seclusion, is primarily concerned with spiritual matters over and above the affairs of this world. Thus, while initiatives that claim 'inspiration' from his teachings (they always deny his direct involvement) take root all across the United States and around the world, Gülen himself remains enigmatically withdrawn on his Pennsylvania estate.

Gülen's reclusiveness developed in earnest only after his move to the United States. Before this time, he had been active in a public capacity in Turkey, both preaching and speaking at dialogue events and meetings. His retreat from public view was undoubtedly precipitated in large part by the controversy surrounding his departure from his homeland, and the criminal charges that were directed at him at the time. It also perhaps suited the narrative that he was suffering from poor health for him to remain behind closed doors. In the intervening years, however, his very reclusiveness has become a key feature of Gülen's charismatic appeal. His followers around the world gather on a weekly basis to hear his regular sermon, which is broadcast digitally from the Pennsylvania estate, but apart from this they rarely see him or hear from him directly.

Coordination of the Movement from Pennsylvania

Gülen's presence on the Pennsylvania estate makes it the geographical pivot point in the movement's organisational structure. Totalling a reported 11 hectares (28 acres) of private land, it functions as much more than Gülen's personal residence, and he is far from its only inhabitant.

Globalisation of the Movement, and Gülen in the USA

Also present on the estate is his group of closest disciples, an all-male cohort comprising high-level students of Islamic theology. These disciples take religious instruction from Gülen directly, who appears to function as their 'master' (*sheikh*, or *mürşit*) in an arrangement that reflects a centuries-old tradition of Islamic learning.[11] Relatively little is known about this arrangement, as access is only very rarely granted to researchers to visit the compound itself. It is, however, referred to in passing by followers of Gülen in other contexts. For example, a university academic in Turkey, who had studied for his PhD in the USA and was loosely affiliated with the movement during his time there, described the practice to me:

> When I was in the USA, I used to take part in *Hizmet* activities [...] I trust them and I like to be involved in what they are doing, and to go to their talks. If you preach in a mosque, you can say a lot and nobody questions it, but I am an academic, and I will ask you what your sources are. The people leading the talks in the movement are excellent theologians – very knowledgeable. The small group who study with Fethullah Gülen in the USA are excellent. I heard one of them give a talk on Sufism in [a given state]. He had excellent English, and I wondered how he had managed that. It was better than mine! Fethullah Gülen wants them to integrate into American society, but they are based at his home in Pennsylvania – that's where they live, with him.[12]

As this excerpt suggests, the inner circle of disciples surrounding Gülen does not remain on the estate with him at all times. Rather, individuals from this elite group are dispatched around the country, and indeed the world, to provide religious instruction and disseminate Gülen's ideas, sometimes to a public audience and sometimes to private groups of his loyal followers in other locations. At one of the schools at which I conducted research in Turkey, for example, teachers reported that their community of followers received periodical visits from an *ağabey* from Pennsylvania. These visits, which were closed to outsiders, would take the form of religious instruction and would involve the whole community of dedicated followers.

The term *ağabey* is used in common Turkish parlance to denote 'older brother', and is also used informally in public interactions. In the movement's terminology, it refers to a male individual who holds responsibility within the Gülen hierarchy, and its female equivalent is *abla*. I heard these terms used regularly by followers such as schoolteachers and students, and examples of the structure and function of the *ağabey/abla* system in the university context were given in Chapter One.

Senior members of staff at Gülen dialogue institutions tended, however, to refrain from using the terms and, in so doing, to distance themselves from the implication of hidden hierarchies that they seem to suggest. When, on one occasion, I pressed the issue with regard to the function of *ağabey*s and *abla*s within the school system, I was told by a senior member of staff at the GYV that 'it's not an institution, and also in daily life you call people *ağabey* and *abla*. But you are a peer tutor (*belletmen*) – that's the term'.[13] This observation was valid in its context, and I often heard the term *belletmen* used by students. The positions of *belletmen* and *ağabey/abla* are, however, slightly different from each other, the former being an individual with academic tutoring responsibilities and the latter an individual entrusted with the personal oversight of a given group of students' moral and religious development. As I showed in Chapter One, each *ağabey* or *abla* is accountable to a superior *ağabey* or *abla* located one increment above them on the movement's hierarchical scale.

Despite this GYV individual's reluctance to acknowledge it, then, a system of hierarchical leadership populated by *ağabey*s and *abla*s extends beyond the schools and universities and permeates the entire movement. The most junior individuals with positions of responsibility are indeed peer tutors in schools and *dershane*s, but they are positioned within a pyramid-like structure of authority that encompasses the entire movement and leads ultimately back to Pennsylvania, to the inner core of disciples and to Gülen himself.

Most of the senior members of the movement's organisations whom I met in Turkey (at both schools and dialogue initiatives) had passed through the Pennsylvania estate at one time or another, although they did not necessarily immediately volunteer this information. Spending a period of time alongside Gülen himself appeared to be one of the formative aspects of preparing an individual for a senior role in the movement. These individuals had not necessarily been members of the inner circle of disciples, who are specialist students of theology. Rather, they had spent time on the estate as Gülen's personal visitors in order to be equipped to take on positions of leadership within the movement's different organisations and initiatives in Turkey and around the world.

The fact that all of these individuals were males suggested that there were no roles at the highest levels of the Gülen hierarchy for women. Female followers of Gülen may function in an '*abla*' role by taking charge of a particular aspect of the movement's organisation at a local or regional level. That is to say, they might organise and lead a regular *sohbet* group, or they might oversee a more junior *abla* who is herself in charge of running a student house. It appears, however, that at the highest levels, women are structurally excluded from positions of leadership, in part because of their disqualification from personal mentoring with Gülen on the Pennsylvania estate. Gülen's immediate circle of companions there is limited to males, reflecting the strict gender segregation that is practised at every level of the movement's activity.

The Movement's Spiritual Home: Turkey

The Gülen Movement has become a fully global phenomenon over the past 20 years, and is now active in approximately 120 countries. Its transnational dimensions do not, however, detract from the fundamentally Turkish nature of the movement. Wherever it is active around the world, the great majority of its adherents are either Turkish nationals or individuals of Turkish origin. Gülen has an inclusive vision for the movement that surrounds him, seeking to welcome people of all creeds and backgrounds into an ecumenical and intercultural initiative dedicated to what he describes variously as the pursuit of 'universal peace' and a commitment to 'shared human values'. The movement does attract sympathisers and participants from other nationalities and other faith groups, and it actively seeks this support through its various dialogue activities as well as its programme of sponsored tours to Turkey.

There are various non-Muslim and non-Turkish university academics – mostly in the USA – who maintain a kind of affiliation with the movement by writing enthusiastically about it, and speaking out in support of its goals and ambitions. Moreover, the movement seems particularly interested in cultivating links with Catholic constituencies, and the university chairs that have been established in recent years in Fethullah Gülen's name in Australia and Belgium are located at universities with Catholic foundations.

Despite these efforts, however, the movement's core affiliates remain overwhelmingly Turkish and Muslim. While individuals from other backgrounds may participate in the activities that are organised by Gülen organisations, it is rare for them to become fully committed followers of Gülen themselves. There are of course exceptions, but there seems to be little evidence to suggest that as the movement has globalised, the demographic of Gülen's core following has become any more diverse or multicultural than its original Turkish Muslim constituency.

We should therefore imagine a global social movement composed overwhelmingly of Turkish citizens (or foreign nationals of Turkish origin), with strong ties to their cultural and religious homeland of Turkey, yet with an administrative structure that is centred in the USA. This administrative hub maintains a constant dialogue with a cadre of high-level leaders who, based in Turkey and elsewhere, receive periodic visits from the *ağabey*s of Gülen's inner circle and also pass intermittently through the estate in Pennsylvania themselves. At the top of the movement's organisational hierarchy sits Gülen himself. Around him, his core followers are organised according to an ascending scale of authority, which, giving structure to the entire movement, reaches its zenith in Pennsylvania. Such is the culture of secrecy that surrounds the Pennsylvania estate that no followers of Gülen would disclose to me the precise amount of detail with which their leader follows the movement's activities, even if they were themselves privy to that information. The movement maintains its narrative that Gülen is merely an 'inspirational' sage and that he does not directly oversee his followers' activities in any way. Yet the pyramid-like structure of accountability that pervades the entire movement and ends with Gülen himself means that he, and his core group of senior affiliates, are undoubtedly aware of what organisations are operational within the movement, who is staffing them and how they are funded.[14]

Cords of Connection between the Movement in Turkey and the USA: Schools

Besides making it the practical centre of the Gülen Movement's organisation, the residency of its leader in the USA also has a significant impact on the movement's internal culture. There are 'cords' that connect the movement in its Turkish homeland to the United States in ways far exceeding administrative oversight, and which shape its very DNA. For while the movement is profoundly Turkish at its core, it nonetheless reflects a high degree of familiarity with contemporary America and American culture. There is a complex, two-way nexus of cultural interaction between Turkey and the USA that sustains and directs it today, and this is visible on a number of different levels. During my fieldwork in Turkey, I observed various ways in which followers of Gülen cultivated and maintained links with the USA. Many of these links were forged through education at both the school and university level. A high proportion of the schoolteachers and university academics whom I encountered had lived for a time in the USA, and opportunities to visit seemed to be prolific. At one of the middle schools at which I carried out fieldwork, for example, regular student trips were offered to destinations in the United States. When I was there in the spring of 2013, colourful posters were on display in the school lobby, advertising a forthcoming summer trip to the East Coast. Students would be hosted by Putnam Science Academy, a successful Gülen school in the Boston area, and would visit New York City and Boston for sightseeing as well as various local science museums and educational events. Unlike the school itself, which was mixed-gender in order to abide by Turkish legal requirements, the trip was gender-segregated and was confined to male students that year. Female students would be eligible to go on a separate trip the following year. The cost of the trip, which would last two weeks, was $4,000 per student.

Kenan, one of the English teachers at the school who was hosting my visits, informed me that bursaries to fund the trip were available to students from lower-income families. In his view, such opportunities were important because they gave students a chance to experience American culture and, particularly, to see the paths in further education that are available to them in the USA. Kenan had lived and studied in the US himself, and his two children had been born in Texas. He was enthusiastic about the time that he had spent there, and was keen for his students as well as his colleagues to have similar experiences:

> I have been a couple of times before on such trips – they run every summer. My family has a ten-year visa for the United States and so it is easy for us to come and go. I would like to go

again this summer, but there are teachers who have not yet been and so they should take priority.[15]

American influences were also visible in the school's teaching staff. A cohort of teachers from the USA had been recruited to teach English, both at the school in question and the others in the same affiliated group. These foreign teachers were, with a very few exceptions, the only members of the teaching staff who were not committed followers of Gülen. They were, however, all evangelical Protestant Christians and thus shared a core value of the movement, which is the defence of religious piety and a socially conservative lifestyle. The American teachers reported that they were well-received by their Gülen school communities, and observed that their shared piety gave them grounds for common understanding.

The movement is, generally speaking, highly uncomfortable with atheistic and materialist currents within the modern world. Reflecting Fethullah Gülen's writings on the subject, however, his followers seem eager to interact with other individuals of faith – particularly of the Christian tradition. This is yet another area in which the movement finds grounds for engagement with an American audience – especially, a conservative evangelical constituency – as reflected by the easy accommodation of the American Christian teachers in the school community.

Universities

If the close connections between the movement and the USA were evident in the middle- and high-school contexts that I observed, they were even more apparent in the universities. At the institution on which I focused my research – a new, private university in the west of Turkey – well over 50 per cent of the faculty staff had studied for PhDs in the USA. Not all of these academics were committed followers of Gülen, but their tenure at a university run by his followers indicated that they were at the very least broadly sympathetic to the movement. Mustafa, the young economics professor mentioned in Chapter Five, was an employee of this university. He related to me how the idea of studying in the USA had originally been suggested to him by the tutors at his Gülen-run *dershane*, who had guided him through the application process:

Globalisation of the Movement, and Gülen in the USA

> I went to a *Hizmet dershane* in [my home city], but I didn't go to a *Hizmet* high school. There was a meeting one day at the *dershane* when we were introduced to the idea of doing a PhD in the United States. They showed us the application process and told us how to go about it. I did my bachelor's degree in Istanbul but then I went to the States for five years to do my doctorate. I used to take part in a lot of *Hizmet* activities while I was there – educational events, cultural events and inter-faith events. Once I broke my fast [in Ramadan] in a Catholic church there. I met my wife in America and both of our children were born there.[16]

Mustafa had been channelled through the Gülenist education network in Turkey, and encouraged to pursue an advanced research degree in the USA. Individuals like him – who are not core affiliates but nonetheless have an allegiance to the movement, having benefited from its secondary-education system – are apparently now being recruited back to Turkey in order to staff emerging Gülenist initiatives in higher education. This is one of the ways in which the movement has both expanded its circle of influence in the university sector and also cultivated further ties with the USA.

The university in question had set out to model itself on the US system, and was proactively recruiting academic staff with graduate degrees from that country. It is not unusual for Turkish private universities to follow the North American system. Bilkent University in Ankara, the first private university to be established in Turkey in 1984, is based on the US model, as are various others that have been founded more recently. Neither is it unusual for high-achieving Turkish students, like their counterparts around the world, to aspire to continue their education in the USA. The dream of an Ivy League PhD is one that inspires many top international graduates. What struck me as distinctive about the Gülen communities that I observed, however, was the emphasis on the USA at all costs, and the relative lack of interest in other Western nations for educational purposes.

A good number of Turkish students undertake doctoral and postdoctoral research at universities in the UK, France, Germany, Australia and elsewhere besides the USA with scholarships provided by TÜBİTAK, the Turkish state-funded body for scientific research.[17] Students are eligible for funding if they secure a place at any university ranked within the top 100 of the Times Higher Education World University Rankings.[18] In 2014–15, universities from 17 countries are included in this list.[19] The qualifications that these students gain from these foreign institutions are highly regarded on their return to Turkey, and generally earn them secure jobs in the academic sector.

The strategy for education that I observed in the Gülen Movement did not reflect the variety of countries and universities that are apparent in the national demographics, but rather was heavily focused on the United States. One rare exception was Metin, the research assistant at Irfan university, who was also mentioned in Chapter Five. Metin had studied for his MA in London, and was very keen to return for his PhD. He seemed happy to have an opportunity to talk about the UK with me, and expressed frustration that the emphasis in the movement – particularly regarding higher education – was always on the USA:

> I spent a year in London doing a Masters in Middle East Studies. I really loved being there, and I'd like to return. But the talk in *Hizmet* is always about America! They love being there, I think they feel really comfortable there. I've seen them in Brussels, Amsterdam, Paris and London and they're much less well organised and widespread in those places than they are in the USA.[20]

While they might be less widespread in these countries, there are nonetheless many Gülen initiatives in Western Europe. Besides an estimated 12 Gülen schools in Germany, there are schools in France, Belgium and the Netherlands, and there is one in the UK. The movement also runs the usual dialogue initiatives all over the continent, with organisations called Dialog in Germany, the Dialogue Society in the UK and Platforme de Paris in France. Yet while these staple Gülen Movement activities are under way in the countries of Western Europe, the point that Metin was highlighting was that movement insiders do not generally feel the same cultural affinity with Western European nations as they do with the USA. Individual followers of Gülen do not come and go between Turkey and Europe in the same way they do between Turkey and America. In Turkey as elsewhere, the United States is often representative in some ways of the West at large – incorporating Western Europe as well as Canada, Australia and other countries.

In the case of the movement, it is clearly the United States specifically in which they are most heavily invested, more so than the other countries in the Western world.

The Appeal of the USA to the Gülen Movement

At a different university in another city, I met Sinan, a young professor of divinity, who offered an explanation for this situation. Sinan was heavily involved in the movement and, like many of its other senior figures whom I encountered in Turkey, had been resident in the United States for a number of years. He had lived in Chicago during his doctoral studies and then had gone on to teach at a university in Texas. While resident in the USA, Sinan had also spent time in conversation with Gülen himself on the estate in Pennsylvania. He confirmed to me that, in recent decades, the movement had deliberately sought to create opportunities for followers and affiliates to leave Turkey in order to live and study in the USA. He also provided an explanation for this agenda:

> Mr Gülen encouraged us to move to the United States as much as possible. America is important, and therefore he put a special emphasis on it. Turkish Muslims are missing in the USA – there are Pakistanis and Arabs, but relatively few Turks. He says that the Turkish interpretation of Islamic values is important, and that the USA is an influential place to emphasise this. But the home of the movement is Turkey, not the USA. The reason it has focused on America rather than anywhere else, for example Europe, is that there are so many different opportunities there. For example, opening schools is easier, as is opening companies. The USA is also more receptive to newcomers than Europe – they do not treat you like aliens or a minority. In Germany, for example, Turkish people are treated like gypsies and their projects are not welcomed.[21]

The open society of the United States, in which newcomers are relatively welcome and free enterprise is easily facilitated, suits the Gülen Movement. It has enabled it to establish more schools there than in any other country besides Turkey, and also to cultivate forums for dialogue that have attracted the patronage and support of some highly influential people in Washington, DC.

Furthermore, unlike in Europe, the movement faces no serious competition in the USA from other transnational Turkish groups. In Germany, which has a Turkish population of approximately 3 million, there are various well-established social and religious foundations catering for the Turkish community and often competing to speak on its behalf. These include firmly established Sunni groups such as the Suleymancıs and Milli Görüş (a branch of political Islam founded in Turkey by former prime minister Necmettin Erbakan), as well as various local and national foundations representing the Alevi minority. The size and complexity of the Turkish population in Germany, as well as in certain other European countries, means that Turkey is already ascribed with certain – often negative – connotations in public consciousness there. Some of these relate to the low socio-economic position of many Turkish communities; others are connected to broader insecurities about Islam and radical Islamist activism.

In the United States, the Gülen Movement is well placed to create its own narrative surrounding Turkey in general and Turkish Islam in particular. The movement tends, wherever it is active, to avoid sustained collaboration with other Muslim groups. By doing this, it avoids burdening itself with the complexities that are often attached to publically associating as a Muslim group. Rather, the movement plays down its Islamic credentials in the public sphere and seeks instead to showcase its ability to engage in secular civil society alongside other faith groups and civic associations. The USA provides an excellent place to do this, and this is something that Gülen himself apparently realised quite some time ago when, as Sinan reported, he began encouraging his followers to establish themselves there.

The Globalisation of the Movement

Gülen's move to Pennsylvania in 1999 coincided with the beginning of a period of rapid expansion in the movement's overseas activities. Up until that time, its presence outside Turkey had been largely limited to the countries of Central Asia and the Balkans, where it had established a great many schools in the 1990s. It had also begun to establish a scattering of schools across Europe and the USA. Since the late 1990s, its presence in these locations has increased considerably and it has also moved into entirely new parts of the world including sub-Saharan Africa and Southeast Asia. The movement has fully consolidated its international presence, and today it is reckoned amongst the largest of all transnational providers of modern education. The relocation of its leader to America served as something of a catalyst toward the movement's globalisation, and helped to complete its transformation into a fully transnational organisation.

An equally significant, although largely unrelated, event was the ascent of the AKP through a landslide election in 2002. The AKP has been in power with a majority government ever since, and during the first two terms of the AKP administration, its unofficial alliance with the Gülen Movement was an important factor behind the party's success. It garnered the support of movement affiliates, who shared a common commitment to social conservatism and the reintegration of Islam into parts of public life. The alliance also benefited the movement itself, and it prospered and expanded during this period as its ventures received state patronage in Turkey and overseas.

The mutually beneficial nature of this alliance can be clearly seen in the context of Africa. Turkey's interest in the whole continent of Africa, including its sub-Saharan nations, is a recent development. Ottoman influence extended only to the north of the continent, and many of the countries with which Turkey has cultivated closer ties in the past decade had no significant involvement with Turkey historically. An important milestone came in 1998, when the Turkish government adopted an Action Plan on Africa.[22] The Gülen Movement capitalised on this initiative, and began that year to open schools in countries including Senegal, Kenya, Nigeria and Tanzania. Its operations on the continent accelerated when the AKP came to power in the following decade, and in the 2000s it opened schools in Ethiopia, Ghana, the Gambia, Mozambique and the Democratic Republic of the Congo, as well as a number of other countries in mainly sub-Saharan Africa. Coincidentally, in 2005, the AKP declared the 'Year of Africa', broadcasting the Turkish government's intention to increase trade and strengthen diplomatic ties with African nations from that time on. In 2008, at the tenth summit of the African Union, Turkey was declared a strategic partner of the continent.

The development of closer links between Turkey and Africa has benefitted the Gülen Movement and the AKP in equal measure. The movement's expansion in Africa, which has been one of its most significant growth markets, has largely coincided with the Turkish state's establishment of new diplomatic missions there, as well as the opening up of new routes to African capitals by Turkish Airlines, a long-time ally of the AKP. A similar pattern is discernible in other parts of the world where the movement has expanded in the twenty-first century. Turkey has accumulated a significant amount of soft power during this time, thanks in large part to the schools of the Gülen Movement and their promotion of Turkish language and culture around the world.

Global Coordination

The rapid global spread of the Gülen Movement since the turn of the century has been undertaken with Gülen resident in the USA. This situation results in a rather complex organisational structure, wherein the movement's leadership is located in America yet its primary pool for recruiting new affiliates is still in Turkey. The bedrock of Gülen activities around the work is education, and probably more of Gülen's core followers are employed in this sector than in any other. The teaching profession is highly esteemed in Gülen's thought, and he exhorts his followers to become teachers, either as a lifelong vocational commitment or as a temporary act of service (*Hizmet*) for a period of perhaps four or five years.

A good proportion of the teachers whom I encountered in the schools in Turkey had spent time teaching in the movement's schools abroad, some of them in very far-flung locations. Aynur, a mathematics teacher in her late forties, had spent a number of years with her husband and young children, first in Turkmenistan and later in the Central African Republic:

Aynur: We were in Turkmenistan for some years, not in the capital but in a city called Mary. My children were both born there. We were really happy there and would like to have stayed longer actually.

CT: *Can you speak the language? What language did you teach in?*

Aynur: It's very close to Turkish, and so it was very easy. I can understand everything but I can't speak it. At the school I taught at, lessons were given in English – but I can't speak English, so I gave mine in a mixture of Turkish and Turkmen. My subject is mathematics and so language is not so important anyway!

CT: *Where did you go after you left Turkmenistan?*

Aynur: We went to the Central African Republic, but we only stayed a few months as it was a very hard country. The children were very small, and they got ill so we had to come back. The school had been there for ten years or so [...]

CT: *You must have formed some very close relationships when you were in these foreign countries?*

Aynur: Yes, you become like family – your colleagues are everything to you. The relationships are very genuine [*samimi*]. We still talk on the phone, and we see some of our old students from Turkmenistan who are now studying in Turkey – some of them are in [our city], so we see them sometimes.[23]

The tight-knit community of which Aynur and her family had been a part in Turkmenistan and the CAR was primarily composed of Turkish nationals and followers of Gülen like themselves. It did not appear to be unusual that Aynur had not learnt to speak the local language, or indeed that she did not speak English. These linguistic shortcomings imposed no limitations on her, as the language of the Gülen teaching community in the international context was Turkish.

Aynur and her family had moved directly from one international location to another. Staff in Gülen schools and other institutions are regularly rotated, according to the reports of some of my interlocutors, on an approximately four-yearly basis. During my fieldwork in Turkey, which spanned two years, I observed a great number of changes in personnel. On my visits to schools or dialogue institutions that were more than a few months apart, I would often find different individuals in post on my return visit. In the school context, this happened on a wide scale after the summer break; in the dialogue context it happened at less obvious intervals, yet over the course of two years, two key individuals from the GYV with whom I was in contact in Ankara and Istanbul switched locations inexplicably and without warning. This posed a challenge to my research, as maintaining continuity with the same informants over the course of more than a few months was rather difficult.

Like other teachers whom I spoke to, Aynur and her family had been moved from Turkmenistan to CAR against their own personal wishes. This practice seemed to be very common. Hatice and İrem, teachers whose stories I have partially related in other chapters, had both been moved to the school that I studied from other parts of Turkey that they had not wanted to leave. Indeed, during the course of my research, Hatice was reassigned locally, moving from a girls' high school to a middle school. She expressed muted unhappiness about the change, telling me that she was unfamiliar with the particular pedagogical challenges presented by younger students, but was evidently in no position to challenge the decision to move her.

The movement of staff around Gülen institutions was coordinated externally, and was not something that the staff themselves appeared to have any influence over. The same practice of rotating staff around locally affiliated groups of schools, as illustrated by Hatice's case, was also seen at a national as well as transnational level – as evidenced by Aynur's story. It was not possible to learn any more about the processes by which these decisions were made, as individual teachers were either unwilling to disclose them or – perhaps equally likely – were unaware of their workings themselves. It seems apparent, however, that the same hierarchical chain of accountability that is partially visible in the *ağabey/abla* system is at work in the allocation of positions in Gülen schools and other institutions. This top-down coordination of the movement's activities, which leads back to Pennsylvania, works in the same way in the international context as it does in Turkey itself.

Conclusion

The reasons behind Fethullah Gülen's decision to flee Turkey in 1999 and take up residence in the United States are still not fully transparent. Depending on which source one consults, the explanation lies either in his failing health, the impending threat of his arrest in Turkey or a covert

CIA plan to shelter him as an American intelligence asset. It is of course possible that all three of these explanations played a part in his emigration. Gülen has, however, proven himself throughout his career to be a consummate strategist and leader. It is quite possible that he rightly identified the USA in the 1990s as a place of influence and future opportunity for the movement, and that his move in 1999 was motivated by a straightforward ambition for its global consolidation and expansion.

The residency of Gülen in America over the past 16 years has indeed had a seismic impact on the growth and evolution of the movement that takes his name. It has not only expanded into the American education market, but it has also spread to other countries and continents. In the second decade of the twenty-first century, it is a fully global entity with an extensive portfolio of material assets, as well as an established presence in intercultural dialogue and diplomacy centred around its base in Washington, DC.

The United States has become pivotal to the movement, not only as the home of its leader and the centre of its adminstrative organisation but also as the greatest influence on its internal culture besides Turkey itself. Gülen has encouraged his followers to capitalise on the new opportunities that have been available to them in the USA, and they have done so very effectively. This kind of strategic ambition is one of the hallmarks of the movement, and has facilitated its growth within less than four decades from a localised Islamic community in Turkey to one of the largest and wealthiest transnational civil-society movements in the modern world.

8

Political Influence and the AKP

On 17 December 2013, a host of influential people close to the ruling AK Party were detained by police as part of a far-reaching corruption investigation.[1] Over 90 individuals, who included wealthy businessmen with connections to the AK Party as well as a municipal mayor and the sons of several cabinet ministers, were questioned on suspicion of bribery, corruption and money laundering. Further damaging allegations were widely rumoured, and an attempt at a second round of arrests on 25 December was only narrowly averted. Prime Minister Recep Tayyip Erdoğan's son, Bilal, was already implicated in the scandal, and the following February, allegations of Erdoğan's own direct involvement were made explicit. Telephone recordings were leaked purporting to show him discussing, with Bilal, the disposal of millions of dollars in apparently illicitly obtained funds. The prime minister was incensed by the allegations and claimed that the recordings had been falsified. He acted quickly and blocked further arrests by passing sweeping legislation that, among other things, increased the government's control over the judiciary as well as the internet, thus effectively stalling the allegations in their tracks.

These events were the most sustained and damaging upset that the AKP had faced in just over a decade in office, and the perpetrator behind them was its one-time friend and ally, the Gülen Movement. While the movement never spoke openly about its role in the arrests, it was widely recognised in the Turkish media that many of the prosecutors and police chiefs who instigated the operation were loyal to Gülen, and that their actions were part of a coordinated plan.[2] Erdoğan labelled the operation an 'attempted coup' on the part of the movement, and alleged that the intention behind it had been to fatally discredit his government and destabilise his position as prime minister.

In the period that has followed, thousands of Gülenist civil servants – including police chiefs, police officers and state prosecutors – around the country have been reassigned, dismissed, and even prosecuted or stripped of their qualifications in a bid to weaken the movement's networks and remove Gülen's followers from influential positions. In 2015, the process was still ongoing. In his public addresses, Erdoğan has declared war on the movement, speaking of a 'parallel state' of Gülen sympathisers who sought to topple a democratically elected government and posed a grave threat to Turkish national security. As the crisis escalated, a warrant was issued for Gülen's arrest on the grounds that he was 'leading an armed terrorist organisation', and extradition arrangements between Turkey and the USA became the focus of public scrutiny. To date, though, no formal extradition request has been made and Gülen remains in the USA – although at the end of 2015, the Turkish government took steps to precipitate his forced return to Turkey in order to stand trial.[3]

Until recent years, the *unofficial* support of Gülen and his followers for the AKP was widely recognised.[4] Gülen himself has historically refrained from speaking out directly on political issues, and the movement that takes his name claims to be a civil-society initiative with no aspirations to attain political power. This narrative is questionable, for the movement is indeed profoundly political; the point is that Gülen's views on this subject have generally been implicitly rather than explicitly expressed, and his political influence has been exerted mainly through indirect channels. However, the developments of December 2013, which represent the culmination of almost two years of sporadic fighting between the Gülen Movement and the AKP amid deteriorating relations, suggest the dawn of a new era. Not only have Gülen's (albeit unofficial) political loyalties changed conclusively but furthermore, the movement appears to have entered a new phase of open political confrontation. By going public with a raft of toxic allegations, it is clear that the Gülenists' intention was to unseat now-President Erdoğan and precipitate a change in the Turkish administration. The move failed, but onlookers are left questioning the movement's avowedly distant relationship from Turkish party politics, and its true agenda in political affairs. The future directions that the movement will take are also in question, now that the era of cooperation and patronage that it received from president Erdoğan's AKP, which has characterised its rapid expansion over the past 15 years, is so firmly over.

Turkish Political Islam

The war that has broken out between Gülen and Erdoğan needs to be understood in light of the historical context for political Islam in Turkey, and the various different strands that exist within Turkish Islamism. With the events of 17 December 2013, the gradual transformation of Fethullah Gülen from close friend of the AKP to its arch-enemy was finally sealed. Cracks in the alliance's veneer had, in fact, been discernible for some time before the eruption of the crisis, and the rift between the two – which is primarily a stand-off between Gülen and Erdoğan – had been developing over the course of years. United originally by their common Islamic piety, the two groups had cooperated closely during the early years of the AKP's tenure, motivated by a shared ambition to weaken Turkey's secularist establishment by downgrading the power of its military elite. Both groups fundamentally resist the Kemalist model for the relegation of Islam to the private sphere and the removal of religious influences from public life. Gülen and his followers supported the AKP's mission, which continues today, to restructure the way in which secularism is enforced in Turkey. Once this goal had been largely achieved, though, the bonds of cooperation weakened and major ideological differences between the two groups, which had been simmering beneath the surface all along, became markedly apparent.

Although they share a pious identity rooted in Hanefi Sunni Islam, the Gülen Movement and the AKP in fact originate from two different religious strands in Turkey that have very different political philosophies, although both derive ultimately from Naqshbandi Sufism.[5] Gülen, following in the twentieth-century tradition of Said Nursi, espouses a kind of Islamist activism that is focused on making gains in the civil and economic spheres rather than the political.[6] That is to say, while his vision is very much predicated on the reintroduction of Islamic themes into public life, he does not seek to do this through organised party politics but rather through the targeted accumulation of influence in society at large. This ambition has underpinned the Gülen Movement's activities in education and the media in particular, and the influence that it has accrued in these areas has, in turn, contributed to the Islamisation of Turkish society in recent years. The movement has also attained influence in the civil service, business and the judiciary, and aspires to steer political agendas through indirect channels. While politics is one area in which they are interested, however, as long as they are making ground elsewhere, it is not *necessarily* the primary focus of interest for Gülen and his followers.

Like Said Nursi, who lent his implicit support to the Democrat Party towards the end of his life and encouraged his followers to be active in the democratic system, Gülen also expects his followers to use their right to vote. In practice, the great majority of Gülens have voted for the AKP, as it has reflected the same core values of social conservatism and religious piety that they hold in high esteem. The crucial point is that neither Gülen nor his followers have ever formally confirmed this alliance, and affiliates of the movement are theoretically free to vote for whomever they choose.

The AKP, meanwhile, is derived from a very different tradition within Turkish Islam, which has a long and complex history but within which Necmettin Erbakan is a pivotal recent figure.[7] Founder of the transnational Islamist movement, Milli Görüş (National Outlook), Erbakan was, like Recep Tayyip Erdoğan, an initiate of the İskenderpaşa Dergahı, a leading Naqshbandi lodge. He inspired and led a number of political parties throughout the late twentieth century, and as leader of the Welfare Party (Refah Partisi) he was prime minister between 1996 and 1997. Erbakan challenged Turkey's commitment to secularism with a political philosophy that sought the partial introduction of Islamic law as well as a strengthening of ties with the Arab nations in place of Turkey's Western allies.[8] He was ousted soon after the 'soft coup' of 1997 when the newly installed president, Süleyman Demirel, ejected him from office, and the Welfare Party was subsequently banned. Rarely do major Turkish political parties disappear entirely from the landscape, however, and the Welfare Party reformed itself and re-emerged the following year as the Virtue Party (Fazilet Partisi). The closure of the Virtue Party in 2001 for the same reasons – that its core principles contravened those of the secular republic – led to its dissolution in turn, and this time it was succeeded by the Justice and Development Party (Adalet ve Kalkınma Partisi, AKP).[9]

The AKP's founders, who include now-President Erdoğan, recognised that the Islamist model that had been attempted by the Welfare and Virtue parties would only ever achieve limited success within a political system that was dominated by a secularist military. The AKP was formed largely under the ideological influence of Abdullah Gül, who, although not reckoned amongst its founding members, was nonetheless its major architect.[10] Gül would become the AKP's first prime minister, and in 2007, succeeded Ahmet Necdet Sezer to become the county's first Islamist president. Gül imagined a new way for a political party to negotiate within the constraints of the secular system while retaining its Islamic credentials. Rooted in Muslim conservatism, the AKP distanced itself from the openly religious rhetoric of its predecessor parties. Rather, it espoused an economically progressive agenda, and an eagerness for Turkey to engage confidently with the European Union and, in turn, with the wider, modern world.[11] By so doing, the AKP appealed to a wide electoral base in 2002, and secured votes not only from a religiously observant constituency but also from those attracted to its confident economic vision for the nation's future. The signficant economic growth that Turkey has experienced since that time has, indeed, been a major factor behind the party's continued success.[12]

Unlike in the countries of the Arab Middle East, political Islam had never traditionally gained a strong popular following in Turkey, and only a relatively small voter constituency supported a Sharia-oriented vision for the future of the State. In the 1990s, the Welfare Party had only secured a sizeable enough percentage of the national vote to govern as part of a coalition government. Granted, this was an era in which the Turkish political scene as a whole was very fragmented and no single party could gain an outright majority. When the AKP swept to power in Turkey in 2002 with 34 per cent of the national vote and a subsequent landslide victory precipitated by the particular structure of the Turkish electoral system, namely the '10per cent threshold',[13] it was a rare instance since 1983 of a single party gaining such a comprehensive overall majority in Parliament.[14] Erdoğan's party secured two-thirds of the seats, and formed a single-party administration that was widely welcomed after a string of failed coalition governments. The Republican People's Party, the party of Turkey's secularist 'father', Mustafa Kemal Atatürk, came second in the election and its members took up their seats as the only party in opposition.

United Around a Common Goal

In the first two terms of the AKP's tenure, one of its primary goals was the internal restructuring of the Turkish state in order to eliminate the political power of the military, which had been constitutionally entrusted with the defence of national security and, by extension, state secularism.[15] The informal alliance that the party had established with the Gülen Movement was based on a shared commitment to this common goal which, in turn, would pave the way for a gradual Islamisation of the public sphere.

The Gülenists' cooperation against the military was invaluable to the AKP, namely through their role in the so-called Ergenekon, Balyoz and Poyrazköy trials. These trials, which began in 2008, were a major onslaught against the secularist establishment in general and the military in particular, and it was widely recognised in Turkey at the time that the driving force behind them was a cadre of police chiefs and prosecutors loyal to Gülen. They alleged that hundreds of individuals, including high-ranking army generals, university professors and opposition lawmakers, were part of a 'deep state' plot to overthrow the AKP government by way of a string of interconnected terrorist attacks. The defendants were tried in a series of high-profile public cases, which gripped the public imagination and spanned five years in total. The allegations were supported by evidence that ranged from tenuous to downright bizarre,[16] yet at their conclusion in 2013, life sentences were nonetheless handed down to many prominent individuals. Foremost amongst these was General İlker Başbuğ, who had previously been Turkey's highest-ranking military officer and head of the armed forces.

In early 2014, however, after the escalation of open conflict between the Gülenists and the AKP, the situation turned around quite dramatically. Since that time, almost all the convicted individuals, including Başbuğ himself, have been released from prison. The evidence supporting their convictions has been shown to have been fabricated, and the Gülen Movement's central role in bringing the cases to court is now generally decried.[17] Unsurprisingly, Gülen and other individuals within the movement continue to deny their pivotal role in the trials, and no explanation or apology has been forthcoming.

While the falsification of evidence that underpinned the trials is now acknowledged, it was, remarkably, almost entirely unquestioned at the time.[18] The trials commanded broad support, not only from a conservative religious constituency but also from the nation's secular intellectuals, most of whom endorsed the narrative that calling the army generals to account, and reining in the political power of the military, paved the way for a new era of fuller democratisation in Turkey. Despite the dubious validity of the evidence presented, a popular narrative argued that by seeking to downgrade the guardianship of the armed forces over the secular state, Turkey was coming into line with EU requirements surrounding freedom of expression and the conditions associated with liberal democracy. In turn, there was much support in Europe and the USA for these moves to apparently liberalise the Turkish political landscape. A Brookings Institution briefing from April 2012, for example, declared that 'the AKP heralds democracy', and described its potential (widely discussed at the time) to serve as a successful model to Arab nations in the wake of the regional uprisings.[19]

In 2010, at the height of the Ergenekon trials and with the core of the secularist establishment already seriously weakened, the government called a referendum seeking a popular mandate for constitutional reform. The date of 12 September was symbolic, being the anniversary of the 1980 *coup d'état*. Despite massive public protests in Ankara, Istanbul and elsewhere by opposition supporters, 58 per cent of voters supported the proposed amendments.[20] The 'yes' vote allowed changes to the constitutional protections afforded to military officers in the aftermath of a coup, paving the way for 93-year-old former president Kenan Evren, the military architect of the 1980 coup, to stand trial.[21] The referendum also gave the government increased control over the judiciary, which, by implication, strengthened the hand of the Gülenists, who had made it a priority to attain positions of authority in the Turkish legal system and were subsequently very well represented there.[22] While there is no evidence that Gülen was the architect of the referendum, he nonetheless lent it his firm support, and broke with tradition to speak out publically to encourage his followers to vote 'yes' and thus to approve the changes.[23]

Gülen's Record on Secular Democracy

The Gülen Movement has justified the support that it lent to the campaign against the military establishment using the same language as many secularist commentators. That is to say, it has defended the value of liberalising Turkish democracy from military guardianship and encouraging the fuller maturation of state secularism. Its major mouthpieces in this endeavour are the national daily *Zaman* and its English-language counterpart, *Today's Zaman*, in which columnists have written regularly on these themes. The same ideas are characteristic of the movement's dialogue activities abroad where, in Western Europe and the USA especially, its discourse on civic engagement as well as its public renunciation of violent or political channels for implementing Islam are major facets of its public identity, and reason for its appeal.[24]

When scrutinised, however, Gülen's public record on the subject of secular democracy is problematic and contains some major contradictions. On the one hand, he claims to recognise the compatibility of Islam and democracy, and argues for the general desirability of democratic systems of governance according to the Islamic texts and traditions:

> each society holds the reins of its fate in its own hands. The prophetic tradition emphasises this idea: 'You will be ruled according to how you are.' This is the basic character and spirit of democracy; an idea which does not conflict with any Islamic principle. As Islam holds individuals and societies responsible for their own fate, people must be responsible for governing themselves.[25]

With regard to democracy and secularism in Turkey in particular, Gülen has said the following:

> The first article of the Turkish Constitution states that [the] 'Turkish state is a republic.' Just after that in the second article, the attributes of this republic are enumerated, and it says,

'Turkey is a democratic, secular, and social state governed by the rule of law.' Again as you know, these two articles cannot be changed, and even a bill to change it cannot be introduced in the parliament. Yes, these two foundations are under guarantees, and you cannot touch them. But, maybe you can improve them, perfect them, and make additions to democracy. *You can open and expand the definition of secularism; you can elevate it to the human horizon to contain more humane values.* You can dwell on the 'social state.' You can dwell on the concept of 'welfare state'; you can work on it and make it a little more humane and a little friendlier. But you can do all of these by remaining objective and benefitting from the developments in the world, then you can improve on them towards perfection.[26]

What Gülen seems to be saying in this passage is that he desires not to dismantle the secular tradition in Turkey and replace it with a religious state, but rather to effect change in the particular *nature* of Turkish secularism. The target of his criticism is very specifically the Turkish Kemalist tradition, which he accuses of being actively opposed to religion rather than neutral towards it. Thus he claims to advocate a more progressive and 'passive' interpretation of secularism, in which public expressions of religion are tolerated despite the State ascribing official status to no religion. In Gülenist discourse, the US model is often held up as a preferable alternative to the Turkish model in this regard. A theoretical framework has been provided by Ahmet Kuru, an American academic who is close to the Gülen Movement, and he sets it out in his book *Secularism and State Policies toward Religion: the United States, France and Turkey*.[27] This book, and Kuru's ideas more widely, were frequently alluded to by high-level movement insiders whom I interviewed in Turkey. In this vein, one such individual in Istanbul summed up his objections to the Kemalist tradition in the following way:

Kemalism is different from secularism, as it is enforced upon the nation and it is anti-religious at its core. The kind of secularism that Fethullah Gülen wants to see is like the secularism that you see in Britain or the USA. In those countries, you can be religious in public places and nobody hassles you about it.[28]

This statement is, however, directly contradicted by some of Gülen's earlier sermons, namely those that he gave in Turkey before he fled to the USA in 1999. Here, he clearly encourages his followers to seek the infiltration and overthrow of the democratic system in Turkey, in order to substitute for it an Islamic state. In a well-known recording that was aired in 1999, he said the following:

> You must move in the arteries of the system without anyone noticing your existence until you reach all the power centres [...] until the conditions are ripe, they [the followers] must continue like this. If they do something prematurely, the world will crush our heads, and Muslims will suffer everywhere, like in the tragedies in Algeria, like in 1982 [in] Syria [...] like in the yearly disasters and tragedies in Egypt. The time is not yet right. You must wait for the time when you are complete and conditions are ripe, until we can shoulder the entire world and carry it [...] You must wait until such time as you have gotten all the state power, until you have brought to your side all the power of the constitutional institutions in Turkey [...] Until that time, any step taken would be too early – like breaking an egg without waiting the full 40 days for it to hatch. It would be like killing the chick inside. The work to be done is [in] confronting the world. Now, I have expressed my feelings and thoughts to you all – in confidence [...] trusting your loyalty and secrecy. I know that when you leave here – [just] as you discard your empty juice boxes, you must discard the thoughts and the feelings that I expressed here.[29]

Gülen denied that this sermon was accurately recorded, and claimed that his message was deliberately distorted in order to discredit him. There is, however, wider evidence of a marked shift in Gülen's teachings around the time of his move to the USA, with the tone and content of his later sermons differing sometimes radically from his earlier material. Sermons from the 1990s, for example, contain some anti-Semitic and anti-Christian teaching, which is in direct contradiction to his more recent emphasis on dialogue and tolerance between faiths.[30] The inconsistency of his preaching record, together with the movement's now-shamed campaign to bring down Turkey's secular establishment through fabricated claims and falsified evidence, mean that, notwithstanding the movement's protestations to the contrary, there must be serious doubts surrounding Gülen's commitment both to secularism and to the free, democratic process.

The Beginnings of the End: Early Signs of a Breakdown in the Alliance

During the AKP's second term in office, tensions began to appear in public between Prime Minister Erdoğan and Fethullah Gülen. These tensions did not manifest themselves in the parliamentary context, for there were only very few Gülenists in cabinet positions. Rather, as tensions rose, they became apparent in broader power struggles as the movement exerted its considerable influence within the police force and the judiciary.

One of the earliest sources of conflict between the two men, and the subject of their first public disagreement, was in the realm of international affairs and concerned Turkey's relationship with Israel. Throughout the twentieth century, Turkey had been a rare regional ally of Israel and relations between the two countries had been generally strong. Since Erdoğan's rise to power, this relationship has deteriorated severely. Various diplomatic spats between the two countries have escalated rapidly, fuelled in part by ideologically driven anti-Israeli rhetoric from the then prime minister himself. The failure of diplomatic relations between Turkey and Israel has been accompanied by a surge in anti-Israeli sentiment in the general public.[31] When Erdoğan publically stormed out of a debate on Gaza with Israeli President Shimon Peres at the Davos World Economic Forum in 2009, he was greeted as a returning hero on his arrival back in Turkey, with cheering crowds waiting for him at the airport.

Gülen's stance on Israel is markedly different from Erdoğan's, being tempered by his stated interest in interfaith dialogue, especially with Jewish and Christian groups. The prime minister's public rhetoric against Israel therefore sat uneasily with Gülen, and while he did not speak out after the Davos affair he did intervene in the Mavi Marmara incident of the following year. This incident, in which nine Turkish activists on a humanitarian flotilla were killed at sea by Israeli soldiers during their attempt to break the blockade on Gaza, led to the expulsion of the Israeli ambassador from Ankara and the suspension of diplomatic relations between the two countries. Gülen spoke out publically, suggesting that the confrontational approach of the activists had been misplaced and that the pursuit of a diplomatic path would have been preferable, both before the crisis and during its aftermath.[32] His position brought him into direct conflict with the prime minister and with public opinion more widely, and although there was only muted public response to an interview that he gave, it was a sign of further trouble to come.

The major deterioration in AKP–Gülen relations came nearly two years later in February 2012, when Gülenist prosecuters sought the arrrest of Hakan Fidan, the head of Turkey's National Intelligence Organisation (Millî İstihbarat Teşkilatı, MİT) and a close personal ally of Erdoğan. Fidan was engaged at the time in secret, high-level talks with Abdullah Öcalan, the highly controversial leader of the Kurdish PKK (Partiya Karkerên Kurdistanê – Kurdistan Workers' Party), who is serving a life prison sentence. The Kurdish issue had been a subject on which the Gülen Movement had differed ideologically from the AKP: being strongly informed by Turkish nationalist ideology, the movement was not a supporter of the government's tentative rapprochement with Kurdish separatists. Erdoğan was able to stop Fidan's arrest by issuing emergency legislation the following day, but the movement's attack on such a high-level AKP ally was perceived as a declaration of open warfare.

It was not long before the government hit back. In October of the same year, the Prime Minister announced his intention to forcibly close down the nation's *dershane* network, an area in which followers of Gülen are heavily invested.[33] According to this new plan, *dershane*s across the country were to be turned into private schools, ostensibly because the government no longer wished to tolerate a parallel system of education provision. The inefficiencies and inequalities of the *dershane* system are not in doubt, but the sudden anouncement of their impending closure came as a shock to many. The Gülen Movement is amongst the foremost providers of *dershane* education in Turkey; large national franchises such as FEM, as well as innumerable smaller operations, provide a valuable source of income to the movement, and also act as its primary recruitment ground. In threatening to close them down, the AKP government knew that it was targeting one of the major arteries of the movement's social and economic power. Gülen reached out and offered to voluntarily turn the movement's *dershane*s over to state control, but the offer was rejected. The date of the planned closures has been revised a number of time since the original announcement, and at the time of writing it remains uncertain.

Against this backdrop of mounting tension, relations between the two groups foundered irretrievably in 2013. In May and June of that year, the Gezi Park riots dominated the national news. Violent protests spread from a park in central Istanbul to Ankara, Izmir and many other major cities across Turkey. The riots began as a small-scale, environmental protest but soon became a national movement focused on opposition to prime minister Erdoğan. Erdoğan responded by ordering a harsh police crackdown, which resulted in multiple deaths and many serious injuries. It also triggered widespread criticism of his handling of the crisis in the international media.[34]

The protesters were drawn from a wide range of social and religious backgrounds, including a group calling itself 'Anti-Capitalist Muslims', but were dominated by individuals of a secular-leaning, educated and urban background. These are not the people of Gülen's core constituency, and he voiced his criticism of the protesters, declaring that their actions were indicative of 'a generation of moral and spiritual decay'.[35] Gülen was also, however, openly critical of the AKP's response to the situation and, in an interview with *Zaman* newspaper he publically condemned its excessive use of force to quash the riots, asking whether 'a shopping mall [was] worth a single drop of blood?'[36] He was not alone in voicing criticism of Erdoğan's heavy-handed approach – indeed, various senior members of the AKP did as well, namely incumbent president Abdullah Gül and deputy prime minister Bülent Arınç. Nonetheless, Gülen's public criticism of the then-prime minister did nothing to improve already deteriortating relations between the two men.

The December 2013 Scandal and its Aftermath

The full escalation of the mounting power struggle between Gülen and his followers and Erdogan's AKP came with the corruption scandal that erupted on 17 December 2013. The Gülenists played their best hand in revealing material that appeared to indicate endemic corruption within the AKP and embezzlement of public funds on a shocking scale. It was a bold move, and a great deal was at stake. The recordings that were leaked a few months later on 24 February 2014, purporting to show the prime minister and his son conspiring to secrete away huge sums of money, were their strongest blow. The veracity of the recordings has never been clearly established, although many, including opposition politicians, believe that they were genuine.[37] What is certain, however, is that the Gülenists obtained them through illegal means by the sustained wiretapping of encrypted government telephone lines.

With the news being disseminated through social media across the entire country in a matter of hours, it was not clear that Erdoğan could survive the scandal. The leader of the opposition, Kemal Kılıçdaroğlu, called on the prime minister to 'either flee the country, take your helicopter, or resign'. Erdoğan remained resolute but local elections were scheduled for only two months later, and it appeared that he and his party were likely to be punished by the electorate for their alleged misdeeds and their involvement in what appeared to be a systemic abuse of political power.

In a remarkable turn of events, however, the AKP secured another strong majority in the local elections of 30 March 2014, claiming over 42 per cent of the national vote, notwithstanding serious allegations of voting irregularities, which may have robbed the opposition of control of several provinces including the capital, Ankara.[38] The Prime Minister's position therefore seemed largely unaffected by the corruption allegations, and the AKP continued with a seemingly strong popular mandate to govern at the local level. Five months later, on 10 August 2014, Erdoğan strengthened his position further still by securing over 50 per cent of the national vote in the country's first presidential election, and this enabled him to step up to the office of president. The main opposition candidate, Ekmeleddin İhsanoğlu who stood for both the CHP (the Republican People's Party) and MHP (the Nationalist Movement Party), secured less than 40 per cent.

President Erdoğan's success in both elections was derived in large part from his ability to turn around the narrative surrounding the corruption allegations and, particularly, the phone recordings: although he flatly denied the allegations, he focused in his response not primarily on the content of the conversations but rather the fact that the Gülenists had acted illegally and subversively in wiretapping his telephone and constructing a misleading 'montage'. Gülen was labelled an enemy of the state, and his followers a dangerous and pernicious force conspiring against a legitimate and democratically elected government. Erdoğan's rhetoric has become increasingly vitriolic with the passage of time, and he has repeatedly likened the Gülen Movement to the *hashshashin*, a medieval Islamic sect known for murders and espionage and referred to in English as the 'Assassins'.[39]

AKP political hegemony has prevailed, although support for President Erdoğan has undoubtedly waned, even within his own party. Nonetheless, a core constituency from the president's support base remains loyal to him, even when faced with serious questions surrounding his leadership. The situation has thus increased the divisions visible in an already polarised political landscape. There have been public protests in response to the scandal in some cities, but these have not on the scale of Gezi Park the previous year, perhaps because they have been met with a similarly overpowering police presence. Further, structural changes have been made in order to control further dissent, and laws were passed in early 2014 that increased the government's control over the judiciary and the intelligence services, as well as tightening internet surveillance. The latter in particular stoked further anger amongst opposition voters but, despite renewed violent street protests, were signed into law by then-president Abdullah Gül.[40]

When he emerged victorious from the March 2014 elections, prime minister Erdoğan vowed to eliminate Gülen and his followers for their attempt to discredit him and his government. In the intervening year, this punishment has been meted out in a variety of forms: firstly, through the sacking or reassignment of thousands of Gülenists in the police force and judiciary (an operation that is ongoing); secondly, and more latterly, through targeted legal action against the movement's key assets and individuals. In December 2014, various senior individuals in the Gülen-affiliated media were amongst 28 people arrested on suspicion of forming a criminal network in opposition to the State. These included Ekrem Dumanlı, the editor-in-chief of the movement's flagship national daily newspaper *Zaman*, as well as Hidayet Karaca, head of the Samanyolu TV media group. Dumanlı was released shortly afterwards, but Karaca remains in custody along with three of his co-defendants.[41]

Another major Gülenist target in Turkey has been Bank Asya, Turkey's largest Islamic lender, which was founded by followers of Gülen in 1996.

The bank was threatened with closure towards the end of 2014, following the withdrawal that year of around $1.6 billion in funds by state-owned firms and institutions.[42] Shareholders loyal to Gülen responded by flooding the bank with deposits in order to keep it afloat, with twice as many deposits recorded in the year to September 2014 than in the previous year.[43] Despite their best efforts, however, on 3 February 2015 – the same day that an opinion piece by Fethullah Gülen, in which he criticised the Turkish administration, was published in the *New York Times*[44] – management of Bank Asya was forcibly taken over by Turkey's Savings Deposit Insurance Fund (TMSF). The grounds given were that insufficient transparency was hindering its proper regulation. Ahmet Davutoğlu, the new prime minister following Erdoğan's accession to the presidency, denied that Bank Asya had been targeted as an act of political retribution, stating that '[the] Bank Asya decision has no political dimension, it is a completely legal decision. The legal criteria are for everyone, for every company.'[45] A few months later, on 29 May 2015, it was announced that, following the earlier handover of its management to the TMSF, the bank's remaining shares had been seized and it had been taken over by the State.[46]

Despite the prime minister's protestations to the contrary, the takeover of Bank Asya was clearly a strategic attack on a major Gülenist asset. Its appropriation by TMSF in February was accompanied in the same month by the cancellation of Gülen's Turkish passport, in a move that suggested that a formal request might soon be made for his extradition from the USA. The reason cited for the passport's cancellation that was communicated to US officials was that it had been obtained by way of a 'false statement'. Since 2014, Erdoğan has repeatedly called for the USA to expel Gülen and send him back to Turkey to face trial for crimes related to terrorism, but the government has yet to make an official request for his deportation and the USA has not offered a response. In March 2014, however, the White House responded firmly to Erdoğan's report that in talks with President Obama, the lattter had 'looked positively' at his request for Gülen's extradition. An official spokesperson was quick to reject this claim, stressing that 'the response attributed to President Obama with regards to Mr. Gülen [was] not accurate'. The US ambassador to Turkey has indicated separately that his government is unwilling to take sides in this Turkish domestic war, and at the time of writing Gülen's imminent deportation from the United States looked unlikely.

While Gülen's own future in the United States may not yet be in doubt, the businesses, media platforms, schools and other ventures run by his followers in Turkey remain under serious and sustained threat of closure. President Erdoğan has pledged to shut down the movement's schools and other activities, and is reported to have ordered local government officials to seize its land and buildings. The Bank Asya affair is likely to be only the tip of the iceberg, and the repercussions of the corruption allegations look set to haunt the Gülen Movement for some time yet. In addition, many senior individuals in the movement continue to face questioning by the police, and, at the time of writing, new arrests and prosecutions are reported on an almost weekly basis.

Implications for the Global Gülen Movement

The movement's institutions in Turkey have not been the only ones to be adversely affected. The President has taken his campaign to dismantle the movement beyond Turkey's borders and into the international arena, petitioning various foreign heads of state to close down Gülen-run schools in their countries. To date, the most success he has had is in Azerbaijan, which was once fertile ground for the movement and home to a significant number of schools. In the summer of 2014, all Gülen-run educational institutions in the country – which included 11 high schools, 14 primary schools and Qafqas University – were shut down.[47] Azerbaijani president Ilham Aliyev declared his intention to preserve the relationship with Ankara at all costs, and apparently acted on Erdoğan's express wishes.

To date, President Erdoğan has had varied success elsewhere. He has made direct appeals to various African governments for them to close their Gülen schools and allow the Turkish state to run alternative institutions. In January 2015, at a news conference in Ethiopia where the movement runs five schools, he told reporters, '[the Gülen Movement] might have established educational institutions, but they will be closed down because the Republic of Turkey education ministry will be providing the needed services for students.'[48] It is unclear how the Turkish state could reasonably replicate the educational provision of the Gülen Movement though, as while it might be financially capable of establishing new schools it would be hard-pressed to replicate the human resources that are central to the success of the global Gülen education project. One of the main reasons for the schools' academic success is the extraordinary commitment of their Turkish teachers, who are motivated to teach (for low pay and often in far-flung locations) by their particular interpretation of Islam and their dedication to Gülen's teachings. Without this cadre of dedicated teachers, as well as the organisational capacity of the Gülenists, it is unclear that the schools could continue in the same way.[49] Nonetheless, the Ethiopian Government, while yet to close the schools down, has indicated that it will respect the wishes of the Turkish Government on the subject. Elsewhere on the continent, in Gabon and Senegal, Gülen schools have reportedly already been closed.

Other countries have been entirely unreceptive to Erdoğan's demands, and on a recent visit to Albania the Turkish President's public declaration that the Gülen Movement was a terrorist organisation and that it should be treated as such was met with a lukewarm reception. The movement runs a number of primary and high schools, two universities and a string of Islamic madrassas in Albania.[50] In May 2015, a spokesperson for the government rejected the demand on the grounds that the Turkish president's request was a political move related to domestic issues, which had no bearing on security in Albania or the wider region. At the time of writing, Gülen educational enterprises in Albania continue to function normally.

In the United States, which has the highest rate of Gülenist activity outside Turkey and is home to Gülen himself, the movement's schools face no imminent threat of statutory closure, despite Erdogan's statement to the American broadcaster PBS in April 2014 that they posed a security threat: 'these elements which threaten the national security of Turkey cannot be allowed to exist in other countries because what they do to us here, they might do against their host'.[51] Gülen has been able to defend himself and the movement against President Erdoğan's accusations in the diplomatic arena through the think tanks and dialogue platforms that the movement runs in Washington, DC, as well as the group of friends and supporters that it has cultivated in Congress.[52] It remains to be seen, however, whether the presence that it has established in this global centre of political power will be sufficient to protect the movement from President

Erdoğan's onslaught, which has the benefit of recourse to official diplomatic channels not only in the United States but around the world.

The Future of the Gülen Movement

Throughout his long career, which began in earnest in the 1960s, Fethullah Gülen has publically emphasised to his followers the primary value of civil-society activism, and has maintained an outward position of political neutrality. That he has exercised indirect political influence through the AKP administration over the past 15 years is not in question. He has, though, remained mostly behind the scenes in doing this while continuing to project an apolitical official persona. At the same time, Gülen has been able to build up a global movement that has appealed to many audiences, especially in the West, precisely because of its emphasis on civic engagement, its reconciliation of Islamic piety with the ideas of secularism and democracy, and because of the activities of his followers in the field of modern education and intercultural dialogue. This arrangement has suited the Gülen Movement, and Gülen himself has found it expedient to retain a low profile in public all the while.

The movement's recent decision to go public in its war with the AKP suggests a major shift in its attitude towards political involvement. Having remained in the shadows for years, Gülen has now acted openly in Turkish politics. It is unclear what the outcome would have been or what the movement's next step would have looked like, had the corruption allegations led to Erdoğan's fall from power. Certainly, there is no evidence to suggest that the movement is planning on entering politics in a formal capacity, or that it harbours aspirations to become a political party to challenge the AKP in its own right. Certainly, to do so might seriously undermine the credibility that it has built up both in Turkey and also in the USA and the international arena.

The movement faces serious challenges in the days ahead, with attacks on its people and institutions in Turkey continuing. On 22 May 2015, close to the time of writing, 31 people close to Gülen were detained in a police operation spanning 19 provinces. These included a former university rector (equivalent to vice-chancellor in the British system), a former vice-president of YÖK (Turkey's Higher Education Board) and various senior members of the legal profession as well as the police. Charging and prosecution by the courts of 12 of the detainees was subsequently sought.[53] This is one example of the ongoing governmental crackdown on the Gülen Movement in Turkey, and there are no signs of it abating.

Political wrangling aside, Gülen himself is now an elderly man apparently beset by poor health, and the issue of his eventual demise raises a host of separate questions surrounding the movement's possible future directions. As far as we know, there is no obvious successor to take his place, and anyway the loyalty that he commands from his followers is derived from his own charismatic persona and would be hard for another leader to replicate. His predecessor, Said Nursi, was keen to avoid his own sanctification by his followers after his death, and is reputed to have requested burial in an anonymous location in order to pre-empt his grave becoming a place of pilgrimage and supplication.[54] In death, Gülen is also likely to attain saintly status for his followers. The fact that his teachings are so well recorded both in written and oral form means that his legacy may well live on for generations to come. It seems inevitable, though, that, like the Nur Movement after Nursi, the Gülen Movement will lose its internal coherence after his death. Different splinter groups therefore seem bound to emerge, which will likely weaken the movement's scope and influence overall.

The possibility of its evolution into an educational movement largely divorced from its political and religious foundations is there, and the Jesuit model is sometimes referred to as a comparison in this respect. Without Gülen himself as the driving motivational force, however, it is hard to imagine that the extraordinary human resources on which it so heavily depends will continue to be available to it, and thus it seems unlikely that the global network of schools could continue to operate so widely and with such a high measure of success. Without a cadre of unusually dedicated teachers and administrators, as well as the movement's unique organisational capacity, its schools would certainly lose their competitive edge.

Like all religious movements, the Gülen Movement is neither static nor universal in nature. Rather, it has emerged and spread in a certain way as a result of particular local and historical circumstances. Since early 2014, however, the movement has been losing ground in Turkey and it potentially stands to forfeit many of the gains it has made in the previous 30 years. One of its great strengths historically has been its ability to understand the times well, and to respond to changes in fortune accordingly. It could well be, however, that with the events of December 2013, the movement overplayed its hand in the Turkish political arena, and the challenges facing it today as a result may yet prove too great for it to overcome.

Afterword

The research for this book was carried out during an extremely volatile period in the Gülen Movement's history, over the course of which its fortunes changed considerably. When I first met many of my fieldwork interlocutors in Turkey in early 2013, the movement was confident, prosperous and flourishing. Although tensions in its relationship with the AKP government were in fact already emerging, they had not yet become explicit, and did not impact on the movement's ability to operate successfully. Today, the situation is quite different. The Gülenists' attempt to publically discredit President Erdoğan in December 2013 was, for the most part, a failure. The result, in the following three years, was the comprehensive downgrading of the movement's power and influence in Turkey, and the loss of the political and economic leverage – and, by extension, much of the social capital – that it once enjoyed.

The full degeneration of relations between the AKP government and the Gülen Movement has never been more apparent than it is on the eve of this book going to press. Turkey is presently reeling from the shock of a violent attempt at a military coup that occurred on the night of 15 July 2016, in which the Gülen Movement is directly implicated. A bloody and chaotic night saw aircraft from a rebel faction within the armed forces attack, amongst other targets, the Turkish intelligence headquarters and the parliament in Ankara, and an embattled President Erdoğan addressing the nation via the 'Facetime' app on his mobile phone, inviting his supporters to come out onto the streets to resist the military takeover – something which thousands of them duly did.[1]

The president made it clear immediately, during this address in the early hours of the morning and at the height of the crisis, that he held Fethullah Gülen and his followers to blame for the coup attempt, and for attempting to violently dismantle Turkey's democratic tradition. Over the course of the night, the government and its supporters repudiated the coup and regained control, but not without the loss of almost 300 lives. Subsequently, tens of thousands of individuals have been either arrested or suspended from their duties across an extremely wide section of Turkish civil society, and a three-month state of emergency has been declared. Turkey has formally requested the extradition of Gülen by the US authorities amid suggestions that the death penalty could be re-introduced as punishment for the plotters.

Gülen soon spoke out in a rare public interview to deny his connection to the coup attempt – although he made a caveat that he could not rule out involvement by his followers in Turkey, on the grounds that (as per his usual official stance) he is unsure who all of those individuals are.[2] While the involvement of the movement and of Gülen himself remains unclear, what is immediately evident is the extent to which the crisis has strengthened President Erdoğan's own position. The events of 15 July 2016 shocked the nation, and the entire political establishment has since rallied around the AKP government to defend its democratic mandate – an act of cross party solidarity that has rarely, if ever, been seen in modern Turkish politics. Support for Erdoğan therefore seems to be consolidating around the failed coup, and public appetite – even amongst his opponents - for military intervention to overturn what, in spite of flaws that are recognised by many, is nonetheless a democratic political order is apparently low.[3] This response marks a departure from the twentieth-century context, when the coup tradition was a central part of Turkish politics and – in 1980 at least – the intervention of the military during periods of political failure and instability was received by many with a muted sense of relief.

The fact that the president so rapidly and confidently attributed the failed coup to Gülen indicates the extreme toxicity of the latter's reputation now in Turkey. It also had immediately visible implications for relations between Turkey and the USA at an international level. The US administration has shown little appetite for meeting Turkey's demands for Gülen's extradition to date; since 15 July 2016, however, it has indicated that it will consider the case if solid evidence of his involvement can be provided. Such evidence may or may not be forthcoming; either way, it is clear that Fethullah Gülen and his on-going presence in the United States have now become a major point of diplomatic tension between the US and its geopolitically strategic NATO ally. Different voices within the Turkish administration have already made it clear that to *not* extradite Gülen would be tantamount to an admission of American involvement in the failed coup itself, allegations with potentially very grave consequences which risk destabilising critical US-Turkish relations at a time of high volatility in neighbouring Syria and the wider Middle East region.

Even before the escalation of this recent crisis, President Erdoğan had already been spearheading a bitter campaign of retribution for the events of December 2013, in which the Gülen Movement had paid a high price for disloyalty to its erstwhile ally. This campaign targeted Gülenist assets and institutions in all of its major spheres of influence. In education, schools across Turkey were subjected to routine police inspections in which their legal and financial status were called into question, and student intake was reported to have dropped by a half in the year 2014–2015. Some of the schools abroad bowed to diplomatic pressure from the Turkish embassy and closed their doors. In healthcare, scores of Gülen-run private hospitals had their contracts with the state's social security institution (SGK) revoked, rendering them effectively incapable of operating. In finance, the movement's major asset, Bank Asya, was removed from Gülenist control in 2014 and appropriated by the government. Finally, in the media, various Gülen-run TV channels and newspapers were forcibly shut down and various senior editors arrested.[4]

On an individual level, too, the movement suffered considerable setbacks, witnessing the full fruition of President Erdoğan's 2014 threat to launch a 'witch hunt' against Gülen and his associates. Dozens of the movement's senior leaders and affiliates – including high ranking police chiefs, journalists and former politicians – were taken into custody to face police investigations. They were alleged to have been involved in a 'parallel state' – now officially designated FETÖ (*Fethullahçı Terör Örgütü*; Fethullah Terror Organisation) - intent on overthrowing the government, and which, according to Erdoğan, harbours violent, terrorist ambitions. Even before the events of 15 July 2016, the president was pursuing the extradition from the United States of Gülen himself: a lawsuit was filed in a Pennsylvania court in December 2015 by the Turkish Embassy in Washington, which appeared to be designed to precipitate Gülen's forced return to Turkey to stand trial for his alleged crimes.[5]

While the movement faced the full force of Erdoğan's wrath and suffered continued losses, the president himself emerged, if not entirely, then mostly unscathed from the December 2013 crisis. In the general election of June 2015, the AKP temporarily lost its parliamentary majority, but this was likely due largely to other factors than the crisis between Erdoğan and Gülen. The government had lost considerable popularity anyway as a result of its heavy-handed response to the Gezi Park riots the previous summer, a situation that was capitalised on in June 2015 by the People's Democratic Party (Halkların Demokratik Partisi, HDP), a Kurdish political party which managed to garner support from disenfranchised voters including the liberal secularist left who had been central to the Gezi protests. After a summer throughout which the Kurdish question became worryingly violent and volatile, though, the HDP was unable to repeat its success in the November re-run of the election, and the AKP won back enough seats to form a majority government (albeit with smaller numbers than before).

The retraction of Gülenist support from the AKP had little impact on the overall election results. There were reports of a new, and rather unlikely, alliance being forged between the movement and the CHP which, although it embodies secularist values that are almost entirely antithetical to the movement,[6] is nonetheless the largest party of opposition and the only potentially serious challenger to the AKP. It seemed improbable, however – especially after the association of the movement with the failed coup of 2016, which CHP leader Kemal Kılıçdaroğlu resolutely condemned - that this alliance would develop in any significant way, and the influence that Gülen has exerted indirectly on the Turkish political scene since the early 2000s is therefore certain to be over. Even if the CHP were to have become a new ally of the movement, it would have been incapable of exerting the same influence through the CHP as it did through its alliance with the AKP. Over the past two decades, the movement has operated within informal networks based on shared conceptions of Muslim piety, networks in which the AKP is active and through which unofficial state patronage was forthcoming to the Gülenists. The CHP does not operate within these same networks and so, even if in the unlikely event that it attained power, it would have offered far less to the Gülen Movement in return for its support.

Like the rest of the movement's interests in Turkey, in the aftermath of the failed coup of July 2016 the Gülen schools are now faced with the prospect of either closure or state appropriation. The schools began to constitute the backbone of the movement's activities, and a crucial vehicle for recruitment, soon after Gülen's initial appearance in Izmir in the 1970s. Over the subsequent four decades, the schooling franchise that Gülen oversaw evolved into one of the most successful and lucrative in

Turkey for the provision of science-focused education. The future of the Gülen schools, and the *dershanes* which ran alongside them in parallel, was already in doubt after the events of December 2013, although they managed to remain operational for nearly three years afterwards. At the time of writing, however, it is becoming clear that they will not survive as Gülenist institutions for much longer; in the immediate aftermath of the 2016 coup attempt, 21,000 teachers within the private education market (many of whom we can assume to be followers of Gülen) had their licenses to teach revoked, and resignations were demanded from university deans across the nation. These purges, along with those in other sectors, stand to affect more people in Turkey than just Gülenists. Indeed, the government has other detractors domestically that are also likely to be caught up in the post-coup climate of score-settling. The Gülen Movement is, nonetheless, likely to be the greatest net loser in the field of education specifically: this is the area in which its most valuable resources have been invested and the operational base through which it has accrued valuable supporters and influence, without which it cannot continue to function effectively.

The legacy that the Gülen schools in Turkey leave for future generations will be revealing. In the almost four decades that they were operational, the schools stayed true to their Nursian-inspired vision of equipping a new generation of pious Muslims in modern science and scientific ways of knowing. On one level, they achieved great successes in this area, both internally within the Turkish education system but also on the international stage in the independently organised 'Science Olympiad' competitions. Yet my research found little evidence to suggest that the schools trained their students to think critically or philosophically about modern science in a way that might herald a new development in the field of science and Islam. Those graduates who pursued scientific paths did so almost exclusively in the areas of engineering, medicine and technology, and only a tiny minority went on to study and contribute to the natural sciences – the field which is most demonstrably in need of rejuvenation in the Muslim world today.[7]

Graduates of Gülen schools have used their scientific education primarily to gain access to a modern, rationalist knowledge economy, and to compete ably in that arena without, crucially, compromising their Muslim piety. This has been Gülen's goal since the early days of the movement, and his followers have played a central role in the re-Islamification of Turkish society to this end. Under the influence of AKP patronage for many years, the Gülen Movement led the way in the emergence of a new class of religiously and socially conservative, but economically mobile, Muslims. Science education has been the cornerstone of the Gülenist project, yet science appears to have provided the *means* of expansion and a vehicle for the accrual of influence rather than the end goal in itself.

It is unclear as yet how followers of Gülen will survive in Turkey in this new era in which the AKP patronage that it once enjoyed has turned to open aggression. Gülen continues, for the most part, to project from his compound in Pennsylvania a public image of a peace-loving sage, committed to dialogue and understanding between peoples, and his responses to Erdoğan's enraged retaliation have (mostly) been characteristically muted. If Gülen resists extradition from the USA and his followers are able, despite diplomatic pressure from the Turkish government, to continue functioning overseas, then it seems likely that the movement will continue to pursue the dialogue-related activities that his followers have established in the US and elsewhere, and that the promotion of Turkishness will remain central to its goals abroad. In Turkey itself, the movement as we know it is undoubtedly fatally wounded, both because of its failure to successfully challenge Erdoğan in December 2013 and because of the president's assured belief that Gülen was the mastermind behind the failed military coup of 15 July 2016. With Erdoğan rapidly consolidating his power in its aftermath, Gülen and his followers now find themselves firmly on the wrong side not only of an increasingly powerful government but also, perhaps just as significantly, of Turkish public opinion.

Said Nursi's ideology of *müspet hareket* (positive action) was designed in the early twentieth century to allow his pious Muslim followers a space in which not only to survive in an assertively secularist regime, but to prosper and influence society around them. The Gülen Movement implemented this ideology extremely effectively for over four decades, but now faces a challenge that Nursi could not have forseen: to continue under conditions of extreme state hostility, when the president himself is no longer secularist but rather Islamist in orientation and when the public mood is highly suspicious of the moods and motivations of Fethullah Gülen and the movement that he inspires.

Notes

Introduction

1 Şerif Mardin, *Religion, Society and Modernity in Turkey* (Syracuse, NY: Syracuse University Press, 2006); Richard Tapper (ed.), *Islam in Turkey: Religion, Politics and Literature in a Secular State* (London: I.B.Tauris, 1991); David Shankland, *Islam and Society in Turkey* (Huntingdon, PA: Eothen Press, 1999).

2 Bernard Lewis, *The Emergence of Modern Turkey* (Oxford: Oxford University Press, 2002); Feroz Ahmad, *The Making of Modern Turkey* (London/New York: Routledge, 1993); Niyazi Berkes, *The Development of Secularism in Turkey* (New York/Abingdon: Routledge, 1998); Erik J. Zürcher, *Turkey: A Modern History* (London: I.B.Tauris, 1997).

3 David Shankland, *The Alevis in Turkey: The Emergence of a Secular Islamic Tradition* (London: RoutledgeCurzon, 2003); Markus Dressler, *Writing Religion: The Making of Turkish Alevi Islam* (Oxford: Oxford University Press, 2013). There are also small Greek Orthodox and Armenian Christian populations, mainly in Istanbul, and very small numbers of Jews and Protestant Christians.

4 The term 'political Islam' has various definitions, but here I take it to mean the official integration of religious and political authority at a national level. On the rise of political Islam in Turkey, see Jenny B. White, *Islamist Mobilisation in Turkey: A Study in Vernacular Politics* (Seattle, WA: University of Washington Press, 2002). On the AKP specifically, see William Hale and Ergun Özbudun (eds), *Islamism, Democracy and Liberalism in Turkey* (London/New York: Routledge, 2010); and Arda Can Kumbaracıbaşı, *Turkish Politics and the Rise of the AKP* (London/New York: Routledge, 2009).

5 On the Naqshbandis in Turkey, see Itzchak Weismann, *The Naqshbandiyya: Orthodoxy and Activism in a Worldwide Sufi Tradition* (Abingdon: Routledge, 2007); and Brian Silverstein, *Islam and Modernity in Turkey* (New York: Palgrave MacMillan, 2011). For an introduction to the Muslim Brotherhood, see Barry Rubin (ed.) *The Muslim Brotherhood: The Organisation and Policies of a Global Islamist Movement* (New York/Basingstoke: Palgrave MacMillan, 2010).

6 Gareth H. Jenkins, 'Falling Facades: The Gülen Movement and Turkey's Escalating Power Struggle', *Turkey Analyst*, vol. 7, no. 1 (15 January 2014).

7 Serif Mardin, *Religion and Social Change in Modern Turkey: The Case of Bediuzzaman Said Nursi* (Albany, NY: State University of New York Press, 1989).
8 John L. Esposito, *Islam and Politics* (New York: Syracuse University Press, 1984), Gilles Kepel, *Muslim Extremism in Egypt: The Prophet and Pharaoh* (Berkeley, CA and Los Angeles: University of California Press, 1984), Olivier Roy, *The Failure of Political Islam* (Cambridge, MA: Harvard University Press, 1994).
9 Mardin, *Religion and Social Change*, p.102.
10 John Hedley-Brooke, *Science and Religion: Some Historical Perspectives* (Cambridge: University of Cambridge Press, 1991); Ian Barbour, *Religion and Science: Historical and Contemporary Issues* (London: SCM Press, 1998); Seyyed Hossein Nasr, *Science and Civilisation in Islam* (Cambridge, MA: Harvard University Press, 1968) and *The Need for a Sacred Science* (London: Curzon, 1993).
11 Mardin, *Religion and Social Change*, pp. 203–16; Yamine Mermer and Redha Ameur, 'Beyond the "Modern": Said Nursi's View of Science', *Islam and Science*, vol. 2, no. 2 (2004), pp. 119–60.
12 Caroline Tee and David Shankland, 'Said Nursi's Notion of Sacred Science: Its Function and Application in *Hizmet* High School Education', *Sociology of Islam* Vol. 1, Issue 3–4 (2014), pp. 209–32.
13 Bekim Agai, 'Fethullah Gülen and his Movement's Islamic Ethic of Education', *Critique: Critical Middle Eastern Studies*, 11:1 (2002), pp. 27–47.
14 Taner Edis, *An Illusion of Harmony: Science and Religion in Islam* (New York: Prometheus, 2007); Nidhal Guessoum, *Islam's Quantum Question: Reconciling Muslim Tradition and Modern Science* (London: I.B.Tauris, 2011).
15 timss.bc.edu/timss2011 (accessed 30 January 2016). See also the recent report edited by Nidhal Guessoum and Athar Osama, *Science at Universities of the Muslim World*, published in October 2015 by the Muslim World Science Initiative and available at muslim-science.com/science-at-universities-of-islamic-world-2 (accessed 30 January 2016).
16 Talal Asad, *Formations of the Secular: Christianity, Islam, Modernity* (Stanford, CA: Stanford University Press, 2003).
17 Philip G. Altbach and Daniel C. Levy (eds), *Private Higher Education: A Global Revolution* (Rotterdam: Sense, 2005).
18 Joshua D. Hendrick, *Gülen: The Ambiguous Politics of Market Islam in Turkey and the World* (New York: New York University Press, 2013). See also M. Hakan Yavuz and John L. Esposito (eds), *Turkish Islam and the Secular State: The Gülen Movement* (New York: Syracuse University Press, 2003); and David Tittensor, *The House of Service: The Gülen Movement and Islam's Third Way* (New York: Oxford University Press, 2014).

19 Salman Hameed, 'Making Sense of Islamic Creationism in Europe', *Public Understanding of Science* 1–12 (2014); Guessoum, *Islam's Quantum Question*.
20 Stefano Bigliardi, *Islam and the Quest for Modern Science: Conversations with Adnan Oktar, Mehdi Golshani, Mohammed Basil Altaie, Zaghloul El-Naggar, Bruno Guiderdoni and Nidhal Guessoum* (Istanbul: Swedish Research Institute in Istanbul, 2014).

1 : Gülen : Leader and Community

1 The main scholarly sources on the Gülen Movement are as follows: Joshua D. Hendrick, *Gülen: The Ambiguous Politics of Market Islam in Turkey and the World* (New York: New York University Press, 2013); M. Hakan Yavuz, *Toward an Islamic Enlightenment: The Gülen Movement* (New York: Oxford University Press, 2013); M. Hakan Yavuz and John L Esposito (eds), *Turkish Islam and the Secular State: The Gülen Movement* (Syracuse, NY: Syracuse University Press, 2003); and *A Special Issue on the Gülen Movement: Sociology of Islam Journal* (Edited by Joshua Hendrick) Volume 1, Issue 3–4, 2014 (Brill).
2 www.herkul.org. His weekly sermon is one of the rare channels of Gülen's teachings that is only available in Turkish and is not offered in translation.
3 His year of birth is recorded in official documentation as 1942, on account of an administrative delay. Gülen's father registered both him and his younger brother, Seyfullah, at the same time two and a half years after Gülen's birth. See Faruk Mercan, *Fethullah Gülen* (Istanbul: Doğan, 2008), pp. 34–5. This discrepancy was not at all unusual in rural Turkey in the 1940s.
4 Halil Inalcık, 'Erzurum', *Encyclopaedia of Islam*.
5 Mercan, *Fethullah Gülen*, p.37.
6 Weismann, *The Naqshbandiyya*.
7 Mardin, *Religion and Social Change*; Şükran Vahide, *Islam in Modern Turkey: An Intellectual Biography of Bediüzzaman Said Nursi* (Albany, NY: State University of New York Press, 2005); Ibrahim M. Abu-Rabi (ed.), *Islam at the Crossroads: On the Life and Thought of Bediuzzaman Said Nursi* (Albany, NY: State University of New York Press, 2003).
8 Ibrahim M. Abu-Rabi (ed.), *Spiritual Dimensions of Bediuzzaman Said Nursi's Risale-i Nur* (Albany, NY: State University of New York Press, 2008).
9 Mercan, *Fethullah Gülen*, p.49. Turkish to English translation here and hereafter my own, unless otherwise indicated.
10 Agai, 'Islamic Ethic'.
11 Ali Ünal and Alphonse Williams, *Advocate of Dialogue: Fethullah Gülen* (Fairfax, VA: The Fountain, 1999), p. 318.
12 Ibid., p. 50.
13 Ibid., p. 310.

14 Fabio Vicini, 'Pedagogies of Affection: The Role of Exemplariness and Emulation in Learning Processes—Extracurricular Islamic Education in the Fethullah Gülen Community in Istanbul', in *Anthropology and Education Quarterly*, Vol. 44, Issue 4 (2013), pp. 381–98.
15 Andrew Mango, *The Turks Today* (London: John Murray, 2004); David Shankland, *Islam and Society*; Zürcher, *A Modern History* (London: I.B.Tauris, 2004).
16 These are Yamanlar Koleji in Izmir, Fatih Koleji in Istanbul and Samanyolu Lisesi in Ankara.
17 The movement's major media corporation is Feza Gazetecilik (Feza Media Group), which owns the national daily newspaper *Zaman* and its English-language counterpart, *Today's Zaman*. Işık Sigorta is an insurance firm run by movement affiliates, and, until its recent takeover by the State, the Islamic lender Bank Asya was a Gülen institution.
18 Berna Turam, 'National Loyalties and International Undertakings: The case of the Gulen community in Kazakhstan', in Yavuz and Esposito (eds), *Turkish Islam and the Secular State*, pp.184–207; Elisabeth Ozdalga, 'Worldly asceticism in Islamic casting: Fethullah Gülen's inspired piety and activism', in *Critique: Critical Middle Eastern Studies*, 9:17 (2000), pp. 83–104.
19 Hendrick, *Gülen*, pp. 144–73.
20 White, *Islamist Mobilisation in Turkey*.
21 The political Islamist ideology of the Welfare Party inspired the development of Milli Görüş, a major Turkish diaspora movement quite distinctive from the global Gülen Movement, espousing a political vision for the future of Islam.
22 Hendrick, *Gülen*.
23 Martin van Bruinessen, 'The Netherlands and the Gulen Movement', in *Sociology of Islam 1* (2013), pp. 165–87.
24 Kristina Dohrn, 'Translocal Ethics: *Hizmet* Teachers and the Formation of Gülen-inspired Schools in Urban Tanzania', in *Sociology of Islam 1* (2013), pp. 233–56.
25 Joshua D. Hendrick, 'Globalisation, Islamic activism and passive revolution in Turkey: the case of Fethullah Gülen', in *Journal of Power*, vol. 2, no. 3 (December 2009), pp. 343–68.
26 Zeki Saritoprak, 'Fethullah Gülen: A Sufi in his own way', in Yavuz and Esposito (eds), *Turkish Islam*, pp. 156–69.
27 M. Fethullah Gülen, *Key Concepts in the Practice of Sufism: Emerald Hills of the Heart*, Volumes 1–4 (Clifton, NJ: Tughra Books, 2011).
28 M. Fethullah Gülen. *Toward a Global Civilisation of Love and Tolerance* (Somerset, NJ: The Light, Inc., 2006), p.1.
29 M. Fethullah Gülen. *Key Concepts in the Practice of Sufism: Emerald Hills of the Heart Vol. 2*, 'I'thar'. Available at en.fgulen.com/sufism-2/2365-ithar-altruism (accessed 30 January 2016).

30 Sufi *tarikats* throughout history have sustained a sometimes complex relationship with wider society, and many of them have been socially active and engaged. What distinguishes them from the Gülen Movement is, however, their rootedness in esoteric ritual practice.
31 Interview in English with a senior management figure at GYV (Gazeteciler ve Yazarlar Vakfı – Journalists and Writers Foundation), March 2013.
32 Hendrick, *Gülen*.
33 There is a considerable literature in Turkish written by movement detractors. The best known of these is Ahmet Şık's *İmamın Ordusu* (The Imam's Army), which was at the centre of a major controversy in 2011 when the author was arrested on charges related to the Ergenekon case. The book was never published in its original form, but a version of it appeared under the title *000Kitap*, or 000Book (Istanbul: Postacı Yayınları, 2011).
34 Hendrick, *Gülen*.
35 The names of all fieldwork informants have been changed.
36 Fieldwork interview, 22 May 2013.
37 The *sohbet* tradition is not unique to the Gülen Movement, but is practised in many Islamic groups in Turkey and elsewhere. The focus of discussion is usually the Qur'an and Sunna of the prophet Muhammad. See Smita Tewari Jassal, 'The Sohbet: Talking Islam in Turkey', in *Sociology of Islam 1* (2013), pp. 188–208.
38 Fieldwork interview, 14 May 2013.
39 Ibid.
40 Berna Turam, *Between Islam and the State: The Politics of Engagement* (Stanford, CA: Stanford University Press, 2007).
41 Fieldwork interview, 22 May 2013.

2 : A Nursian Spiritual Framework for Modernity

1 An authoritative hagiography of Said Nursi is provided by Vahide, *Islam in Modern Turkey*. See also Mardin, *Religion and Social Change*; and Ibrahim M. Abu-Rabi (ed.), *Islam at the Crossroads: on the life and thought of Bediüzzaman Said Nursi* (Albany, NY: State University of New York Press, 2003).
2 There is some confusion over the date of Nursi's birth, with some sources giving 1876 and others 1877. Vahide gives 1877. See *Islam in Modern Turkey*, fn. 1, p. 353.
3 Bernard Lewis, *The Emergence*; Stanford J. Shaw and Ezel Kural Shaw, *History of the Ottoman Empire and Modern Turkey, Volume 2* (Cambridge: Cambridge University Press, 1977); Erik Zürcher, *Turkey: A Modern History* (London: I.B.Tauris, 2004).
4 Mardin, *Religion and Social Change*, and Vahide, *Islam in Modern Turkey*. See also Zeynep Akbulut Kuru and Ahmet T. Kuru, 'A political Interpretation of Islam: Said Nursi's Faith-Based Activism in Comparison with Political Islam and Sufism', in *Islam and Christian-Muslim Relations*, 19.1, 99–111.

5. See for example *Munazarat* (The Dialogues).
6. Said Nursi, *Mektubat* (The Letters) (Istanbul: KLMN Yayınları, 1996), p. 368.
7. Vahide, *Islam in Modern Turkey*, p. 335.
8. The hostility of the Turkish state to Nursi and his first disciples is also said to have contributed to the consolidation and early growth of the movement.
9. Nursi himself followed etiquette, and publicly rejected this honorific title. See Said Nursi, *The Reasonings: A Key to Understanding the Qur'an's Eloquence* (Clifton, NJ: The Light Inc., 2008), p. 3.
10. Encyclopaedia of Islam: 'Mujaddid'.
11. Colin Turner and Hasan Horkuç, *Said Nursi* (London: I.B.Tauris, 2009), pp. 47–8.
12. Vahide, *Islam in Modern Turkey*, pp. 101–10.
13. Berna Turam, *Between Islam and the State: The Politics of Engagement* (Stanford, CA: Stanford University Press, 2007).
14. Said Nursi, *The Letters*, vols 1–2 (Izmir: Kaynak, 1998).
15. Ibrahim M. Abu-Rabi (ed.), *Spiritual Dimensions of Bediuzzaman Said Nursi's Risale-i Nur* (Albany, NY: State University of New York Press, 2008).
16. Mustafa Sungur in Sahiner, *Aydinlar Konusuyor*, p. 399. Quoted in Vahide, *Islam in Modern Turkey*, p. 167.
17. Fieldwork interview, 14 May 2013.
18. Serif Mardin expands on this point further. See *Religion and Social Change*.
19. Mermer and Ameur, 'Beyond the "Modern"', pp. 119–60.
20. See Said Nursi, *The Words: the reconstruction of Islamic belief and thought* (Clifton, NJ: The Light Inc., 2010), pp. 179–90.
21. Peter Harrison, '"The Book of Nature" and Early Modern Science', in Klaas van Berkel and Arjo Vanderjagt (eds), *The Book of Nature in early Modern and Modern History* (Leuven: Peeters, 2006).
22. See Nasr, *Science and Civilisation*, pp. 23–4.
23. Nursi, *The Words*, p. 146.
24. Ibid., p. 141.
25. This is not at all an unusual worldview in the Muslim context. Rather, Nursi was restating this position in response to Turkish secularism.
26. Nursi, *The Words*, p. 170.
27. Erol Nazim Gulay, 'The Theological Thought of Fethullah Gulen: Reconciling Science and Islam', unpublished MPhil thesis, St Antony's College, University of Oxford, May 2007.

3 : The Gülen Movement's Science-focused Schools

1. When I had visited the school in the early summer of 2013, the teachers had been legally obliged to remove their scarves upon entering the school building in the morning and not put them on again until they left. A de facto change in the law had come about since my previous visit, and the female

teachers were now able to retain their headscarves throughout the course of the school day.
2 Some of the material in this chapter has been previously published elsewhere. See Tee and Shankland, 'Said Nursi's Notion of Sacred Science', pp. 209–32. For further studies on the structure of Gülen schools, see also Agai, 'Islamic Ethic'; and Kristina Dohrn, 'Translocal Ethics: *Hizmet* Teachers and the Formation of Gülen-inspired Schools in Urban Tanzania', in *Sociology of Islam* 1 (2013) pp. 233–56.
3 A brief consultation of websites of the Gülen schools in Turkey reveals considerable success in this area. See, for example, details of students' acceptance to prestigious courses and universities on graduation from Samanyolu Lisesi in Ankara: www.samanyolu.k12.tr/Page/Index/10 (accessed 30 January 2016).
4 Mandatory state education is provided for children in Turkey between the ages of six and 18. Since reforms implemented in 2012, this is now divided into four years each of primary, middle and secondary schooling.
5 Followers of Gülen run the FEM *dershane* franchise, which is one of the largest of its kind in Turkey and known for its high-quality product. (www.fem.com.tr – accessed 30 January 2016). In 2013, the AKP government announced the abolition of the *dershane* system and the imminent closure of its facilities across the country. This decision was widely interpreted as an attack on the Gülen Movement, which is a major actor in this sector, and foreshadowed the major public rift that has since developed between President Erdoğan and Fethullah Gülen. The *dershane*s remain under threat of closure at the time of writing.
6 The focus of the *dershane* is to equip students for entry in the annual exams, which are administered nationally and which determine the highly competitive university-entrance process. These are the YGS (Yüksekögretime Geçiş Sınavı – Examination for Entrance to Higher Education) and the LYS (Lisans Yerleştirme Sınavı – Degree Placement Exam).
7 Joshua Hendrick calls this 'strategic ambiguity'. See Hendrick, *Gülen*.
8 See the following websites for more details: www.fatihokullari.k12.tr; http://lise.nilufer.k12.tr/; http://www.samanyolu.k12.tr/; http://www.yamanlar.k12.tr/ (accessed 30 January 2016).
9 See 'What is the movement's chief priority?' at en.fgulen.com/about-gulen-movement/3841-what-is-the-movements-chief-priority (accessed 30 January 2016).
10 For example, the nationwide network of prestigious TED (Türk Eğitim Derneği – Turkish Education Association) schools. See www.ted.org.tr (accessed 30 January 2016).
11 There are three main streams in the state high-school education sector, and students attend either a general high school, an Anatolian (*Anadolu lisesi*) high school or a vocational (*meslek lisesi*) high school. Academic standards are

highest at Anatolian high schools, which are considered the most prestigious and often have a science focus (*Anadolu Fen lisesi*).

12 See http://www.aljazeera.com.tr/haber/ortaokul-ve-lisede-basortusu-serbest (accessed 30 January 2016).
13 www.haberturk.com/gundem/haber/1016445-zorunlu-din-dersi-icin-karar-verildi (accessed 30 January 2016).
14 İren Özgür, *Islamic Schools in Modern Turkey: Faith, Politics and Education* (Cambridge: Cambridge University Press, 2012).
15 See www.haberturk.com/gundem/haber/911943-imam-hatip-liseleri-rekora-kosuyor (accessed 30 January 2016).
16 For a sceptical secularist perspective on the Imam Hatip reforms, see www.cumhuriyet.com.tr/haber/egitim/88123/Haydi_kizlar_iHL_ye_.html (accessed 30 January 2016).
17 The AKP government took its first steps towards changing the law governing the so-called 'co-efficient system' (which prevented graduates of vocational and Imam Hatip high schools from entering university on equal terms with their mainstream counterparts) in July 2009. The law was changed to allow for full equality in December 2011. See Özgür, *Islamic Schools*, pp. 137–40.
18 A theology degree in Turkey leaves one with few career options besides high-school teaching or the religious vocations.
19 The number of female students at Imam Hatip schools now outnumbers males. Given that females are ineligible for the vocations for which these schools traditionally prepared students (imams and preachers), this rise in female participation has fuelled secularists' suspicions that the government's agenda is to make religious forms of education mainstream within Turkish society. The change in law facilitating equal university entrance for Imam Hatip graduates appears to have confirmed these suspicions.
20 The research was completed just before the eruption of a major and acrimonious row between the Gülen Movement and the AKP government. This row, which had in fact been developing for some time, was made explicit on 17 December 2013 with the publication by movement affiliates and sympathisers of allegations of high-level governmental corruption. At the time of writing, the movement is in a much less confident position than it was during the research period, having since seen, in the wake of 17 December, numerous acts of retaliation launched against it and its assets by the Turkish government.
21 *Tesettür* is a conservative style of female Islamic dress favoured by pious Muslim women in urban Turkey. It generally features a smart, floor-length coat over a long, loose skirt and blouse, and either a silk or thick, cotton headscarf pinned tightly around the face. While a few female followers of Gülen choose to wear all-black coats and headscarves, none of them choose the billowing black *çarşaf* (literally, 'sheet') covering, which includes the facial *niqab* and is worn only by a very small minority of Turkish women.

22 Fieldwork interview, 19 November 2013.
23 Ibid.
24 Ünal and Williams, *Advocate of Dialogue*; Agai, 'Islamic Ethic'.
25 Robert W. Hefner, and Muhammad Qasim Zaman, (eds), *Schooling Islam: The Culture and Politics of Modern Muslim Education* (Princeton, NJ: Princeton University Press, 2007).
26 Gülen quoted in Ünal and Williams, *Advocate of Dialogue*, pp. 308 and 312.
27 Fieldwork interview, 19 November 2013.
28 Fieldwork interview, 14 November 2013.
29 Conversation between the author and girls in a ninth grade chemistry class, girls' school in Kelebek, 22 May 2013. *Sahur* is the early-morning meal eaten shortly before sunrise during Ramadan. It is common to share *iftar* (the meal eaten at sunset) with friends and neighbours in Turkey, but visiting someone's house to share *sahur* is unusual. The girls found this quite amusing and reported it enthusiastically.
30 Fieldwork interview, 19 November 2013.
31 Fieldwork interview, 14 November 2013.
32 Lesson observation at Kelebek, 22 November 2013.
33 The approach of the schools, and the Gülen Movement more widely, to biological evolution is addressed in the following chapter.
34 Fieldwork interview, 19 November 2013.
35 The Science Olympiads originated in the 1930s in the Soviet Union, which sought to raise its standards and international competitiveness in the fields of science and technology. The competitions developed in the Eastern Bloc countries during subsequent decades, with the first International Olympiad in mathematics being held in Romania in 1959. Western nations began to take part in the 1970s, but the events are still largely dominated by the ex-Soviet Bloc countries and by China. See Berna Arslan, 'Pious Science: The Gülen Community and the Making of a Conservative Modernity in Turkey', unpublished PhD thesis, University of California in Santa Cruz, 2009, Appendix 1. Also, see Özlem Kocabaş, 'Scientific Careers and Ideological Profiles of Science Olympiad Participants from Fethullah Gülen and other Secondary Schools in Turkey', unpublished MA thesis, Middle East Technical University, Department of Sociology, 2006, Appendix A.
36 www.tubitak.gov.tr/sites/default/files/2203_dereceler_istatistikler.pdf (accessed 8 July 2013).
37 Türkiye Bilimsel ve Teknolojik Araştırma Kurumu (Foundation for Scientific and Technological Research of Turkey).
38 For example, the website of Fatih Koleji in Istanbul lists 93 student medal winners in the International Science Olympiads between 1992 and 2015. See www.fatihokullari.k12.tr/Sayfa/uluslararasi-olimpiyat/66 (accessed 30 January 2016).

39 See the website of any major Gülen high school in Turkey, all of which include a prominent section listing their successes in the Science Olympiads.
40 Mathematics is the only branch in which an Olympiad is organised at a national level for middle-school students. National Olympiads are organised in all five branches for high-school students.
41 Fieldwork interview, Kelebek boys' high school, 9 April 2013.
42 It was not possible to visit the girls' high school at Yunus, but their website shows that it is active in the International Science Olympiads, where one (female) student was recently selected for the Turkish national team in mathematics. While the research at Kelebek suggested that substantially more investment was made in training male than female students for the Olympiads, it would be premature to draw any far-reaching conclusions based on this one case study. Arslan, however, also finds evidence of gender inequality in the way Olympiad students are taught in Gülen schools, with boys being prioritised over girls (Arslan 2009: 455).
43 Alumni networks play an important role in the internal organisation of the Gülen Movement. Schools stay in close contact with their graduates, facilitating regular reunions and meetings. The interpersonal connections that are fostered and maintained in this way characterise the many other activities with which the Gülen Movement is involved.
44 Fieldwork interview, Yunus boys' high school, 3 June 2013.
45 Schools train their own students in preparation for the national Science Olympiad events, in which qualification for the Turkish national team is decided. TÜBITAK then assumes responsibility for training the national team, which goes on to compete in the five International Science Olympiads.

4 : Creationism in Gülenist Thought

1 Fieldwork interview, November 2013.
2 M. Fethullah Gülen, *Yaratılış Gerçeği ve Evrim* (Istanbul: Nil Yayınları, 2003).
3 'What is the reason for the persistence of Darwinism in the General Culture of the Masses, Though Many of Darwin's Hypotheses Have Been Challenged and Even Disproved?'. Available at http://www.en.fgulen.com/questions-and-answers/2129-what-is-the-reason-for-the-persistence-of-darwinism-in-the-general-culture-of-the-masses-though-many-of-darwins-hypotheses-have-been-challenged-and-even-disproved (accessed 30 January 2016).
4 www.fgulen.com/en (accessed 30 January 2016).
5 Some of the contributors to these publications are drawn from the American creationist movement. See, for example, the Turkish translation of an article by Duane T. Gish entitled 'Creation and Evolution in Education' at www.sizinti.com.tr/konular/ayrinti/egitimde-yaratilis-ve-evrim.html (accessed 30 January 2016).

6 This is one of the rare forums in which Gülen has written regularly since the early days of the movement. The magazine continues to feature a regular editorial by Gülen, but some material is now replicated from earlier work.
7 'Introduction' in Gülen, *Yaratılış Gerçeği*. Available at http://fgulen.com/tr/fethullah-gulenin-butun-eserleri/iman/fethullah-gulen-yaratilis-gercegi-ve-evrim/11771-Fethullah-Gulen-Giris (accessed 30 January 2016). English translation my own.
8 Ernst Mayr and William B. Provine (eds), *The Evolutionary Synthesis: Perspectives on the Unification of Biology* (Cambridge, MA: Harvard University Press, 1998). See also Ulrich Kutschera and Karl J. Niklas, "The modern theory of biological evolution: an expanded synthesis", *Naturwissenschaften* 91 (2004), pp. 255–76.
9 Gülen, *Yaratılış Gerçeği*. http://fgulen.com/tr/fethullah-gulenin-butun-eserleri/iman/fethullah-gulen-yaratilis-gercegi-ve-evrim/11779-Fethullah-Gulen-Madde-Tesaduf-ve-Kendi-Kendine-Olma-Iddialari (accessed 30 January 2016).
10 'Introduction' in ibid. This idea has also been addressed in anthropological literature. The biological anthropologist Jonathan Marks, for example, has argued that 'every generation of evolutionary biologists has various political ideologies attached to the fairly simple Darwinian propositions that (1) species are genealogically connected and (2) the primary cause of adaptation is natural selection. How do we know this? Because every previous generation indeed has tethered their ideologies to their Darwinism.' See 'Evolutionary Psychology is Neither', published by the Evolution Institute, 22 March 2015. Available online at evolution-institute.org/article/evolutionary-psychology-is-neither/?source=tvol (accessed 30 January 2016).
11 There is an extensive literature on this subject, but see for example the relevant chapter on evolution in John Hedley Brooke, *Science and Religion: Some Historical Perspectives* (Cambridge: University of Cambridge, 1991); and Simon Conway Morris, 'Creation and Evolutionary Convergence', in J.B. Stump and Alan G. Padgett (eds), *The Blackwell Companion to Science and Christianity* (New Jersey: John Wiley & Sons, Ltd, 2012, pp. 258–69). On the reception of evolution in the Muslim context, see the work of Salman Hameed as well as Fern Elsdon-Baker's article, 'Creating creationists: The influence of "issues framing" on our understanding of public perceptions of clash narratives between evolutionary science and belief', in *Public Understanding of Science* (2015), pp. 422–39.
12 Non-human evolution (i.e. microbial and/or animal evolution) is often regarded as unproblematic by Muslims, but the research carried out on this subject to date has not successfully differentiated in this way. I am grateful to Salman Hameed for this observation.
13 The textbook was called *Tarih ve Medeni Bilgiler* (History and Civilised Knowledge). See Ümit Sayin and Aykut Kence, 'Islamic Scientific Creationism: A New Challenge in Turkey', *Reports of the National Center for Science Education*, vol. 19 issue 6 (November–December 1999), pp. 18–20 and 25–9.

14 Qur'an 2.34. Translated by M.A.S. Abdel Haleem (Oxford: Oxford University Press, 2004).
15 John D. Barrow. *Impossibility: The Limits of Science and the Science of Limits* (Oxford: Oxford University Press, 1998).
16 Fieldwork interview, 25 November 2013.
17 http://www.theguardian.com/science/2006/mar/17/scienceprizes.g2 (accessed 30 January 2016).
18 'Results' (*Netice*) in Gülen, *Yaratılış Gerçeği*.
19 See the materials produced by the Institute for Creation Research, based in Dallas, Texas: www.icr.org (accessed 30 January 2016).
20 'The Myth Collapses: The Theory of Evolution', *Fountain*, Issue 24, October–December 1998.
21 Guessoum, *Islam's Quantum Question*, p. 275. Emphasis my own. The same point is made by Michael Ruse in *Darwinism and its Discontents* (Cambridge: Cambridge University Press, 2006).
22 There is a rare, sustained discussion of evolution in light of the Qur'an in the final chapter of *Yaratılış Gerçeği*, which is entitled 'Kur'ân-ı Kerim'de ve Hadis-i Şeriflerde Yaratılış' (Creation in the Qur'an and Hadith).
23 This is also a common strategy employed by Christian creationists in the USA.
24 For a reading of the Qur'an that accommodates evolution, see D. S. Adnan Majid, 'Qur'anic Interpretative Latitude and Human Evolution: A Case Study', *Al-Bayan – Journal of Qur'an and Ḥadith Studies* 12 (2015), pp. 95–114. See also the chapter on evolution in Guessoum, *Islam's Quantum Question*.
25 The Qur'an 32.5.
26 Qur'an 3.59; 38.71.
27 This biological descent is also said to be described in the Qur'an in the verse that refers to the creation of man through a 'drop of fluid', i.e. sperm. See Qur'an 23.13.
28 See Majid, 'Qur'anic Interpretative Latitude', pp. 98–100.
29 Riaz Hassan, 'On Being Religious: Patterns of Religious Commitment in Muslim Societies', *Muslim World*, vol. 97 (2007), p. 466.
30 Veysel Kaya, 'Can the Quran Support Darwin? An Evolutionist Approach by Two Turkish Scholars after the Foundation of the Turkish Republic', *Muslim World*, vol. 102 (April 2012), pp. 357–70.
31 Ibid.
32 See Guessoum, *Islam's Quantum Question*, pp. 305–8, which refers to the doctoral thesis of Mahfuz A. Azzam on this subject, published in Arabic and entitled *The Principle of Biological Evolution in the Works of the Classical Muslim Philosophers* (Beirut, Lebanon: al-Mu'assassah al-Jami'iyyah li-d-Dirassat wa-l-Nashr wa-t-Tawzi', 1996). See also Kaya, 'Can the Qur'an Support Darwin?' pp. 368–69.

33 See the entry on the history of evolution in the *Internet Encyclopaedia of Philosophy*: www.iep.utm.edu/evolutio (accessed 30 January 2016).
34 For a comprehensive analysis of Adnan Oktar and his group, see Anne Ross Solberg, 'The Mahdi Wears Armani: An Analysis of the Harun Yayha Enterprise', Södertörn doctoral dissertations, 2013. For a brief introduction to Oktar's ideas on Islamic creationism, see Martin Riexinger, 'Turkey', in Stefaan Blancke, Hans Henrik Hjermitslev and Peter C. Kjaergaard (eds), *Creationism in Europe* (Baltimore, MD: Johns Hopkins University Press, 2014); and Stefano Bigliardi, 'Who's Afraid of Theoscientography? An Interpretive Hypothesis on Harun Yahya', *Zygon: Journal of Religion and Science* Vol. 49 Issue 1 (2014), pp. 66–80.
35 Hameed, 'Making Sense of Islamic Creationism'.
36 www.irtiqa-blog.com/2008/05/muslim-creationist-adnan-oktar.html (accessed 30 January 2016).
37 Harun Yahya, *The Evolution Deceit: The Scientific Collapse of Darwinism and Its Ideological Background*. Available at www.harunyahya.com/en/books/974/The-Evolution-Deceit (accessed 30 January 2016).
38 See www.atlasofcreation.com/ (accessed 30 January 2016).
39 Harun Yahya, 'Introduction: Why the Theory of Evolution', in Yahya, *The Evolution Deceit*. Available at http://www.harunyahya.com/en/books/974/The-Evolution-Deceit/chapter/3286/Introduction-Why-the-Theory-of-Evolution (accessed 30 January 2016).
40 This show is broadcast live on the A9 TV channel which the Harun Yahya organisation runs. See harunyahya.co/a9-tv-canli-yayin-izle/ (accessed 30 January 2016). Extracts from it are also archived and widely available on YouTube.
41 See Solberg, 'The Mahdi Wears Armani', p. 10, where she explains that 'Oktar's shows [...] contravene most notions of Islamic modesty, and instead resemble popular daytime variety-TV shows on Turkish commercial channels. Yet, these shows are presented as religious programmes that aim to preach the message of Islam.'
42 This individual was a university professor who had studied to doctoral level in the USA.
43 'Introduction' in Gülen, *Yaratılış Gerçeği*.
44 Sayin and Kence, 'Islamic Scientific Creationism'. See also Taner Edis, 'Islamic creationism in Turkey', *Creation/Evolution*, 14 (1) no. 34 (1994), pp. 1–12.
45 Fieldwork interview with a physics teacher at a Gülen school, 19 November 2013.
46 The official website of the International Biology Olympiad states that 'each Biology Olympiad exam will have 20 per cent of the questions devoted to Genetics and Evolution'. See biolympiads.blogspot.co.uk/2014/08/genetics-and-evolution.html (accessed 30 January 2016).
47 Jeffrey Guhin, 'Why Worry about Evolution? Boundaries, Practices, and Moral Salience in Sunni and Evangelical High Schools', *Sociological Theory* (forthcoming).

48 For example, Blue Dome Press and Tughra Books, both based in New Jersey.
49 The Rumi Forum in Washington, DC is one of the most active and prominent Gülen initiatives in the USA. It was founded as an interfaith dialogue centre in 1999 and its principal aim is 'to promote peace in the world and contribute to a peaceful coexistence of the adherents of different faiths, cultures, ethnicities and races'. See www.rumiforum.org/about/about-rumi-forum.html (accessed 30 January 2016).

5 : Higher Education, Networking and Careers in Science

1 Guessoum and Osama (eds), *Science at Universities of the Muslim World*; Edis, *An Illusion of Harmony*, pp. 13–32. See also the TIMSS (Trends in International Mathematics and Science Study) report of 2011, which provides statistical evidence of the deficit in scientific research in many Muslim-majority nations: timss.bc.edu/timss2011/international-results-science.html (accessed 30 January 2016).
2 Not its real name.
3 These three students took part in a group discussion attended by six foreign students as well as İbrahim and a female university administrator. The remaining students were from Tajikistan (x 2) and Mali. The conversation took place in English, apart from the occasional interjection from İbrahim in Turkish. All the students spoke good Turkish, having learnt it at their Gülen high schools in their home countries.
4 Some interviews with students (such as the one with Arif, Majid and Rustam) were arranged and monitored by İbrahim, but on other occasions I was able to speak with them freely and without oversight. Students were noticeably more reluctant to talk about certain issues during the monitored interviews – for example, details of life in the *ışıkevleri*, or student houses. When I asked the group questions on this subject, their answers were hesitant and short and the students frequently looked to İbrahim for affirmation that they should continue. I learnt very little about the *ışıkevi* system from these exchanges, but rather more from informal and unsupervised chats with students.
5 These include Gediz University in Izmir, Süleyman Şah University in Istanbul, Turgut Özal University in Ankara, Antalya International University, Mevlana University in Konya and Melikşah University in Kayseri.
6 Epoka and Beder universities in Albania, Burç University in Bosnia, the International Black Sea University in Georgia, Işık University in northern Iraq, Lumina University in Romania and the International Turkmen–Turk University in Turkmenistan. Until its closure by the authorities in 2014, the movement also ran Qafqaz University in Azerbaijan.

7 Fieldwork interview, 14 November 2013.
8 This is explained in Chapter One. For a complementary account of tiers of allegiance within the movement, see Hendrick, *Gülen*.
9 *Vakıf* universities are not-for-profit foundations with charitable status. Özel universities, by contrast, are private, profit-making institutions. Money invested in a *vakıf* (foundation) is liable only for limited taxation in Turkey, and thus wealthy businesspeople with substantial cash savings benefit from investing in this way. Investors may, furthermore, choose to award lucrative contracts for the construction of the university either to their own companies or to those in their close circle, thereby increasing their financial rewards further still.
10 A digital map that shows the complex web of personal, institutional and political connections that sustain the new generation of private universities in Turkey has been researched and presented by Burak Arıkan and Zeyno Üstün at Koç University: http://burak-arikan.com/ozeluniversiteler/ (accessed 30 January 2016). The rate at which new private universities have been opening has been the subject of derision in some parts of the anti-AKP popular press. See, for example, Mehmet Türker's article, 'University or Corner Shop?!' in *Sözcü*, 19 January 2013: www.sozcu.com.tr/2013/yazarlar/mehmet-turker/universite-mi-bakkal-dukkani-mi-193542 (accessed 30 January 2016).
11 Philip G. Altbach, 'The Private Higher Education Revolution: An Introduction', in Altbach and Levy (eds), *Private Higher Education*, pp. 1–12.
12 Selen Altınsoy, 'A Review of University Facilities in Turkey', CELE Exchange 2011/6, OECD 2011. Available at www.oecd.org/edu/innovation-education/centreforeffectivelearningenvironmentscele/48358175.pdf (accessed 30 January 2016). At the time of writing in early 2015, the founding of five new universities (three of them state, two of them *vakıf*) had just been announced: www.cnnturk.com/haber/turkiye/bes-yeni-universite-kurulacak?utm_content=buffer48887&utm_medium=social&utm_source=twitter.com&utm_campaign=buffer (accessed 30 January 2016).
13 Fieldwork interview, 14 November 2013.
14 This is different from the Gülen schools, where (although some movement outsiders are employed, especially in the schools abroad) the great majority of the teaching as well as administrative staff are core affiliates of the movement.
15 Fieldwork interview, 21 May 2013.
16 In fact, the question is also applicable to other Gülen-run initiatives, where a non-Turkish audience can often access Gülen products without realising their informal affiliation with Gülen. The Gülen schools in other countries that attract non-Turkish students are one example, and the online, English-language newspaper *Today's Zaman* is another. There is no official mention of Gülen on the pages of *Today's Zaman*, and a casual visitor might simply be wishing to

access English-language reporting on Turkish current affairs without understanding the implications of the newspaper's links to Gülen.
17 This was because of their voluntary donation of a portion of their monthly salary back to the school.
18 A national network of private schools ranging from kindergarten to high school, run by the Gülen Movement: www.anafen.com (accessed 30 January 2016).
19 The largest national network of *dershane*s in Turkey, run by the Gülen Movement. The FEM Dershaneleri chain has a very good reputation and attendance at its courses is desirable to many: www.fem.com.tr (accessed 30 January 2016).
20 Fieldwork interview, May 2013.
21 Ibid.
22 These two are often grouped together in Turkish universities, under faculties entitled *Fen-Edebiyat* (Science and Literature).
23 See, for example, the websites of the following post-2000 *vakıf* universities: Istanbul Şehir University, Özyeğin University, TOBB (Türkiye Odalar ve Borsalar Birliği) University of Economics and Technology, and Izmir University of Economics.
24 Social Science is also a growth area in the Turkish higher-education market. Istanbul Şehir University, for example, established in 2008, has made Social Science its focus and has established a strong reputation in a short space of time. Within the Gülen Movement, Süleyman Şah University in Istanbul, established in 2010, focuses entirely on Social Science subjects.
25 For a discussion of the various problems facing scientific research in the contemporary Muslim world, see Guessoum, *Islam's Quantum Question*; and Edis, *An Illusion of Harmony*. See also Guessoum and Osama (eds), *Science at Universities of the Muslim World*.
26 The preference for engineering over medicine was explained in light of students' aspirations to study at postgraduate level in the USA or Europe. Medical qualifications from foreign countries are not recognised in Turkey, and thus to practise as a doctor one must have qualified at a Turkish university. For careers in engineering, there are no such restrictions – and, indeed, a degree from the USA or Europe in this field is a mark of prestige.
27 Fieldwork interview, April 2013.
28 Editorial, *Nature*, Vol 444, Issue no. 7115 (2 November 2006). Available at www.nature.com/news/specials/islamandscience/index.html (accessed 30 January 2016). For a discussion of critical thinking in education more broadly, see R. T. Pithers and Rebecca Soden, 'Critical thinking in education: a review', in *Educational Research* 42:3 (2000), pp. 237–49.

29 The 'Golden Age' narrative is prevalent in discussions surrounding science and Islam, and invokes the Middle Ages, when Islamic societies led the world in many areas of intellectual enquiry, including scientific experimentation. See George Saliba, *Islamic Science and the Making of the European Renaissance* (Cambridge, MA: MIT Press, 2007).

6 : Intercultural Dialogue

1 www.gyv.org.tr (accessed 30 January 2016).
2 Another is the daily newspaper, *Zaman*.
3 Ian Markham, *Engaging with Bediuzzaman Said Nursi: A Model of Interfaith Dialogue* (Farnham, Surrey: Ashgate, 2009); Sophia Pandya and Nancy Gallagher (eds), *The Gülen Hizmet movement and its transnational activities: case studies of altruistic activism in contemporary Islam* (Boca Raton, FL: BrownWalker Press, 2012); Greg Barton, Paul Weller and İhsan Yılmaz (eds), *The Muslim World and Politics in Transition: Creative Contributions of the Gülen Movement* (London: Bloomsbury, 2013). See also the chapter entitled 'The Theology of Interfaith Dialogue' in M. Hakan Yavuz, *Toward an Islamic Enlightenment*, pp. 173–97.
4 This conversation, like most of my fieldwork, took place shortly before the public row that erupted between the movement and President Erdoğan in December 2013. It is somewhat speculative to assume either way, but I am not clear whether my interlocutors would be as accessible or comfortable in conversation at the time of writing.
5 The Alevis are a non-Sunni Muslim minority group in Turkey whose religious tradition and culture relies heavily on music and the performance of sung poetry. See Shankland, *The Alevis in Turkey*.
6 Said Nursi, *The Letters (2)*, p. 141 (The Twenty-sixth Letter, 'the second topic'), p.262 (The Twenty-ninth Letter, the fifth section); Nursi, *The Words*, p. 430 (The Twenty-fifth Word).
7 Nursi, *The Words*, pp. 425–26 (The Twenty-fifth Word).
8 Said Nursi, *The Rays: Reflections on Islamic Belief, Thought, Worship and Action* (Clifton, NJ: The Light Inc.), p. 324 (The Thirteenth Ray). We are told in a footnote that people of the 'interregnum' are 'those who live at a time or place where the acquisition of true knowledge about the Straight Path is impossible for them'.
9 John Hick (d. 2012) was a highly influential theologian and philosopher who developed the idea of religious pluralism.
10 Ian Markham, *Engaging with Bediuzzaman Said Nursi*, p. 64.
11 www.rumiforum.org. The movement also founded the similar, but rather smaller, Dialogue Society in London in 1999, www.dialoguesociety.org (both accessed 30 January 2016).

12 www.thedialoginstitute.org (accessed 30 January 2016).
13 www.guleninstitute.org/about-gulen/mission/ (accessed 30 January 2016).
14 The most prominent of these are John Esposito and John Voll at Georgetown University. In Texas, Helen Rose Ebaugh at the University of Houston is very supportive of the movement and has written a book, *The Gülen Movement: A Sociological Analysis of a Civic Movement Rooted in Moderate Islam* (Dortrecht: Springer Netherlands, 2009).
15 Gülen, *Toward a Global Civilisation*, pp. 74–5. The original publication date is given online at en.fgulen.com/about-fethullah-gulen/251-fethullah-gulens-speeches-and-interviews-on-interfaith-dialogue/1341-dialogue-with-the-people-of-the-book-jews-and-christians (accessed 30 January 2016).
16 Erkan M. Kurt (ed.), *A Fethullah Gülen Reader: So That Others May Live* (New York: Blue Dome Press, 2013), p. 6.
17 Fieldwork interview, 23 May 2013.
18 This observation is also made by Hakan Yavuz. See Yavuz, *Toward an Islamic Enlightenment*, p. 191.
19 A reference to an early interfaith conference that was held by the movement in the city of Şanlıurfa.
20 Fieldwork interview, 13 January 2015.
21 www.abantplatform.org (accessed 30 January 2016). See also Etga Ugur, 'Organising Civil Society: The Gülen Movement's Abant Platform' in Barton et al. (eds), *The Muslim World and Politics in Transition*, pp. 47–64.
22 Hendrick, *Gülen*.
23 akdim.org/tr/ (accessed 30 January 2016).
24 Besides the Dialogue Society, which has small local branches in 11 cities outside of London, followers of Gülen in the UK also run the Axis Educational Trust, providing additional tutoring services to school children. The trust is also linked to the only Gülen-run school in the UK, Wisdom School in the North London borough of Haringey (shortly to move to a larger new site in Hendon, West London). See www.axiseducationaltrust.org and www.wisdom-school.org.uk/ (both accessed 30 January 2016). The movement also runs the Mevlana Rumi Mosque in Edmonton, London, which was opened in 2009 and houses the Anatolian Muslim Society, which was founded a few years previously in 2004. See mevlanarumimosque.org and www.rumicentre.org.uk/?tmlmstf=article&id=12 (both accessed 30 January 2016).
25 On the movement in the Netherlands, see Martin van Bruinessen, 'The Netherlands and the Gülen Movement', *Sociology of Islam* 1 (2013), pp. 165–87.
26 www.loveisaverbmovie.com/movie (accessed 30 January 2016). The movement has produced various films for popular audiences. For a short analysis of two of them, see Fabio Vicini, 'Representing Islam: Cinematographic Productions of

the Gülen Movement', in Lea Nocera (ed.), *The Gülen Media Empire: The Monographs of Arab Media Report* (Rome: Reset S.r.l, 2015).

27 http://www.rumiforum.org/upcoming-events/ (accessed 30 January 2016).

28 Bayram Balcı, 'The Gülen Movement and Turkish Soft Power', Carnegie Endowment for International Peace opinion piece, 4 February 2014. Available at http://carnegieendowment.org/2014/02/04/g%C3%BClen-movement-and-turkish-soft-power (accessed 30 January 2016).

29 Mehmet Aslan, 'The International Turkish Language Olympiads (ITLOs): Educating for Intercultural Dialogue and Communication', *Sociology and Anthropology* 2 (4) (2014), pp. 125–36.

30 Ibid., p. 129.

31 On Erdoğan's announcement, see www.sabah.com.tr/gundem/2014/03/21/erdogan-turkce-olimpiyatlari-bitti, and on the movement's response, see www.kure.tv/izle/12-turkce-olimpiyatlari-2014-almanya-kapanis-finali-2014 (both accessed 30 January 2016).

32 Gülen blamed the Gezi Park protests on the 'moral decay' of a generation. See fgulen.com/en/fethullah-gulens-works/thought/the-broken-jug/35970-fethullah-gulen-the-protests-of-taksim-gezi-park-and-the-root-of-the-problems (accessed 30 January 2016). He was also critical of the government's harsh response to the protests.

33 Gülen writes a considerable amount of poetry, and some of it has been set to music. A popular English-language album, which is sold alongside his books in participating bookstores, is entitled 'Rise Up: Colors of Peace' and was released in 2013.

34 Aslan, 'The International Turkish Language Olympiads', p. 129.

35 Other AKP dignitaries present were finance minister Ali Babacan, Ankara mayor Melih Göçek and education minister Nabi Avcı, as well as two local businessmen who had provided funding for the event.

36 Precise figures are unavailable, because the Alevis are not officially recognised and therefore do not appear in state census data. See Shankland, *The Alevis in Turkey*; Elise Massicard, *The Alevis in Turkey and Europe: Identity and Managing Territorial Diversity* (Oxford: Routledge, 2012).

37 Talha Köse, 'The Alevi Opening and the Democratisation Initiative', SETA Policy Report, 3 March 2010. Available at arsiv.setav.org/public/HaberDetay.aspx?Dil=tr&hid=28900&q=alevi-opening-and-the-democratisation-initiative (accessed 30 January 2016).

38 These were the granting of legal status to Alevi places of worship, the removal of compulsory religious education in schools, and state funding for the salaries of Alevi religious leaders.

39 İzzettin Doğan speaks for some Alevis but not for all, a situation that reflects the heterogeneity that is one of the great problems facing the community and

its quest for recognition in Turkey. Many Alevis were strongly opposed to the joint construction projects and staged violent protests at the Mamak site, which were condemned by Doğan and his associates at the Cem Vakfı.

7 : Globalisation of the Movement, and Gülen in the USA

1. The most insightful and comprehensive summary of the Gülen Movement in the United States to date is provided by Joshua D. Hendrick. See his chapter 'Strategic Ambiguity and Its Discontents (i.e., the Gülen Movement in the United States)', in *Gülen*, pp. 206–31.
2. The BBC's Tim Franks gained a rare interview with Gülen on his private compound in January 2014. See www.bbc.co.uk/news/world-europe-25885817 (accessed 30 January 2016).
3. One of the prominent voices on this subject in the USA is Sibel Edmonds, an ex-FBI translator and whistle-blower; see her blog www.boilingfrogspost.com. Another is the freelance American journalist, Claire Berlinski. See her article, 'Who is Fethullah Gülen?' in *City Journal*, Autumn 2012; available at www.city-journal.org/2012/22_4_fethullah-gulen.html. (Both accessed 30 January 2016).
4. The case is documented by James C. Harrington in his book, *Wrestling with Free Speech, Religious Freedom, and Democracy in Turkey: The Political Trials and Times of Fethullah Gülen* (Lanham, MD: University Press of America, 2011).
5. harmonytx.org/AboutUs.aspx (accessed 30 January 2016).
6. Pioneer Charter School of Science in Boston, for example, was recently ranked top in its state for Grade 10 science and technology. See www.pioneercss.org/apps/pages/index.jsp?uREC_ID=231073&type=d&pREC_ID=447852 (accessed 30 January 2016).
7. See the *60 Minutes* documentary that was made by CBS News in May 2012: www.cbsnews.com/news/us-charter-schools-tied-to-powerful-turkish-imam (accessed 30 January 2016).
8. Hendrick notes that the very 'strategic ambiguity' that serves the movement well in the Turkish context is precisely the source of its problems in terms of public perception in the USA. *Gülen*, pp. 217–31.
9. Nancy Gallagher, '*Hizmet* Intercultural Dialogue Trips to Turkey', in Sophia Pandya and Nancy Gallagher (eds), *The Gülen Hizmet Movement and its Transnational Activities: Case Studies of Altruistic Activism in Contemporary Islam* (Boca Raton, FL: BrownWalker Press, 2012), pp. 73–96.
10. Nocera (ed.), *The Gülen Media Empire*.
11. For an anthropological account of these traditional structures of learning in a Sufi context, see Michael Gilsenan's *Saint and Sufi in Modern Egypt: An Essay in the Sociology of Religion* (Oxford: Clarendon Press, 1973).

12 Fieldwork interview, winter 2013.
13 Fieldwork interview, spring 2013.
14 I am grateful to Joshua Hendrick for his insights on this subject.
15 Fieldwork interview, spring 2013.
16 Fieldwork interview, winter 2013.
17 The numbers of scholars receiving state support for doctoral and postdoctoral work has soared in recent years, with over 1,000 registered in 2013. See www.milliyet.com.tr/yurt-disina-gonderilen-genc-egitimdunyasi-1839651/ (accessed 30 January 2016).
18 www.tubitak.gov.tr/sites/default/files/2213_ilan_2015_.pdf (accessed 30 January 2016).
19 www.timeshighereducation.co.uk/world-university-rankings/2014–15/world-ranking (accessed 30 January 2016).
20 Fieldwork interview, winter 2013.
21 Ibid.
22 www.mfa.gov.tr/turkey-africa-relations.en.mfa (accessed 30 January 2016).
23 Fieldwork interview, May 2013.

8 : Political Influence and the AKP

1 See www.bbc.co.uk/turkce/haberler/2014/12/141212_17_25_aralik_operasyonu_neler_oldu_10_soruda (accessed 30 January 2016).
2 The following day's headlines made it clear that the involvement of the Gülen Movement in the operation was widely understood. The national daily *Cumhuriyet* reported on the crisis with front-page headlines 'Pimi Çektiler' (They've pulled the pin on the grenade) and '*Cemaat* "Şah" Dedi' (The movement said 'checkmate'). See Osman Can, 'The Structural Causes of Political Crisis in Turkey', *Insight Turkey*, Vol. 16 / No. 2 (2014), pp. 33–41.
3 Julian Pecquet, 'Turkey Lobbyists Bring Ankara's War with Gülen to Washington', *Al Monitor*, 30 December 2015. Available at www.al-monitor.com/pulse/originals/2015/12/turkey-lobby-gulen-movement-us.html (accessed 30 January 2016).
4 Berna Turam, *Between Islam and the State: The Politics of Engagement* (Stanford, CA: Stanford University Press, 2002).
5 Weismann, *The Naqshbandiyya*.
6 Vahide, *Islam in Modern Turkey*; Mardin, *Religion and Social Change*.
7 White, *Islamist Mobilisation in Turkey*. See also the same author's chapter, 'Milli Gorus' in Frank Peter and Rafael Ortega (eds), *Islamic Movements of Europe: Public Religion and Islamophobia in the Modern World* (London: I.B.Tauris, 2014).
8 Phillip Robins, 'Turkish Foreign Policy under Erbakan', *Survival: Global Politics and Strategy*, 39:2 (1997), pp. 82–100.

9 Hardliners from the Virtue Party formed the more traditionally Islamist Felicity Party (Saadet Partisi) at the same time, which has had limited success and has never passed the 10 per cent threshold to gain representation in Parliament.
10 Gerald Maclean, *Abdullah Gul and the Making of the New Turkey* (Oxford: Oneworld, 2014).
11 Hale and Özbudun (eds), *Islamism, Democracy and Liberalism*.
12 Ersin Kalaycıoğlu, 'Justice and Development Party at the Helm: Resurgence of Islam or Restitution of the Centre-of-Right Predominant Party?', in Birol Yeşilada and Barry Rubin (eds), *Islamisation of Turkey Under the AKP Rule* (Abingdon: Routledge, 2010); Ziya Öniş, 'The Triumph of Conservative Globalism: The Political Economy of the AKP Era', *Turkish Studies* 13:2 (2012), pp. 135–52.
13 In order for a political party to gain any seats in the Turkish Parliament, it must gain at least 10 per cent of the total national vote. This requirement prohibits smaller parties from entering Parliament, and there are frequent calls to abolish it. The most recent attempt to do so was quashed in January 2015. See www.reuters.com/article/2015/01/06/us-turkey-election-threshold-idUSKBN0KF1DJ20150106 (accessed 30 January 2016).
14 The other instance was in 1987, when the centre-right Motherland Party won 36.3 per cent of the vote and 292 seats in Parliament.
15 William Hale, *Turkish Politics and the Military* (Abingdon: Routledge, 1993).
16 www.newyorker.com/news/daily-comment/show-trials-on-the-bosphorus (accessed 30 January 2016).
17 Dani Rodrik, 'The Plot Against the Generals'. Available at https://www.sss.ias.edu/files/pdfs/Rodrik/Commentary/Plot-Against-the-Generals.pdf (accessed 30 January 2016). Taha Özhan, 'An Operation Against the Gülen Movement', SETA opinion piece, 25 July 2014. Available at setav.org/en/an-operation-against-the-Gülen-movement/opinion/16190 (accessed 30 January 2016).
18 An early report indicating that the evidence did not stand up to scrutiny was written by Gareth Jenkins: 'Between Fact and Fantasy: Turkey's Ergenekon Investigation', Silk Road Paper, August 2009. Available at www.silkroadstudies.org/resources/pdf/SilkRoadPapers/2009_08_SRP_Jenkins_Turkey-Ergenekon.pdf (accessed 30 January 2016).
19 www.brookings.edu/research/papers/2012/04/24-turkey-new-model-taspinar (accessed 30 January 2016).
20 There were some irregularities surrounding the referendum, which required a single 'yes' or 'no' to 26 unrelated questions.
21 www.theguardian.com/world/2012/apr/04/turkey-1980-coup-kenan-evren (accessed 30 January 2016).
22 Halil Karaveli, 'Coups and Class: Why Turkish Democracy Is Derailed', *Turkey Analyst* vol. 8, no. 10 (May 2015).

23 www.herkul.org/bamteli/kuvvetin-cilginligi-ve-referandum-firsati (accessed 30 January 2016).
24 See the work of the Dialogue Society in London, which includes panel discussions on human rights, freedom of expression and countering radicalisation: www.dialoguesociety.org/discussion-forums.html (accessed 30 January 2016).
25 Gülen, *Toward a Global Civilisation*, p. 222.
26 F. Gülen quoted by Doğu Ergil in *Fethullah Gülen and the Gülen Movement in 100 Questions* (Blue Dome Press, 2012). Emphasis my own.
27 Ahmet T. Kuru, *Secularism and State Policies toward Religion: The United States, France and Turkey* (Cambridge: Cambridge University Press, 2009).
28 Fieldwork interview, spring 2013.
29 Turkish channel ATV, 18 June 1999. English translation quoted by Rachel Sharon-Krespin in 'Fethullah Gülen's Grand Ambition: Turkey's Islamist Danger', *Middle East Quarterly* (Winter 2009), pp. 55–66.
30 See the blog by Pınar Doğan and Dani Rodrik, in which some of Gülen's early sermons with anti-Semitic as well as anti-Christian content are translated into English: http://balyozdavasivegercekler.com/2012/11/05/fethullah-Gülen-the-jews-and-hypocrisy/ (accessed 30 January 2016).
31 The recent hit television series *Kurtların Vadisi* (Valley of the Wolves) is one of the most successful of all time, and has inspired spin-off films. Plotlines draw on Turkish nationalism generally and anti-Israeli sentiment in particular.
32 www.youtube.com/watch?v=th4OF_2ddBo (accessed 30 January 2016).
33 www.yeniasir.com.tr/politika/2012/10/07/dershaneler-kapanacak (accessed 30 January 2016).
34 www.theguardian.com/world/2013/may/31/istanbul-protesters-violent-clashes-police (accessed 30 January 2016).
35 www.herkul.org/herkul-nagme/323-nagme-taksim-gezi-parki-hadiseleri-ve-problemlerin-temeli/ (accessed 30 January 2016).
36 www.ntv.com.tr/arsiv/id/25505281 (accessed 30 January 2016).
37 www.reuters.com/article/2014/02/25/us-turkey-erdogan-idUSBREA1N1ZX20140225 (accessed 30 January 2016).
38 www.mcclatchydc.com/2014/04/09/223936/turkish-election-irregularities.html (accessed 30 January 2016).
39 www.milliyet.com.tr/hashasiler-kimdir-hashasi-ne/siyaset/detay/1821968/default.htm (accessed 30 January 2016).
40 www.aljazeera.com/indepth/features/2014/02/new-internet-law-turkey-sparks-outrage-201422312144687859.html (accessed 30 January 2016).
41 Nocera (ed.), *The Gülen Media Empire*.
42 uk.reuters.com/article/2015/02/11/asya-katilim-lawsuit-idUKL5N0VL35A20150211 (accessed 30 January 2016).

Notes to Pages 177–184

43 www.bloomberg.com/news/articles/2015-02-04/turkey-s-in-an-uproar-here-s-what-s-happening- (accessed 30 January 2016).
44 www.nytimes.com/2015/02/04/opinion/fethullah-gulen-turkeys-eroding-democracy.html (accessed 30 January 2016).
45 www.reuters.com/article/2015/02/04/bankasya-regulator-idUSL6N0VE0GZ20150204 (accessed 30 January 2016).
46 www.reuters.com/article/2015/05/29/bankasya-watchdog-idUSL5N0YK4ZB20150529 (accessed 30 January 2016).
47 www.cumhuriyet.com.tr/haber/dunya/84539/Gülen_okullarina_kapatma_karari.html (accessed 30 January 2016).
48 www.reuters.com/article/2015/01/22/us-ethiopia-turkey-erdogan-Gülen-idUSKBN0KV1MA20150122 (accessed 30 January 2016).
49 The centrality of teacher commitment to the Gülen-school model, and its concomitant success, is discussed at length in Chapter Three.
50 Albania appears to be the only country where the movement runs Islamic madrassa-style schools, whose curricula emphasise Arabic and the study of the Qur'an. Followers of Gülen were invited to take on the management of five madrassas in Albania in the early 2000s, taking over the role from Arab groups who had run them previously. See www.sema.edu.al (accessed 30 January 2016).
51 www.huffingtonpost.com/2014/04/29/erdogan-extradite-Gülen_n_5231320.html (accessed 30 January 2016).
52 See, for example, the report entitled 'The Persecution of the *Hizmet* (Gülen) Movement in Turkey: A Chronicle' published by the Rethink Institute in Washington, DC in December, 2014. Available at www.rethinkinstitute.org/persecution-*Hizmet*-gulen-movement-turkey-chronicle (accessed 30 January 2016).
53 www.todayszaman.com/national_31-detainees-released-12-referred-to-court-for-arrest-in-konya-based-probe_381625.html (accessed 30 January 2016).
54 Vahide, *Islam in Modern Turkey*, p. 335.

Afterword

1 www.theguardian.com/world/video/2016/jul/15/erdogan-facetime-turkey-coup-attempt (accessed 19 July 2016).
2 www.nytimes.com/2016/07/17/us/fethullah-gulen-turkey-coup-attempt.html?_r=0 (accessed 19 July 2016).
3 It should be noted that, according to some news outlets, expressions of support for the failed coup on social media have resulted in police interrogation and arrest. See www.hurriyetdailynews.com/two-arrested-in-turkey-for-praising-failed-coup-attempt-on-social-media-.aspx?pageID=238&nID=101858&NewsCatID=341 (accessed 21 July 2016).

4 In a particularly dramatic piece of public theatre, in October 2015 the offices of Gülenist media group Koza-İpek were stormed by police and its TV channels KanalTürk and Bugün TV were forcibly closed down while broadcasting live on air.
5 www.al-monitor.com/pulse/originals/2015/12/turkey-lobby-gulen-movement-us.html (accessed 5 January 2016).
6 They do, however, share a common commitment to Turkish nationalism and are both strongly opposed to the official recognition of Turkey's Kurdish minority.
7 Nidhal Guessoum and Athar Osama (eds), *Science at Universities of the Muslim World*. Report commissioned by Muslim World Science Initiative, October 2015. Available for download at www.muslim-science.com (accessed 9 January 2016).

Bibliography

All internet addresses were last accessed on 30 January 2016 if not indicated otherwise.
Abdel Haleem, M.A.S. (tr.), *The Qur'an* (Oxford: Oxford University Press, 2004).
Abu-Rabi, Ibrahim, *Islam at the Crossroads: on the life and thought of Bediüzzaman Said Nursi* (Albany, NY: State University of New York Press, 2003).
_____ (ed.), *Spiritual Dimensions of Bediüzzaman Said Nursi's Risale-i Nur* (Albany, NY: State University of New York Press, 2008).
Agai, Bekim, 'Fethullah Gülen and his Movement's Islamic Ethic of Education', *Critique: Critical Middle Eastern Studies*, 11:1 (2002), pp. 27–47.
Ahmad, Feroz, *The Making of Modern Turkey* (London/New York: Routledge, 1993).
'Almanya Kapanış Finali 2014', *Küre TV*, 21 June 2014. Available at www.kure.tv/izl e/12-turkce-olimpiyatlari-2014-almanya-kapanis-finali-2014
Altbach, Philip G., 'The Private Higher Education Revolution: An Introduction', in Philip G. Altbach and Daniel C. Levy (eds), *Private Higher Education: A Global Revolution* (Rotterdam: Sense, 2005).
_____ and Daniel C. Levy (eds), *Private Higher Education: A Global Revolution* (Rotterdam: Sense, 2005).
Altınsoy, Selen, 'A Review of University Facilities in Turkey', in *CELE Exchange* 2011/6. Available at www.oecd.org/edu/innovation-education/centreforeffec-tivelearningenvironmentscele/48358175.pdf
Arslan, Berna, 'Pious Science: The Gülen Community and the Making of a Conservative Modernity in Turkey', unpublished PhD thesis, University of California in Santa Cruz, 2009.
Asad, Talal, *Formations of the Secular: Christianity, Islam, Modernity* (Stanford, CA: Stanford University Press, 2003).
Aslan, Mehmet, 'The International Turkish Language Olympiads (ITLOs): Educating for Intercultural Dialogue and Communication', *Sociology and Anthropology* 2 (4) (2014), pp. 125–36.
Balcı, Bayram, 'Fethullah Gülen's Missionary Schools in Central Asia and their Role in the Spreading of Turkism and Islam', *Religion, State and Society* Vol. 31, No. 2 (2003).
_____ 'The Gülen Movement and Turkish Soft Power', Carnegie Endowment for International Peace opinion piece, 4 February 2014.
Barbour, Ian, *Religion and Science: Historical and Contemporary Issues* (London: SCM Press, 1998).

Bibliography

Barrow, John, *Impossibility: The Limits of Science and the Science of Limits* (Oxford: Oxford University Press, 1998).

Barton, Greg, Paul Weller and İhsan Yılmaz, *The Muslim World and Politics in Transition: Creative Contributions of the Gülen Movement* (London and New York: Bloomsbury, 2013).

Berkes, Niyazi, *The Development of Secularism in Turkey* (New York/Abingdon: Routledge, 1998).

Berlinski, Claire, 'Who is Fethullah Gülen?', *City Journal*, Autumn 2012. Available at www.city-journal.org/2012/22_4_fethullah-gulen.html

'Beş yeni üniversite kurulacak', *CNN Turk*, 1 April 2015. Available at www.cnnturk.com/haber/turkiye/bes-yeni-universite-kurulacak?utm_content=buffer48887&utm_medium=social&utm_source=twitter.com&utm_campaign=buffer

Bigliardi, Stefano, *Islam and the Quest for Modern Science: Conversations with Adnan Oktar, Mehdi Golshani, Mohammed Basil Altaie, Zaghloul El-Naggar, Bruno Guiderdoni and Nidhal Guessoum* (Istanbul: Swedish Research Institute in Istanbul, 2014).

⎯⎯⎯ 'Who's Afraid of Theoscientography? An Interpretative Analysis on Harun Yahya', *Zygon: Journal of Religion and Science* vol. 49 issue 1 (2014), pp. 66–80.

⎯⎯⎯ 'The Contemporary Debate on the Harmony between Islam and Science: Emergence and Challenges of a New Generation', *Social Epistemology: A Journal of Knowledge, Culture and Policy* (2015).

Can, Osman, 'The Structural Causes of Political Crisis in Turkey', *Insight Turkey*, Vol. 16 / No. 2 (2014), pp. 33–41.

Carroll, Jill, *A Dialogue of Civilizations: Gülen's Islamic Ideals and Humanistic Discourse* (Somerset, NJ: The Light Publishing, 2007).

Çetin, Muhammed, *The Gülen Movement: Civic Service Without Borders* (New York: Blue Dome Press, 2010).

Conway-Morris, Simon, 'Creation and Evolutionary Convergence', in J. B. Stump and Alan G. Padgett (eds), *The Blackwell Companion to Science and Christianity*, (New Jersey: John Wiley and Sons, Ltd, 2012).

Dohrn, Kristina, 'Translocal Ethics: *Hizmet* Teachers and the Formation of Gülen-inspired Schools in Urban Tanzania', *Sociology of Islam* Vol. 1, Issue 3–4 (2014), pp. 233–56.

Dreher, Sabine, 'What is the *Hizmet* Movement? Contending Approaches to the Analysis of Religious Activists in World Politics', *Sociology of Islam* Vol. 1, Issue 3–4 (2014), pp. 257–75.

Dressler, Markus, *Writing Religion: The Making of Turkish Alevi Islam* (Oxford: Oxford University Press, 2013).

Ebaugh, Helen Rose, *The Gülen Movement: A Sociological Analysis of a Civic Movement Rooted in Moderate Islam* (New York: Springer, 2010).

Edis, Taner, 'Islamic Creationism in Turkey', *Creation/Evolution* vol. 14 (1) nr. 34 (1994), pp. 1–12.

_____ *An Illusion of Harmony: Science and Religion in Islam* (New York: Prometheus, 2007).

Elsdon-Baker, Fern, 'Creating Creationists: The influence of "issues framing" on our understanding of public perceptions of clash narratives between evolutionary science and belief', *Public Understanding of Science* 1–18 (2015).

Encyclopedia of Islam, Second Edition. Eds P. Bearman, Th. Bianquis, C. E. Bosworth, E. van Donzel and W.P. Heinrichs (Leiden: Brill, 1960–2005).

'Erdoğan: Türkçe Olimpiyatları bitti', *Sabah*, 21 March 2014. Available at www.sabah.com.tr/gundem/2014/03/21/erdogan-turkce-olimpiyatlari-bitti

Ergene, Mehmet Enes, *Tradition Witnessing the Modern Age: an analysis of the Gülen movement* (New Jersey: Tughra Books, 2009).

Ergil, Doğu, *Fethullah Gülen and The Gülen Movement in 100 Questions* (New Jersey: Blue Dome Press, 2012).

Esposito, John L., *Islam and Politics* (New York: Syracuse University Press, 1984).

_____ and İhsan Yılmaz, *Islam and Peacebuilding: Gülen Movement Initiatives* (New York: Blue Dome Press, 2010).

Franks, Tim, 'Fethullah Gülen: Powerful but reclusive Turkish cleric', article for BBC News, 27 January 2014. Available at www.bbc.co.uk/news/world-europe-25885817

Gallagher, Nancy, '*Hizmet* Intercultural Dialogue Trips to Turkey', in Sophia Pandya and Nancy Gallagher (eds), *The Gülen Hizmet Movement and its Transnational Activities: case studies of altruistic activism in contemporary Islam* (Boca Raton, FL: BrownWalker Press, 2012).

Gilsenan, Michael, *Saint and Sufi in Modern Egypt: An Essay in the Sociology of Religion* (Oxford: Clarendon Press, 1973).

Gish, Duane T., 'Creation and Evolution in Education'. Available at www.sizinti.com.tr/konular/ayrinti/egitimde-yaratilis-ve-evrim.html

Guessoum, Nidhal, *Islam's Quantum Question: Reconciling Muslim Tradition and Modern Science* (London: I.B.Tauris, 2011).

_____ 'Revive Universities of the Muslim World', *Nature* vol. 526 (29 October 2015), pp. 634–36.

_____ and Athar Osama (eds), *Science at Universities of the Muslim World*, report of the Muslim World Science Initiative, 2015. Available at muslim-science.com/science-at-universities-of-islamic-world-2

Guhin, Jeffrey, 'Why Worry about Evolution? Boundaries, Practices and Moral Salience in Sunni and Evangelical High Schools', *Sociological Theory* (forthcoming, 2016).

Gulay, Erol Nazim, 'The Theological Thought of Fethullah Gülen: Reconciling Science and Islam', unpublished MPhil thesis, St Antony's College, University of Oxford, May 2007.

Bibliography

Gülen, M. Fethullah, *Towards the Lost Paradise* (Istanbul: Kaynak, 1998).

_____ Yaratılış Gerçeği ve Evrim (Istanbul: Nil Yayınları, 2003).

_____ *Toward a Global Civilization of Love and Tolerance* (Somerset, NJ: The Light Inc., 2006).

_____ 'What is the reason for the persistence of Darwinism in the General Culture of the Masses, Though Many of Darwin's Hypotheses Have Been Challenged and Even Disproved?', 5 January 2006. Available at en.fgulen.com/questions-and-answers/2129-what-is-the-reason-for-the-persistence-of-darwinism-in-the-general-culture-of-the-masses-though-many-of-darwins-hypotheses-have-been-challenged-and-even-disproved

_____ *Key Concepts in the Practice of Sufism: Emerald Hills of the Heart*, volumes 1–4 (Clifton, NJ: Tughra Books, 2011).

_____ 'The protests of Taksim Gezi Park and the root of the problems', 14 June 2013. Available at fgulen.com/en/fethullah-gulens-works/thought/the-broken-jug/35970-fethullah-gulen-the-protests-of-taksim-gezi-park-and-the-root-of-the-problems

Hale, William, *Turkish Politics and the Military* (Abingdon: Routledge, 1993).

_____ and Ergun Özbudun (eds), *Islamism, Democracy and Liberalism in Turkey: The Case of the AKP* (Abingdon: Routledge, 2010).

Hameed, Salman, 'Bracing for Islamic Creationism', *Science*, vol. 322 (2008).

_____ 'Muslim creationist Adnan Oktar sentenced to 3 years in prison', Irtiqa: A Science and Religion Blog, 10 May 2008. Available at www.irtiqa-blog.com/2008/05/muslim-creationist-adnan-oktar.html

_____ 'Making Sense of Islamic Creationism in Europe', *Public Understanding of Science* (November 2014), pp. 1–12.

Harrington, James, *Wrestling with Free Speech, Religious Freedom and Democracy in Turkey: The Political Trials and Times of Fethullah Gülen* (Lanham, MD: University Press of America, 2011).

Harrison, Peter, 'The "Book of Nature" and Early Modern Science', in Klaas van Berkel and Arjo Vanderjagt (eds), *The Book of Nature in Early Modern and Modern History* (Leuven: Peeters, 2006).

Hart, Kimberly, *And then We Work for God: Rural Sunni Islam in Western Turkey* (Stanford, CA: Stanford University Press, 2013).

Hassan, Riaz, 'On Being Religious: Patterns of Religious Commitment in Muslim Societies', *Muslim World*, vol. 97 (2007).

'Haydi kızlar İHL'ye!', *Cumhuriyet*, 1 June 2015. Available at www.cumhuriyet.com.tr/haber/egitim/88123/Haydi_kizlar_iHL_ye_.html

Hedley-Brooke, John, *Science and Religion: Some Historical Perspectives* (Cambridge: University of Cambridge Press, 1991).

Hefner, Robert W. and Muhammad Qasim Zaman (eds), *Schooling Islam: The Culture and Politics of Modern Muslim Education* (Princeton, NJ: Princeton University Press, 2007).

Hendrick, Joshua D., 'Globalisation, Islamic activism, and passive revolution in Turkey: the case of Fethullah Gülen', *Journal of Power*, Vol. 2, No.3 (December 2009), pp. 343–68.

_____ *Gülen: The Ambiguous Politics of Market Islam in Turkey and the World* (New York: New York University Press, 2013).

_____ 'Approaching a Sociology of Fethullah Gülen', *Sociology of Islam* Vol. 1, Issue 3–4 (2014), pp. 131–44.

'History of Evolution', *Internet Encyclopedia of Philosophy*. Available at www.iep.utm.edu/evolutio

Hunt, Robert and Alp Aslandoğan (eds), *Muslim Citizens of the Globalized World* (Somerset, NJ: The Light Publishing, 2007).

'İmam hatip liseleri rekora koşuyor', *HaberTurk*, 13 January 2014. Available at www.haberturk.com/gundem/haber/911943-imam-hatip-liseleri-rekora-kosuyor

Jenkins, Gareth H., 'Between Fact and Fantasy: Turkey's Ergenekon Investigation', Silk Road paper, August 2009.

_____ 'Falling Facades: The Gülen Movement and Turkey's Escalating Power Struggle', *Turkey Analyst*, vol. 7, no. 1 (15 January 2014).

Kalaycıoğlu, Ersin, 'Justice and Development Party at the Helm: Resurgence of Islam or Restitution of the Centre-of-Right Predominant Party?', in Birol Yeşilada and Barry Rubin (eds), *Islamization of Turkey under the AKP Rule* (Abingdon: Routledge, 2010).

Karaveli, Halil, 'Coups and Class: Why Turkish Democracy is Derailed', *Turkey Analyst* vol. 8, no. 10 (2015).

Kaya, Veysel, 'Can the Qur'an Support Darwin? An Evolutionist Approach by Two Turkish Scholars after the Foundation of the Turkish Republic', *Muslim World* vol. 102 (2012), pp. 357–70.

Kepel, Gilles, *Muslim Extremism in Egypt: The Prophet and Pharaoh* (Berkeley, CA and Los Angeles: University of California Press, 1984).

Kocabaş, Özlem, 'Scientific Careers and Ideological Profiles of Science Olympiad Participants from Fethullah Gülen and other Secondary Schools in Turkey', unpublished MA thesis, Middle East Technical University, Department of Sociology, Ankara, 2006.

Köse, Talha, 'The Alevi Opening and Democratization Initiative', SETA policy report, 3 March 2010.

Kumbaracıbaşı, Arda Can, *Turkish Politics and the Rise of the AKP* (London/New York: Routledge, 2009).

Kurt, Erkan (ed.), *A Fethullah Gülen Reader: So That Others Might Live* (New York: Blue Dome Press, 2013).

Kuru, Ahmet, *Secularism and State Policies toward Religion: The United States, France and Turkey* (Cambridge: Cambridge University Press, 2009).

Bibliography

Kuru, Zeynep Akbulut and Ahmet T. Kuru, 'Apolitical Interpretation of Islam: Said Nursi's Faith-Based Activism in Comparison with Political Islam and Sufism', *Islam and Christian-Muslim Relations*, 19.1 (2008), pp. 99–111.

Kutschera, Ulrich and Karl J. Niklas, 'The modern theory of biological evolution: an expanded synthesis', *Naturwissenschaften* 91 (2004), pp. 255–76.

Lewis, Bernard, *The Emergence of Modern Turkey* (Oxford: Oxford University Press, 2002).

Maclean, Gerald, *Abdullah Gul and the Making of the New Turkey* (Oxford: Oneworld, 2014).

Majid, D. S. Adnan, 'Qur'anic Interpretative Latitude and Human Evolution: A Case Study', *Al-Bayan – Journal of Qur'an and Hadith Studies* vol. 12 (2015), pp. 19–114.

Mango, Andrew, *The Turks Today* (London: John Murray, 2004).

Mardin, Şerif, *Religion and Social Change in Modern Turkey: The Case of Bediuzzaman Said Nursi* (Albany, NY: State University of New York Press, 1989).

_____ *Religion, Society and Modernity in Turkey* (Syracuse, NY: Syracuse University Press, 2006);

Markham, Ian, *Engaging with Bediuzzaman Said Nursi: A Model of Interfaith Dialogue* (Farnham, Surrey: Ashgate, 2009).

Marks, Jonathan, 'Evolutionary Psychology is Neither', article for The Evolution Institute, 22 March 2015. Available at evolution-institute.org/article/evolutionary-psychology-is-neither/?source=tvol

Martin, M. O., I. V. S. Mullis, P. Foy and G. M. Stanco, *TIMMS International Results in Science* (Chestnut Hill, MA: TIMSS & PIRLS International Study Center, Boston College, 2012).

Massicard, Elise, *The Alevis in Turkey and Europe: Identity and Managing Territorial Diversity* (Oxford: Routledge, 2012).

Mayr, Ernst and William B. Provine (eds), *The Evolutionary Synthesis: Perspectives on the Unification of Biology* (Cambridge, MA: Harvard University Press, 1998).

Mercan, Faruk, *Fethullah Gülen* (Istanbul: Doğan, 2008).

Mermer, Yamine and Redha Ameur, 'Beyond the "Modern": Said Nursi's View of Science', *Islam and Science*, vol. 2, no. 2 (2004), pp. 119–60.

'The Myth Collapses: The Theory of Evolution', *Fountain*, Issue 24 (October–December 1998).

Nasr, Seyyed Hossein, *Science and Civilization in Islam* (Cambridge, MA: Harvard University Press, 1986).

_____ *The Need for a Sacred Science* (London: Curzon, 1993).

Nocera, Lea (ed.), *The Gülen Media Empire* (Rome: Reset S.r.l., 2015).

Nursi, Said, *Mektubat* (The Letters) (Istanbul: KLMN Yayınları, 1996).

_____ *The Letters*, volumes 1–2 (Izmir: Kaynak, 1998).

_____ *Munazarat* (The Dialogues) (Istanbul: KLMN Yayınları, 2007).
_____ *The Reasonings: A Key to Understanding the Qur'an's Eloquence* (Clifton, NJ: The Light Inc., 2008).
_____ *The Rays: Reflections on Islamic Belief, Thought, Worship and Action* (Clifton, NJ: The Light Inc., 2010).
_____ *The Words: the reconstruction of Islamic belief and thought* (Clifton, NJ: The Light Inc., 2010).
Öniş, Ziya, 'The Triumph of Conservative Globalism: The Political Economy of the AKP Era', *Turkish Studies* 13:2 (2012), pp. 135–52.
'Ortaokul ve lisede başörtüsü serbest', *Al-Jazeera Turk*, 23 September 2014. Available at www.aljazeera.com.tr/haber/ortaokul-ve-lisede-basortusu-serbest
Özdalga, Elisabeth, 'Worldly asceticism in Islamic casting: Fethullah Gülen's inspired piety and activism', *Critique: Critical Middle Eastern Studies*, 9:17 (2000), pp. 83–104.
Ozgur, Iren, *Islamic Schools in Modern Turkey* (Cambridge: Cambridge University Press, 2012).
Özhan, Taha, 'An Operation Against the Gülen Movement', SETA opinion piece, 25 July 2014.
Özyürek, Esra, *Nostalgia for the Modern: State secularism and everyday politics in Turkey* (Durham, NC/London: Duke University Press, 2006).
Pandya, Sophia and Nancy Gallagher (eds), *The Gülen Hizmet Movement and its Transnational Activities: case studies of altruistic activism in contemporary Islam* (Boca Raton, FL: BrownWalker Press, 2012).
Pecquet, Julian, 'Turkey Lobbyists Bring Ankara's War with Gülen to Washington', *Al Monitor*, 30 December 2015. Available at www.al-monitor.com/pulse/originals/2015/12/turkey-lobby-gulen-movement-us.html
Peter, Frank and Rafael Ortega (eds), *Islamic Movements of Europe: Public Religion and Islamophobia in the Modern World* (London: I.B.Tauris, 2014).
Pithers, R. T. and Rebecca Soden, 'Critical thinking in education: a review', *Educational Research* 42:3 (2000), pp. 237–49.
Riexinger, Martin, 'The Islamic Creationism of Harun Yahya', *Masaryk University Journal of Law and Technology* 2.2 (2008), pp. 99–112.
_____ 'Turkey', in Stefaan Blancke, Hans Henrik Hjermitslev and Peter C. Kjaergaard (eds), *Creationism in Europe* (Baltimore, MD: Johns Hopkins University Press, 2014).
Robins, Phillip, 'Turkish Foreign Policy under Erbakan', *Survival: Global Politics and Strategy*, 39:2 (1997), pp. 82–100.
Rodrik, Dani, 'The Plot Against the Generals', at Balyoz Davası ve Gerçekler (blog by Pınar Doğan and Dani Rodik). Available at balyozdavasivegercekler.com/2014/06/26/the-plot-against-the-generals
Roy, Olivier, *The Failure of Political Islam* (Cambridge, MA: Harvard University Press, 1994).

Bibliography

Rubin, Barry (ed.), *The Muslim Brotherhood: The Organisation and Policies of a Global Islamist Movement* (New York/Basingstoke: Palgrave Macmillan, 2010).

Ruse, Michael, *Darwinism and its Discontents* (Cambridge: Cambridge University Press, 2006).

Saliba, George, *Islamic Science and the Making of the European Renaissance* (Cambridge, MA: MIT Press, 2007).

Sarıtoprak, Zeki, 'Fethullah Gülen: A Sufi in his own way', in M. Hakan Yavuz and John L. Esposito (eds), *Turkish Islam and the Secular State: The Gulen Movement* (Syracuse, NY: Syracuse University Press, 2003), pp. 156–69.

Sayın, Ümit and Aykut Kence, 'Islamic Scientific Creationism: A new Challenge in Turkey', *Reports of the National Center for Science Education*, vol. 19 issue 6 (1999).

'Science and the Islamists', editorial, *Nature*, vol. 444, issue 7,115 (2 November 2006). Available at www.nature.com/nature/journal/v444/n7115/full/444001a.html

Sevindi, Nevval, *Contemporary Islamic Conversations: M. Fethullah Gülen on Turkey, Islam and the West* (Edited and with an Introduction by Ibrahim M. Abu-Rabi; translated by Abdullah T. Antepli) (New York: State University of New York Press, 2008).

Shankland, David, *Islam and Society in Turkey*. (Huntingdon, PA: Eothen Press, 1999).

_____ *The Alevis in Turkey: The Emergence of a Secular Islamic Tradition* (London: RoutledgeCurzon, 2003).

Sharon-Krespin, Rachel, 'Fethullah Gülen's Grand Ambition: Turkey's Islamist Danger', *Middle East Quarterly* (Winter 2009), pp. 55–66.

Shaw, Stanford J. and Ezel Kural Shaw, *History of the Ottoman Empire and Modern Turkey, Volume 2* (Cambridge: Cambridge University Press, 1977).

Şık, Ahmet, *Kitap* (000Book) (Istanbul: Postacı Yayınları, 2011).

Silverstein, Brian, *Islam and Modernity in Turkey* (New York: Palgrave Macmillan, 2011).

Solberg, Anne Ross, *The Mahdi Wears Armani: An Analysis of the Harun Yahya Enterprise*, Södertörn doctoral dissertations, 2013.

Tapper, Richard (ed.), *Islam in Turkey: Religion, Politics and Literature in a Secular State* (London: I.B.Tauris, 1991).

Tee, Caroline and David Shankland, 'Said Nursi's Notion of Sacred Science: Its Function and Application in *Hizmet* High School Education', *Sociology of Islam* Vol. 1, Issue 3–4 (2014), pp. 209–32.

Tewari Jassal, Smita, 'The Sohbet: Talking Islam in Turkey', *Sociology of Islam* Vol. 1, Issue 3–4 (2014), pp. 188–208.

Times Higher Education World University Rankings (2014–15). Available at www.timeshighereducation.co.uk/world-university-rankings/2014-15/world-ranking

Tittensor, David, *The House of Service: The Gülen Movement and Islam's Third Way* (New York: Oxford University Press, 2014).

Turam, Berna, *Between Islam and the State: The Politics of Engagement* (Stanford, CA: Stanford University Press, 2007).

_____ 'National Loyalties and International Undertakings: The case of the Gülen community in Kazakhstan', in Yavuz and Esposito (eds), *Turkish Islam and the Secular State*, (Syracuse, NY : Syracuse University Press/ London: Eurospan, 2013) pp. 184–207.

Türker, Mehmet, 'Üniversite mi bakkal dükkanı mı?!', *Sözcü*, 19 January 2013. Available at www.sozcu.com.tr/2013/yazarlar/mehmet-turker/universite-mi-bakkal-dukkani-mi-193542

'Turkey-Africa Relations', Republic of Turkey Ministry of Foreign Affairs. Available at www.mfa.gov.tr/turkey-africa-relations.en.mfa

Turner, Colin and Hasan Horkuç, *Said Nursi* (London: I.B.Tauris, 2009).

Ugur, Etga, 'Organising Civil Society: The Gülen Movement's Abant Platform', in Barton et al., *The Muslim World and Politics in Transition: Creative Contributions of the Gülen Movement* (London and New York: Bloomsbury, 2013).

Ünal, Ali and Alphonse Williams (eds), *Advocate of Dialogue: Fethullah Gülen* (Fairfax, VA: The Fountain, 1999).

'US Charter Schools Tied to Powerful Turkish Imam', '60 Minutes', CBS News, 13 May 2012. Available at www.cbsnews.com/news/us-charter-schools-tied-to-powerful-turkish-imam

Vahide, Şükran, *Islam in Modern Turkey: An Intellectual Biography of Bediüzzaman Said Nursi* (Albany, NY: State University of New York Press, 2005).

Van Bruinessen, Martin, *Agha, Sheikh and State: On the Social and Political Organization of Kurdistan* (Utrecht: University of Utrecht, 1978).

_____ 'The Netherlands and the Gülen Movement', *Sociology of Islam* Vol. 1, Issue 3–4 (2014), pp. 165–87.

Vicini, Fabio, 'Gülen's Rethinking of Islamic Patterns and Its Socio-Political Effects', in Yılmaz, İhsan (ed.), *Muslim World in Transition: contributions of the Gülen Movement/conference proceedings* (London: Leeds Metropolitan University Press, 2007).

_____ 'Pedagogies of Affection: The Role of Exemplariness and Emulation in Learning Processes: Extracurricular Islamic Education in the Fethullah Gülen Community in Istanbul', *Anthropology and Education Quarterly*, Vol. 44, Issue 4 (2013), pp. 381–98.

_____ 'Representing Islam: Cinematographic Productions of the Gülen Movement', in Nocera (ed.), *The Gülen Media Empire*. (Rome: Reset-Dialogues on Civilisations, 2015), p.93

Walton, Jeremy F., 'Is *Hizmet* Liberal? Mediations and Disciplines of Islam and Liberalism among Gülen Organizations in Istanbul', *Sociology of Islam* Vol. 1, Issue 3–4 (2014), pp. 145–64.

Bibliography

Weismann, Itzchak, *The Naqshbandiyya: Orthodoxy and Activism in a Worldwide Sufi Tradition* (Abingdon: Routledge, 2007).

Weller, Paul and İhsan Yılmaz (eds), *European Muslims, civility and public life: perspectives on and from the Gülen Movement* (New York and London: Continuum International Publishing Group, 2012).

White, Jenny B., *Islamist Mobilisation in Turkey: A Study in Vernacular Politics* (Seattle, WA: University of Washington Press, 2002).

_____ 'Milli Görüş', in Peter and Ortega (eds), *Islamic Movements of Europe*.

Wood, Gary and Tuğrul Keskin, 'Perspectives on the Gülen Movement', *Sociology of Islam* Vol. 1, Issue 3–4 (2014), pp. 127–30.

Yahya, Harun, *The Evolution Deceit: The Scientific Collapse of Darwinism and its Ideological Background* (Istanbul: Vural Yayıncılık, 1997).

_____ *The Atlas of Creation*. Available at www.atlasofcreation.com

Yavuz, M. Hakan, *Toward an Islamic Enlightenment: The Gülen Movement* (Oxford: Oxford University Press, 2013).

_____ and John L. Esposito (eds), *Turkish Islam and the Secular State: the Gülen Movement* (Syracuse, NY: Syracuse University Press/London: Eurospan, 2003).

Yılmaz, İhsan (ed.), *Muslim World in Transition: contributions of the Gülen Movement/conference proceedings* (London: Leeds Metropolitan University Press, 2007).

'Yurt dışına gönderilen genç beyinlerde rekor artış', *Milliyet*, 20 February 2014. Available at www.milliyet.com.tr/yurt-disina-gonderilen-genc-egitimdunyasi-1839651

'Zorunlu din dersi için karar verildi', *HaberTürk*, 6 December 2014. Available at www.haberturk.com/gundem/haber/1016445-zorunlu-din-dersi-icin-karar-verildi

Zürcher, Erik, *Turkey: A Modern History* (London: I.B.Tauris, 1997).

Index

abla/ağabey (*abi*) (hierarchies within the Gülen Movement) 29–33, 68, 109, 148–50, 160.
Adalet ve Kalkınma Partisi (AKP, Justice and Development Party), 2, 6, 9, 59–60, 105, 128, 135, 137–38, 157–58, 162–68, 172–76, 180, 183–86.
Alevis, 2, 120, 136–38, 156.
Anatolian Tigers, 19.
Atatürk, Mustafa Kemal, 2–3, 14, 36, 38, 58, 84, 95, 167.
atheism/atheist materialism, 4, 17, 46, 81, 83–5, 92–3, 121.

Bank Asya, 6, 145, 176–78, 183.
Başbuğ, General İlker, 167.
'Book of Nature', 46.

cemaat (religious community), 1, 24.
cemevi-mosque projects, 137–38.
charismatic authority
    Gülen, Fethullah, 13, 146, 181.
    Nursi, Said, 43.
charter schools in the USA, 21, 142–4.
Christianity
    Christian creationism, 88–90.
    Christian–Muslim relations, 120–25, 136, 152, 171–2.
    and the West, 4, 142.

corruption scandal (17 December 2013), 6–7, 134, 162–64, 183.
coup d'état
    of 1980, 18–19, 50, 93, 168.
    of 1997 ('postmodern coup'), 20, 165.
    of 15 July 2016 (attempted), 183, 184, 185, 188.
Cumhuriyet Halk Partisi (CHP, People's Republican Party), 36, 175, 184–85.

Davutoğlu, Ahmet, 177.
democracy, 49, 127, 129, 168–69, 180.
Demokrat Partisi (DP, Democratic Party), 39.
dershane(ler) (supplemental tutoring centres), 18, 32, 56, 70, 100, 104, 110, 148, 152–53, 173, 185, 193 n.5.
Dialogue Society, London, 131–32, 154, 209 n.24.
Diyanet İşleri Başkanlığı (DİB, Directorate of Religious Affairs), 16, 19, 59, 90, 136.

engineering
    as a graduate career, 76, 85–6, 101–02, 112–15, 202 n.26.
    in Nursian thought, 48.
Erbakan, Necmettin, 2, 20, 165–66, 190 n.21.

Index

Erdoğan, Recep Tayyip, 6, 60, 128, 134, 141, 145, 162–66, 172–80, 183–84, 186.
Ergenekon trials (also Balyoz and Poyrazköy trials), 167–68.
European Union (EU), 166.
evolutionary theory, 5, 9, 79–98.
Evren, General Kenan, 18, 168.

Fatih, Koleji, 57, 195 n.38.
Fatih University, 105–07.
fedakarlık (self-sacrifice), 62–3, 76.
FEM Dershaneleri, 110, 173.

Gazeteciler ve Yazarlar Vakfı (GYV, Journalists and Writers Foundation), 8, 119–28, 135, 148, 159.
gender etiquette, 7–8, 53, 62–3, 78, 128, 149, 151, 196 n.42.
Gezi Park riots, 128, 134, 174–76, 184, 204 n.32.
globalisation, 9, 20, 98, 156–57.
Golden Generation, 17, 60, 140.
Gül, Abdullah, 166, 174, 176.
Gülen, Fethullah
 biography, 13–16, 20–1, 140–41, 146.
 charisma, *see* charismatic authority
 educational philosophy, 17–18, 57–8, 64.
 influence of Nursi, Said , 35, 49–50, 120–22.
 leadership, 26, 68, 79, 94–5, 135, 147.
 Sufism, 14, 21–3.

Halkların Demokratik Partisi (HDP, People's Democratic Party), 184.
himmet (charitable giving), 27–8, 32.

Hizmet (service), 24, 27–8, 30, 49, 64, 158.

ibn Arabi, 45.
Imam-Hatip Okulları (Imam-Hatip Schools), 59–60.
International Science Olympiads, 9, 61–2, 72–7, 96, 113, 195 n.35.
*ışıkevler*i ('Houses of Light'), 29–32, 109, 200 n.4.
Islamophobia, 130–33.
Israel, 172–73.

judiciary
 government relations with, 162, 168, 176.
 Gülen Movement influence in, 2, 165, 172, 176.

Kemalism
 Darwinism, 84.
 Gülen Movement's views on, 142, 164, 170.
 Nursi, Said's relationship with, 3, 36–7, 40, 49.
Kemal, Mustafa, *see* Atatürk, Mustafa Kemal.
khalifa, 84–5.
Kurds in Turkey, 173, 184.

Lisans Yerleştirme Sınavı (LYS, Degree Placement Exam), 73, 115, 193 n.6.

Mardin, Şerif, 3.
Maududi, Abul A'la, 37.
Mavi Marmara incident, *see* Israel.
medical science
 as a graduate career, 112–14, 185, 202 n.26.
 in Nursian thought, 48.

Medrese 57–8.
Milliyetçi Hareket Partisi (MHP, Nationalist Movement Party), 175.
MÜSIAD, 20.

namaz (ritual prayer), 62, 67, 111.
Naqshbandi brotherhood
    Gülen, Fethullah, 14.
    Nursi, Said, 41.
    political philosophy, 2, 164–65.
Nasr, Seyyed Hossein, 46.
national curriculum
    religion, 59.
    science, 61, 74, 84, 96.
Nilüfer Lisesi, 57.
Nursi, "Bediüzzaman" Said
    biography, 2–3, 35–42.
    Nursian thought, *see* Risale-i Nur Külliyatı.

Ottoman Empire, 14, 21, 36, 112, 119–20, 136, 157.
Özal, Turgut, 18, 50, 91.

Pennsylvania, 13, 25, 68, 122, 131, 140–1, 146–50, 155–56, 160, 184.
police force
    arrests following 17 Dec 2013, 162–63, 176, 178, 180–81, 183–84, 210 n.1.
    Gezi Park riots, 134, 174.
    Gülen Movement influence in, 2, 167, 172.
positive action (*müspet hareket*), 2, 15, 23, 40–1, 50, 186.

Qur'an, the, 26, 38, 40, 42–4, 46–7, 49, 84–5, 88–91, 124–26.
Qutb, Sayyid, 3, 37.

recruitment, 32–4, 74–7, 105–09, 115, 153, 158, 173, 185.
Refah Partisi (RP, Welfare Party) *see* Erbakan, Necmettin.
religious mentoring, 18, 55, 67–8, 76.
Rethink Institute, 145.
Risale-i Nur Külliyatı (Epistle of Light)
    Christian–Muslim relations, 121.
    function as text, 26, 36, 42–5, 67–8.
    Gülen, Fethullah, 15, 21, 35, 49–50.
    philosophy of education, 17.
    philosophy of science, 36–7, 45–9.
    political philosophy, 3, 41.
Rumi Forum, 21, 122–23, 134, 144–45, 200 n.49.

Samanyolu Lisesi, 57, 75, 193 n.3.
Samanyolu media group, 145, 176.
secularism
    AKP, the 129, 164–69.
    Gülen, Fethullah, 142, 169–72, 180.
    Nursi, Said, 37–8, 47, 120–21.
    science, 4, 84.
    in Turkish history, 2, 165.
Sharia, 2, 40, 166.
Shi'ism, 136.
Sızıntı/The Fountain (magazines), 80–1, 88.
sohbet(ler) (reading groups), 15, 26, 35, 67–9, 149, 191 n.37.
strategic ambiguity, 5, 24.
Sufism (*tasavvuf*)
    Gülen, Fethullah, 13–14, 21–3
    Nursi, Said, 41–5.
    as rationale for dialogue, 122–23, 132–33.
    Sufi orders (*tarikatlar*), 2, 24, 164, 191 n.30.

Index

Tanzimat reforms, 37.
technology, 48–9, 99, 115, 185–86.
tesettür (Turkish Islamic female dress), 25, 30–1, 53, 62–3, 94, 120, 128, 194 n.21.
TÜBITAK, 72–6, 153.
Turkish-Islamic synthesis, 18–19.
Turkish Language Olympiads (*Türkçe Olimpiyatları*), 134–36.

TÜSIAD, 20.
TUSKON, 20.
vakıf (foundation) universities, 105, 112, 201 n.9.
Yahya, Harun, 91–4, 199 n.34.
Yamanlar Koleji, 57, 75.
Young Turks, 38.
Zaman/Today's Zaman (newspapers), 145, 169, 174, 176, 201 n.16, 210 n.1.